WE, THE JURY

DECIDING THE
SCOTT PETERSON CASE

WE, THE JURY

DECIDING THE
SCOTT PETERSON CASE

WRITTEN BY

GREG BERATLIS, JUROR NO. 1

TOM MARINO, JUROR NO. 2

MIKE BELMESSIERI, JUROR NO. 4

DENNIS LEAR, JUROR NO. 5

RICHELLE NICE, JUROR NO. 7

JOHN GUINASSO, JUROR NO. 8

JULIE ZANARTU, JUROR NO. 9

WITH FRANK SWERTLOW
& LYNDON STAMBLER

PHOENIX BOOKS

ISBN: 1-59777-536-3
Library of Congress Cataloging-In-Publication Data Available

Book Design by: Sonia Fiore

Printed in the United States of America

Phoenix Books
9465 Wilshire Boulevard, Suite 315
Beverly Hills, CA 90212

10 9 8 7 6 5 4 3 2 1

TABLE OF CONTENTS

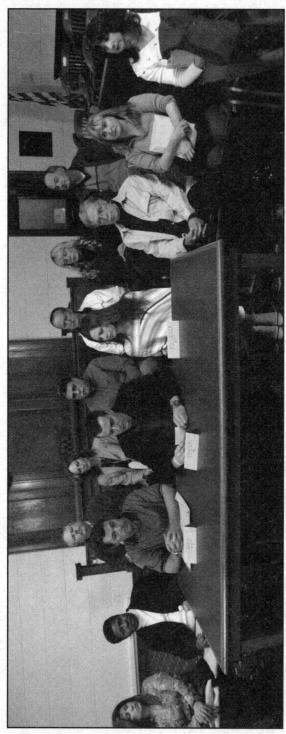

The Peterson jury gathered for a press conference at the San Mateo County Courthouse after they recommended the death penalty for Scott Peterson who was found guilty of murdering his wife, Laci, and thier unborn son, Conner. The group was composed, but many were in tears before announcing the death penalty for the double murder.
Front row from left to right: Lorena Gonzalez, Fairy Sorrell, Greg Beratlis, Steve Cardosi, Richelle Nice, Dennis Lear, Julie Zanartu, Debbie Germenis.
Back row from left to right: John Guinasso, Mary Mylett, Michael Belmessieri, Michael Church, Kristy Lamore, Thomas Marino.

Photo Credit: Modesto Bee/Polaris

WE, THE JURY:

GREG "ZANE" BERATLIS
JUROR NO. 1

TOM "MARIO" MARINO
JUROR NO. 2

MIKE "TREADHEAD" BELMESSIERI
JUROR NO. 4

DENNIS "MONTARA" LEAR
JUROR NO. 5

RICHELLE "RICCI" NICE
JUROR NO. 7

JOHN "BILL" GUINASSO
JUROR NO. 8

JULIE "JOE" ZANARTU
JUROR NO. 9

INTRODUCTION

The 2002 Christmas Eve murders of Laci Peterson and her unborn son, Conner, quickly emerged as the first major criminal trial to capture the imagination of the American public in the 21st Century. Scott Peterson, a handsome but enigmatic fertilizer salesman from Modesto, wasn't a celebrity like Michael Jackson or Robert Blake, both of whom were embroiled in legal battles at the same time, but he became the center of a vortex of events that culminated in his murder convictions and death sentence. Peterson was not a charismatic football star like O.J. Simpson, but his bad boy sex appeal was evident to anyone sitting in the courtroom. Although they were repulsed by his actions, many female reporters were drawn to his physical presence. He was tall, dark and handsome, and an outlaw. These are compelling ingredients that stirred the public's fascination.

Peterson and his wife, Laci, were from Modesto, not big cities like Los Angeles or New York where the murder of a pregnant woman at Christmas would generate tabloid fury. Yet, there was something about this case that touched people in a different way. This was a quintessential American story, perhaps even the dark side of the American Dream. Scott and Laci seemed like the perfect couple, but as this murder mystery unfolded, their love story became a gothic nightmare that sold magazines and newspapers and became a headline story for cable news channels night after night. More than two years after Peterson's conviction, news that a female juror had become the convicted killer's pen pal generated a flurry of attention in the media. Little things like the sale of the Peterson home in Modesto still make news.

By comparison, Michael Jackson's child molestation case faded into obscurity just as quickly as the singer disappeared into the sands of the Middle East. Jackson and the crimes he was accused of had "the ick factor," something so ugly that the public tuned out, especially after he was acquitted. The abrasive Robert Blake was just another out of work actor in a city of out of work actors and waiters. Peterson may be in jail, but he still receives bags of fan mail and marriage proposals. Like Darth Vader, he has become the dark side of stardom.

Peterson's killings haunt us, just as they haunt the 12 strangers from San Mateo County who formed the jury that convicted him and banished him to death row. These strangers, six men and six women, never imagined the effects this trial would have on them. It is doubtful the media ever anticipated the Peterson case would become the sensation that it did. When it did, coverage became non-stop.

"Timing is everything," said Loyola Law Prof. Laurie Levenson. "This case happened during Christmas. A whole town went out looking for Laci instead of having Christmas dinner."

There was much more, though.

"You had an attractive victim, a whodunit, sex and an affair," Levenson said. "It became a moment that captured the history of what was going on in California."

For Bay Area defense lawyer Daniel Horowitz, the Peterson case was like a medieval passion play, a biblical battle between good and evil. With such allegorical characters, it is no surprise the trial captured the imagination of the American public.

The casting was perfect. "You had Laci, the angelic, perfect woman, as the victim, a Mother Mary kind of figure," said Horowitz. "Then you had the seductive girlfriend, who Gloria Allred ultimately spun as a good person but who didn't have to be. Finally, you've got Scott Peterson who is the smiley-faced, sweet devil but he's pure evil. It hit all the hot buttons. They're the elements that novels and soap operas are made of. I don't think there were any grays. That's the whole point."

The jury, Horowitz said, became like a Greek chorus, especially after convicting Peterson and recommending the death penalty. The Peterson case also shattered the myth of the storybook marriage.

"Women identified overwhelmingly with Laci, beyond belief really," Horowitz said.

Stan Goldman, a Loyola Law Professor who analyzed the case for Fox News, stated whenever a Peterson story aired the ratings at Fox News Channel spiked, mostly among young women, a highly prized demographic the channel rarely attracted.

This saga of good and evil also shattered the American Dream of the perfect couple in their perfect little house. Juror Richelle Nice considered the murders a betrayal. "Who could you trust?" she wondered. Others wondered too.

"He was a very good-looking guy," Goldman said. "Especially the one picture of Laci with that big smile made her very appealing. There's something about it. It's the cautionary tale. It's what your mother warned you about if you were a little girl. Don't trust a man just because he smiles at you and looks good. Hence the interest from young women. I think it was a typical kind of cautionary tale with a tragic ending."

When an eight-month pregnant woman disappeared on Christmas Eve, the search for her heightened media attention and hooked the audience.

"Then to find out that the grieving husband was the primary suspect made the case very personal for a lot of women," Goldman said. "It's the classic cliché. It's the car wreck you can't take your eyes off of. Once you get into it, you've got to find out how it ends."

Goldman recalled sitting next to a seasoned 40-something female reporter during the preliminary hearing. "He is a hunk," the reporter told Goldman when Peterson walked into the courtroom.

Bemused, Goldman said, "If these were homely people, this case would have never had legs."

Like the slow speed chase in the O.J. Simpson case or the film clips of JonBenét Ramsey as a beauty queen, people were mesmerized by the images of Scott, Laci and Amber Frey.

"It was like a sitcom with these good looking people that they started to care about," Goldman said. "They cared about Laci. Maybe a few people cared about Scott, although I doubt that many. They were fascinated."

Peter Shaplen, the veteran TV news producer who was the media coordinator at the Peterson and Jackson trials, said the story of Laci and Scott became a complex and unfolding drama, driven by a young woman with a captivating smile. She and Scott also fit the media's ideal for a perfect victim and villain.

"She was pretty, she was white, she was pregnant, she was suburban and she was middle class," he said, "and it was Christmas and Scott was the perfectly handsome villain. Even women in the media found him sexy and irresistible and you would hear them saying, 'I'd like to do him.' And there was a lull in the news."

But what the story had most of all was Laci, and it was not merely her smile on her missing persons poster that captivated the country. It was Laci, herself.

"She was everyone's kid sister," he said. "She was every woman's best girlfriend or the date every guy wanted to take home to his mother. To women, she was pretty, but not too pretty. To men, she had a certain allure that made her desirable. She was approachable and she was vulnerable. She had that old time glamour that Hollywood stars like Joan Crawford and Bette Davis had and that made them stars for decades. She was real."

Peterson also had his role in the psychodrama. If Laci was the perfect heroine, Scott was the villain.

"Scott was a cad to women and an SOB," Shaplen said. "Even during his trial, he never lost his smirk. You wanted to rub sand in his face."

Shaplen said the media and the public didn't respond to Michael Jackson and his troubles because of his alleged crimes of child abuse and his own lifestyle. People couldn't relate to him the way they could to the middle class couple from Modesto.

"Michael was always weird," he said. "He had a weird lifestyle; his ranch was weird and so were the sycophants around him."

But for reporters who met Peterson shortly after his wife's disappearance at a media center at the Red Lion Inn in Modesto, Peterson was a man on the run. He was ice, emotionally detached, always suspiciously darting away from the cameras. His excuse was, "It's about Laci, not about me." The conclusion that most journalists began to make was simply something was wrong, and that feeling came across to the public that followed his elusive moves. This isn't the way a grieving husband behaves after his wife has vanished. Moreover, many reporters wondered how a man whose pregnant wife was so close to birth would claim to have gone fishing when his wife could have easily gone into labor. It was villainy and easy to understand.

Some journalists began to reach a chilling conclusion, typified by questions shouted out at Peterson such as, "Why did you kill Laci?" The icy Peterson never answered, but the public, especially women, were hooked, just as if he had become a star.

"There are different kinds of lures with these cases," said USC Prof. Leo Braudy, a pop culture expert and author of *The Frenzy of Renown: Fame and Its History.* "Stars like Michael Jackson and Robert

Blake are people you think you know already. They are the seamy side of show businesses, the world of glitz and glamour."

For Braudy celebrities are distant, one to two steps removed from the common man; the Petersons weren't.

"The Peterson case is more of a suburban world filled with the good family," Braudy said. "They were the nice couple down the street, but you now find out what was going on behind the curtains. It hits closer to home. When it comes to celebrities, people are more detached. It's about sins and malfeasance. They sort of deserve what happens to them in some way. To maintain their adoration for a celebrity, the celebrity has to walk the straight and narrow, and if they breach this agreement, there is a desire to stomp on them."

The Petersons were an American ideal on the surface—a nice home, good looking and a child on the way at Christmas. It was a postcard.

"They seemed to have a good life, but there were maggots underneath that façade," said the cultural historian. "Scott was like a member of your family, but he has disappointed you. Suddenly, some horrible family secret is erupting at Christmas."

Even these jurors were captivated by the ideal look that the Petersons presented, at first, but after more than six months of weighing the evidence, the men and women who were going to decide Peterson's fate contemplated the same question the media had been asking for months: "Why did you kill Laci?"

This book is an inside look at the Peterson trial through the eyes of seven jurors, two women and five men. These were decent people, plucked out of their daily lives, never really aware of what they would face during the trial and the traumatic effect it would have on their lives.

Their story is filled with twists and turns that not even a Hollywood scriptwriter could have created. Three of their colleagues on the panel were dismissed, including a foreman who was a doctor and a lawyer. Those who remained became prisoners of the judicial system they were trying to serve. It was as if they were criminals themselves. A bailiff constantly monitored their movements in the jury box to see if they were taking too many notes or too few or whether they were dozing. During deliberations, they were driven to and from the courthouse in a sheriff's van filled with shackles for prisoners. They lived in a kind of judicial version of solitary confinement. They were unable to speak about the trial to anyone, even their families. They had to be constantly on guard for private eyes who might be shadowing them, ready to pounce and cause a mistrial if they discovered an indiscretion.

After the jurors reached that cataclysmic decision about the fate of Peterson, they continued to be victims of the jury system. They are wracked by nightmares, flashbacks, and physical pain from the traumatic stress they suffered. Shockingly, San Mateo County does not offer counseling to aid jurors who suffer from post-traumatic stress disorder.

These seven jurors have no regrets about what they faced and their decision to convict Peterson and send him on a journey to his death. Unlike the Jackson jury, they have never second-guessed their decisions. They don't waffle. Despite arguments, disagreements and philosophical differences, they concluded unequivocally that Peterson committed a double murder and deserved the ultimate punishment the state reserved for such heartless killers.

This book tells the reader why a man they originally perceived as the "All-American Boy" was actually a cold-blooded killer. There was no rush to judgment. Throughout the trial, they looked for every possible avenue that would acquit him. But after scrutinizing and listening to the evidence, they came to the same resounding conclusion that the prosecution did. He did it.

The "All-American Boy" was the personification of evil. If they thought he was innocent, despite what the public or the media thought, Peterson would have walked out of the courtroom a free man.

Anne Bremner, a former Seattle prosecutor and a frequent TV legal analyst on the Peterson case, isn't surprised by this jury and its decisions.

"When picking a jury," Bremner says, "pick bowlers. I want common sense, grounded, middle class and no nonsense people. In a murder trial, you want people with common sense."

This is the story of the common sense of seven jurors—a Teamster, a Marine veteran, a mother of four, a biotech clinical trial inspector, a retired airline mechanic, a retired postman and an engineer who coaches youth football.

"This is the dark side of the American dream," said Prof. George Bisharat, a criminal procedure specialist at the University of California's Hastings College of the Law in San Francisco. "People saw the unfolding tragedy as if their own lives could take a wrong turn into a morbid and bizarre environment. It is as if their fundamental values were betrayed. This is because they could relate to Laci and Scott and so could these jurors."

CHAPTER 1:
VERDICT DAY

"I looked down. My tears were hitting the floor.
When he said the word 'unanimous,' we all cried."
—Richelle Nice, Juror No. 7

In the Redwood City courtroom where Scott Peterson awaits the verdict in a murder trial that had captivated the nation for more than five months, even the toughest-looking bailiff turns white.

"I can't breathe," the courtroom cop gasps as he tugs at the collar of his wool tunic.

He's right. The drama sucks the air out of the room. Within minutes, a jury of six men and six women from San Mateo County would reveal their verdict in the murders of Peterson's wife Laci and his unborn son, Conner.

Just before the lunch break on that warm and sunny Friday, Nov. 12, 2004, Judge Alfred Delucchi announced that the jury had reached a verdict. Everyone understood the gravity of the situation. More than a dozen bailiffs were inside the packed courtroom in case trouble erupted once the decision was read.

It had been a tough trial. Peterson's charismatic defense attorney, Mark Geragos, dominated the opening months of the saga of lust, obsession and personal irresponsibility. Would the prosecution led by Rick Distaso and co-counsel Dave Harris become "The Little Engine That Could" and relentlessly chug over the mountain and win over a jury that had been wracked by disputes that led to the dismissal of three jurors? Or would the jury agree with Geragos that there was no evidence, except for one strand of hair that might have been Laci Peterson's, to connect Scott to the crime?

Geragos needed a big win. He had lost the Winona Ryder shoplifting case in Beverly Hills in 2002. Then in early 2004, Geragos abruptly left the Michael Jackson child molestation case and was replaced by Thomas Mesereau, Jr. Geragos, who came from a family of LA lawyers, used his baritone voice to keep spectators and the media awake during the early days of the case. The prosecution presented a phalanx of expert witnesses who would discuss such scintillating subjects as the history of concrete. Geragos, who wore designer suits and flashy ties, was the ringmaster; all eyes went to him when he spoke. He even told jokes and made quips, which would come to haunt him as the trial progressed.

At night, he smoked cigars with reporters and sipped $20 shots of single malt Scotch at Vino Santo, an Italian restaurant near the courthouse. He would adjourn to the posh Marriott hotel in San Mateo for more smokes and cocktails. Geragos was living large in his suite while Scott Peterson sat locked away in his cell.

In the courtroom, sitting behind Geragos in the gallery, were a number of beautiful young women in miniskirts. After the trial, some of the jurors would remark that they thought Geragos might have been attempting to distract them during key testimony by prosecution witnesses. Johnny Cochran had played the "race card." Was Geragos playing the sex card?

"One woman came in and sat down on the edge of her seat with a short skirt, and one bent down one time and her thong was showing," Richelle Nice, Juror No. 7, said. "There was the one day she walked in with those high-heeled boots on."

"I guess it was Geragos' idea of a distraction, but it didn't work," said Mike Belmessieri, Juror No. 4.

Geragos relentlessly turned prosecution witnesses into defense witnesses with his rapier-like cross-examinations.

Conversely, the prosecutors, from the farmlands of Modesto, didn't crack jokes or trade quips with the judge; to them there was nothing funny about a double murder. Grim and low-key, Distaso, the monkish-looking senior deputy district attorney from Stanislaus County, and his team delivered their case methodically and often tediously. The prosecutors kept away from the media, working steadily on their case every afternoon at the more modest Marriott Towne Place Suites in Redwood City.

The view from their hotel overlooked San Francisco Bay that was a constant reminder of their duty. This was where the horrifying remains of Laci and her baby had been found amidst the flotsam and jetsam on a desolate beach along the Richmond shore.

It all began when Laci went missing on Christmas Eve, 2002. Her husband Scott, a handsome, enigmatic Modesto, Calif., fertilizer salesman, the Willy Loman of manure, said he had driven 90 miles to go fishing while his eight-and-a-half-month pregnant wife prepared their home for Christmas and the arrival of the son whom she desperately wanted.

The Peterson trial turned Redwood City into a center of national media attention with its non-stop cable news reports and punditry about the murder of Laci. Laci's iconic missing persons posters featured her as a smiling and bubbly, 27-year-old substitute teacher. But now, after listening to scores of witnesses, opening and closing arguments, DNA reports and after staring at the chilling photographs of the victims' remains, the jury had reached its verdict.

If Peterson is found guilty in the first degree for the murders, there would be a second phase in the case—penalty. The jurors would have to decide if Peterson should be sentenced to death or spend life in prison. There were no other options. If Peterson is acquitted on this autumn afternoon, he would walk out the doors of the courthouse and into the sunlight a free man, perhaps with the kind of arrogant smirk he flashed throughout the trial.

Some media cynics were stunned when Judge Delucchi said the verdict would be read at 1:15 p.m. They thought that Delucchi, who had already dismissed three members of the jury, might possibly drop another one. Some wags began mocking the trial, calling it a new reality show, *Survivor: Redwood City.*

"The winner is the last juror on the island," one reporter quipped.

Most legal observers anticipated the jury, riddled with strife since beginning deliberations nine days earlier, would reach a decision the next week. But this was a Friday, and juries are notorious for coming back with a verdict at the end of the week to avoid another weekend of sequestration.

Now Geragos, who is in Santa Ana, Calif., working on another case, looks as uncaring as his client. His lieutenant, Pat Harris, would have to take the verdict. As the verdict approaches, the public begins filling the courtyard outside the courthouse. Many followed the trial; some had even waited in line during the dewy early morning hours each day to get one of the rare public seats.

Peter Shaplen, the media coordinator during the trial, recalled an eerie mood. "It was a cross between Times Square after VE-Day and Madame La Farge at the guillotine," the veteran news producer said. "It was kind of a carnival. This was the big event and they wanted to be present; they wanted to hear it first; they wanted to be there physically, and not hear it on the news. They somehow felt Laci's murder was personal and they were connected to the outcome. It was pro-guilty. 'Vengeance is ours,' sayeth the Lord."

Shaplen estimated that the crowd was about 60 percent women and predominantly middle-aged. One woman wheeled her paraplegic son into the throng. "She put her child in the midst of this jostling crowd, which is like putting him into a crowded New York City subway," Shaplen said.

But what if the verdict went the other way? What if the jury decided that the prosecution's circumstantial case against Peterson was empty? Would there be violence, a riot?

Deputies in the courtroom were already fearful that Laci's father, Dennis Rocha, might try to attack Peterson, or that Ron Grantski, Sharon Rocha's longtime companion, might strike out at Peterson, too. The opposing families might come to blows.

But in the courtyard, which was lined with media tents from such news organizations as NBC, CNN, Fox and Court TV, the authorities played a different hand. Unlike what would happen at the Michael Jackson trial months later where metal fences and barbed wire turned the Santa Barbara County Courthouse into a stalag, San Mateo authorities used a single strand of yellow crime scene tape to keep the crowd from the courthouse steps. Air One, a lone police helicopter, hovered above to monitor the crowd.

"Deputies were out in the plaza, but there was a conscious decision not to make this a police state or show a heavy hand," Shaplen said. "They did not bring out the bicycle fences or have deputies stand shoulder to shoulder. The only thing they insisted upon was that the top steps into the building be kept clear."

A calm hung over the growing crowd. "There was a weird confidence that they, the jury, would do the right thing and convict Peterson; the *vox populi* had Scott guilty," Shaplen said.

* * *

But the crowd had no idea how difficult it was for the jury to reach a conclusion. Juror No. 2, Tom Marino, a retired postman, mentioned during *voir dire* that as a devout Catholic he might have issues with imposing the death sentence. He sought guidance from his parish priest, who told him there are two sets of laws—man's laws and God's laws and there should be no problem with following the laws of man.

"I was surprised I was picked," Marino said. "I could see why the defense would. I could see why they liked that I had a problem with the death penalty. But the prosecution?"

During the guilt phase, Marino wanted to make sure that every member of the jury was convinced that Peterson was guilty of first-degree murder—beyond a reasonable doubt, as the law required. He scrutinized a white board in the jury room listing the issues in the case and played devil's advocate.

"Gee," he said. "You have no murder weapon; you really don't have a murder scene. What kind of motive? Do you think he did it to live with Amber Frey? I don't think so. I don't think that was the motive. I am the last holdout; tell me, convince me."

They tried.

"They all went through it in their heads and talked and I could see they were sure," he said. "'Okay,' I told them, 'you're comfortable with that; you're relaxed.' I mean, they were sure. I took the heat. I wanted to make sure everybody was comfortable with this decision."

He was, too.

Marino was the last juror to signal that he was ready to make a decision. What the jurors didn't know was that Marino had ana-lyzed the prosecution and the defense cases and concluded that Peterson was a cold-blooded killer.

"I looked at every issue from point A to point Z," he said. "What do we know for sure? We know, for sure, that Scott was the last person to see Laci, other than her sister the night before at the barbershop. That was point A. The last point, point Z, was the bodies washing up on the shore. So what happened from A to Z? I tried to look for one thing that would get him off, but I figured there's a straight line from Scott to the bodies washing up on shore.

"I was looking for one offshoot, anything. Maybe he was seen on the golf course, or maybe he made a phone call at a certain hour from his office or from anywhere. I was looking for some out for him, an alibi, just a minute thing that said there is doubt, and then we started deliberating and there wasn't one offshoot. There wasn't one thing. I was trying to find something, but there was nothing there."

During deliberations, the jurors had been sequestered at the Crowne Plaza Hotel in Foster City, about 20 minutes up U.S. 101 from Redwood City. It, too, overlooked the Bay where Laci and Conner had been hidden under a blanket of seawater for months. Soon, this hastily assembled small family would break up and move on, much in the way a movie company bonds into a family and breaks up after the final scene is shot.

"We had sent the verdict to the judge just before lunch. Then, we had lunch in the courtroom as usual, but it was much quieter now. The tension was building," said Juror No. 5, Dennis Lear, a retired United Airlines mechanic. "After lunch, they finally took us back to the deliberation room, and the tension got worse. After all these months, we had become used to the regimen of knowing what to expect. This day was the unknown."

Inside the jury room, the hours tick away toward the verdict. "It seemed like it was forever," recalled Julie Zanartu, Juror No. 9, a biotech clinical trial inspector for Genentech. "We made our decision and now we had to wait and wait. It was agonizing. We had been through this for so long, and we finally agreed. We were ready. We knew things were going on outside in the plaza; we could hear it. We looked out the windows in the courtroom and we could see people gathering. It was scary. I wanted to get out of there."

Jurors broke down crying; they hugged each other in support. Lunch was served in the courtroom where Peterson would soon learn his fate. Nice was so overwhelmed with emotion, she could not eat, but others did. "We sat in the empty courtroom that soon would be filled with family and media, and some onlookers," she said. "One side would be hurt, but both sides have already been so hurt. How much more can they take?"

John Guinasso, Juror No. 8, is a burly parking lot facility supervisor in San Francisco whom Geragos accused of being a "stealth juror," a ringer who had already made up his mind that Peterson was guilty. Throughout the trial, Guinasso folded his arms below his chest and stared stone faced at Geragos and Peterson.

"We had a one-and-a-half hour wait until all the participants were in the courtroom," Guinasso said. "In the meantime, we would look out the window of the deliberations room and hear and see helicopters hovering. Sheriff's Department cars were scrambling around to get into position to prepare for any type of verdict."

As the months went by, the jurors, who often split off in groups of twos and threes, joked about Geragos who paraded into and out of the courtroom with a John Wayne-like strut. Gradually, some of them bonded. But once they began their deliberations and sequestration, they were anything but united. There were arguments at the courthouse; jurors were dismissed, including the first foreman. Alternates were brought into the deliberations as replacements, and every time there was a change, the deliberations had to start over. The process was taking its toll. Laci and Conner were not the only victims in this case.

The tension continues to grow. "Most of the jurors kept to themselves," Guinasso said. "Some cried and were comforted by other jurors. I, like others, needed some time for me. The deliberations took a toll on my mental state. Many of us were completely exhausted by the end of the guilt phase of the trial. I remember seeing Juror No. 12 (the blonde-haired Kristy Lamore), crying hysterically in the corner of the room and muttering to herself. It was very tough, but it was the right verdict. There were no celebrations, no high fives, no congratulatory gestures in this room. These deliberations were thorough. If anything was going to condemn Scott Peterson, it was the legal process, not any one of us."

"There were butterflies in my stomach," Zanartu said. "I was creeped out seeing all the people in the plaza. It was like being at a rock concert. I wasn't in my right mind at that point. I just wanted to go home. I didn't know what was going to happen. I was concerned about how Scott's family was going to react."

Nice became emotional as the time for the announcement neared. It was not surprising. She openly wept at the sight of the autopsy photos of the remains of Laci and Conner. While the foreman, Steve Cardosi, a paramedic-firefighter from Half Moon Bay, Calif., tallied the final vote, she rested her head on the table.

"I looked down. My tears were hitting the floor. When he said the word 'unanimous,' we all cried," she said. "Mary Mylett, Juror No. 10, grabbed me as I sobbed into her chest. We double-checked that everyone was on the same page. We were."

Jenne Carnevale, a petite and attractive bailiff who had been their caretaker during the trial, knocks on the door. It is time to enter the courtroom. Shaken, Richelle Nice asks Guinasso for support. "She asked me if she could hold my hand once we sat in our respective chairs," he said. "She was very nervous and emotional, more at that moment than any time in the deliberation room."

"I was shaking like crazy, the tears wouldn't stop," Nice said. "John became my rock, I held on to his hand for dear life. I know he couldn't feel it because I couldn't feel mine."

The size of the security force shocks Nice as she enters the courtroom. "Oh my Lord! What is going to happen? What did they think might happen?"

Also waiting in line to get into the courtroom, Gloria Allred, the attorney for Amber Frey, the Fresno massage therapist who had a brief romance with Peterson, looks concerned. "I pray for justice," says Allred, whose client helped indict her ex-lover by taping his lupine telephone calls that were filled with countless lies and deceptions.

Minutes before 1 p.m., the line outside the courtroom parts for Sharon Rocha, Laci's grieving mother who quickly moves through the queue, wearing a lavender jacket and black slacks. A sobbing woman on a nearby court bench reaches to touch her arm. She misses. Sharon's eyes are somewhere else. Beside her are her son Brent, Laci's half-sister Amy and Ron Grantski, her longtime companion, who had been like a stepfather to Laci and Sharon's other children. Dennis Rocha, Laci's father, looks down and enters the courtroom. Laci's sobbing girlfriends complete the extended family.

The bailiff tugging at his wool tunic is not the only one inside the courtroom needing a breath of air. At 1:05 p.m., Jackie Peterson, Scott's mother, who suffers from a chronic lung disease, rushes out of the courtroom. Perhaps Jackie, like her husband Lee, who is surprisingly absent from the courtroom, is too overwhelmed to hear if her son is guilty of first or second degree murder.

"Maybe she is going out to buy a coffin," one spectator whispers.

But Jackie, who has only 20 percent of her lung capacity, comes back. She needed a new oxygen bottle to help her through the ordeal that is about to unfold. Dressed in black, she says nothing as she rushes to her seat just in time to see Judge Delucchi enter his courtroom.

No one is smiling at the prosecution's table. Senior Deputy DA Distaso, who had made an impassioned closing argument for Peterson's conviction, sits at the prosecution table, as does his co-counsel Dave Harris, whose relentless cross-examination of fertility expert Dr. Charles March helped derail Geragos' case. Their supervisor, Chief Deputy DA Birgit Fladager, who helped steady the case, is with them.

Stanislaus County District Attorney James Brazelton had arrived earlier in the day, tipping off the courtroom that something serious might be coming up, but just what no one really knew until Delucchi jolted the crowd that a verdict had been reached.

As the jurors quickly file into the courtroom, some don't even think to glance at the pale-looking Peterson, who has lost so much weight during the trial that his blue designer suit no longer fits. "I looked briefly at Scott as I passed the table that he and his attorney were seated at; I also looked very briefly at both the Peterson and the Rocha families, and thought, 'Today, there will be justice,'" said Belmessieri, Juror No. 4.

Everyone is in the courtroom, it seems, except for Geragos and Lee Peterson.

"Where is Mr. G?" Nice wonders. "Oh my, where is Scott's dad? What the hell is going on? I keep thinking they are going to walk in any time now. It never happened."

"I did notice the absence of Mr. Geragos and Lee Peterson," Belmessieri added. "I thought how terrible it would be for his father to hear of the verdict over a telephone call or some news broadcast. I hoped that his mother and father would not suffer a heart attack or something. I remember thinking, 'God help them.'"

Guinasso maintained the routine he used throughout the trial. "I never looked at the defense or prosecution table, and made a habit of turning my head to the left as I walked by," he said. "But once I sat in my seat, I looked first at Sharon Rocha and her family and saw that she was very nervous."

Geragos' absence stunned him, too. "It was as if he had conceded the trial in my mind," he said. "If I were Scott, I could not feel very confident. I never looked at the Peterson family, and to this day I don't know why."

Lear, originally an alternate, had spent much of the trial sitting in the far reaches of the back row. When he became Juror No. 5, replacing the ousted foreman, he moved closer to the gallery. "My new seat as Juror No. 5 made me uncomfortable being so far up front," he said. "As Alternate No. 1, I was tucked back in the corner and could look out at the families and the gallery without them noticing me. In this seat, I felt I was on display. I concentrated on Scott and Marylin, the clerk, but from this angle I only got a profile of Peterson. From my old seat, I saw a frontal view of him."

Lear looks at the judge for help. "I watched Delucchi for any sign when he read the verdict to himself. No indication; he's done this before, I thought," Lear said.

Juror No. 11, Fairy Sorrell, the lone African-American juror, tips off what might come next. She smiles at Sharon Rocha, at her children and at Laci's girlfriends.

Across the room, Scott Peterson, who had flashed a macabre smile when he entered the courtroom, talks to Pat Harris at the defense table, and then retreats into his inscrutable façade. "I didn't expect him to react," Zanartu said. "He never reacted to anything during the trial. He sort of smirks. I don't think he ever expected what was coming next."

Jackie Peterson seems in pain as she sucks oxygen into her nose through a tube. Beside her is her daughter, Janey.

Judge Delucchi asks the foreman, Juror No. 6, Steve Cardosi, one of the youngest jurors, to hand the verdict forms to a bailiff. The judge opens the document, reads it and grimly hands it to his clerk Marylin Morton, beginning the legal ritual.

"We, the jury, in the above entitled cause," Morton read, "find the defendant Scott Lee Peterson guilty of the crime of murder of Laci Denise Peterson...."

Murder One!

A gasp of bittersweet joy comes from the Rocha side of the room. Then a quieter one. Outside the courtroom, cries of jubilation shoot out from the crowd of more than 1,000 people, then cheering and whooping at the news.

Sharon Rocha sobs.

For baby Conner, the clerk declares that Peterson is guilty too, but this time it is "guilty in the second degree."

Sharon Rocha sobs so hard that her son, Brent, puts his left arm around her and squeezes her shoulder. Laci's girlfriends are also in tears.

Peterson and his clan are silent.

"Once the verdict of Murder One was read for the killing of Laci Peterson, I heard a tremendous sigh, and then tears from Sharon Rocha and family," Belmessieri said. "This continued as Murder Two for Baby Conner was read. I felt sad watching them and said to myself that the only comfort I could provide them was being part of the judicial process and being part of the guilty verdict, and for her and her family to know that justice was done."

It is not by accident that the Rochas' response is muted. "The DA asked the family not to make any public display of emotion," Shaplen said.

District Attorney Brazelton reaches over and puts his hand on the shoulder of Modesto Police Det. Craig Grogan, the lead investigator into the double murder, as if to say that he did a good job putting the case together.

Across the room, Jackie Peterson's head slumps down and she cries. One of Geragos' young assistants sobs.

But not Scott Peterson. Convicted of two murders and now facing a possible death penalty by lethal injection, he shows no emotion. There is no scream of self-defense, no indignation, no pounding on the table declaring his innocence, just a dead, trance-like stare.

Pat Harris asks the judge to poll the jurors. One by one they agree with the verdicts. Peterson peers at the jurors as the polling unfolds.

"I was afraid my voice would crack so I concentrated on Marylin," Lear said. "When Marylin read the verdict and Sharon started sobbing, it really hit me. I was afraid I was going to start crying as some members of the jury were already doing."

"I couldn't stop crying," Nice said. "Laci and Conner won. They didn't want him to get away with this and he didn't. Now Scott's life will forever be changed. The look in his eyes was emptiness. I saw the darkness. Without John Guinasso, I'm sure I would have passed out."

Nice looks at Peterson. Pat Harris still has his arm around him. "Scott sat there, as if to say 'Oh well, they are still dead and I still have my life, plus a chance to get out.' That was the look I saw, stone cold, no remorse. Even if he hadn't done it, why was there no outburst? Or is he just incapable of showing any of that?"

Belmessieri, a Catholic like the defendant, had been looking for a sign of Peterson's guilt or innocence. "Often during the trial I prayed for some huge sign of innocence or guilt that would make it easier for us," he said. "Every night before I went to sleep I prayed for guidance and strength to do my duty."

When pressed to make momentous decisions, men and women often reach deep into their souls to find answers. "I reminded myself of the core values that I learned as a Marine—Honor, Courage, Commitment—and how they applied to the trial and my part in it," Belmessieri said. "I wanted to do nothing less than the right thing for the right reasons. There was no way that I would want to find an innocent man guilty of the murder of his wife and unborn son. It would be the greatest injustice I could ever imagine. I could never live with myself."

But he is at peace with his decision. "Of course, I also did not want to allow a guilty man to go free," Belmessieri said. "When I responded to the questions regarding my vote for guilt and my vote for death, I had no doubt then, nor do I now that I had made the right decision."

Belmessieri stares at the now convicted stone-cold killer. He found what he was seeking. "I never saw that sign of divine intervention, but I know what I saw in Scott's eyes. It was the affirmation that we had done the right thing. There was a blackness in his eyes, much like looking into the eyes of a Great White Shark. Cold, hard, and void of any emotion."

By this time, Marino has no doubts that he had reached the right decision. But Peterson once again surprises him.

"Scott still had that same empty expression on his face that he had throughout the trial," said Marino. "I only had a chance to glance at him during this time because I was also concerned about how the Petersons and Laci's family would react. I was thinking that maybe his reaction would be one of disbelief, as if, 'How could they find me guilty?' but instead it was just that same unconcerned face and that half-smile. There was more reaction to the verdict from his mother than from Scott. When we walked out of the courtroom, he was talking to Harris, as if the verdict was no big deal."

It is 1:30 p.m. The verdict has taken less than 15 minutes. Delucchi clears the courtroom of spectators and journalists before the Rocha and Peterson families could leave. The Petersons exit by a side door. When they emerge into the courtyard, they are booed and denounced as the parents of a murderer.

The Rochas leave the courtroom just as they arrived— through the front door. Sharon's eyes are red and filled with tears. They leave the building through an underground garage. Sobbing, red-faced, teary in the courtroom, once she gets into the car that is driven by Grantski, Sharon looks out the window and smiles. So does Grantski.

Just before he had dismissed the jurors, Delucchi thanks them but gives them a stern admonishment. He warns them not to discuss the verdict, and he continues the gag order over them until the sentencing phase of the trial is completed. Because of the double murder conviction, Peterson is eligible for the death penalty. That part of the murder trial would begin Nov. 30, 18 days after the conviction.

A bailiff leads the jurors down to a room on the street level where they look out at the crowd in the courtyard. The impact of their decision and their ordeal to reach their verdict strikes them in ways they never had imagined. Post-traumatic stress has begun.

"How many people make a decision in life like that?" Greg Beratlis, a Pacific Gas & Electric engineer, said. "Just coming to that decision of guilty or not guilty had us all just crying. It was such agony."

"That was a man's life," Richelle added.

"People were still crying, but it was a relief," Lear said. "There were chills up an down my spine. We still didn't know about the crowds outside. We saw some people but a very limited number. The bailiffs hustled us to the bus to the Crowne Plaza. I saw some of the crowd. I couldn't believe the numbers of bodies in the court-yard. At first, I thought they where angry but then I realized they were cheering. I really thought that was sick."

The ride, Nice recalled, was solemn, quiet. Some called their families on cell phones. She wondered why there was a police escort protecting their bus along Route 101. "Our bus comes out and we are told to make a dash," she said. "We heard all the screams, all the thank yous, but we just kept our heads down and got on the bus."

"We heard cheers outside in the plaza and laughter; it was a mess. None of us felt like celebrating, we wanted to get home to our families, whom, I think, we learned to appreciate more. I know I did, do."

"It was disgusting. We were all hurt," added Beratlis.

He fears this scene might repeat itself again when he has to vote on the death penalty. "I was hoping the whole thing would be over like tomorrow," he said. "The last thing I wanted to do was go back into that courtroom."

"I thought it was bush league," Guinasso said. "As the bus continued to the hotel, I made a startling assessment. Maybe they were cheering the process, and not because it was Scott Peterson, but simply because justice was done."

The mood at the Crowne Plaza is somber. "Once we were at the hotel, we gathered our bags from the rooms," Guinasso said. "We had to gather toiletries and other accessories. Again as we left, there were not any congratulations. We said good bye to one another, knowing that we had to go through this one more time."

For 18 days, they would return to their no longer private lives until they have to be back in court to decide on life or death for Peterson. The cocoon in which they had been sheltered is cracking open. Home, at last, the emotionally drained Nice pulls her sons to her.

"I dropped to my knees and hugged my kids and wouldn't let go," Richelle said. "I think I kind of scared them, I held on so tight. I just cried. I still had no idea what was coming next."

Scott Peterson could guess. It is already 12-0 for Murder One for Laci and 12-0 for Murder Two for Conner. In the upcoming weeks, the jurors would also feel the impact of their decisions.

"Nobody thinks about Post Traumatic Stress Disorder (PTSD) coming after a trial," said Howard Varinsky, the prosecution's jury consultant. "Marriages are affected, but nobody expects this. People will come away from a trial like this as if they had been in a battle zone. They will be very changed people. These people will become victims when they have to decide on the death of someone."

CHAPTER 2:
JURY DUTY

"They picked the most dysfunctional jury."
—Richelle Nice, Juror No 7

"I was amazed at the group that they came up with;
the jury pickers did a good job."
—Tom Marino, Juror No. 2

In Feb. 2004, more than 1,500 San Mateo County residents began receiving letters summoning them to the Redwood City Courthouse to begin the jury selection process in the murder trial of Scott Peterson.

The jury dragnet was expected to last five days, followed by the *voir dire* that would see both sides questioning each potential juror in front of a courtroom filled with reporters, spectators, family members of the victims and the accused killer. The final phase would be handled by a computer—the "Big Spin," as Judge Alfred Delucchi liked to call the electronic selection of finalists who would face a final round of challenges.

The goal was to produce 12 jurors and six alternates, the required number for a case in which the defendant could face the death penalty. Geragos had already succeeded in changing the venue from Modesto to Redwood City. The lawyer pressed for yet another venue change, probably hoping for Los Angeles, where he has his office and home, but Delucchi rejected the request.

Like so much about the Peterson trial, there was always a glitch that surfaced, even with the simple mailing out of a jury summons. This was the case for John Guinasso, the San Francisco parking lot facility supervisor who would survive this pageant to become Juror No. 8. His jury summons was sent to a Redwood City residence where his ex-wife lives, and she eventually passed it along to him. There was no mention of Scott Peterson in his summons. When he arrived at the courthouse on March 9, 2004, he filled out a lengthy juror questionnaire for an upcoming trial.

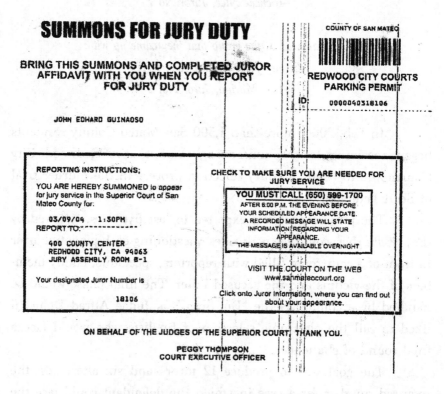

John Guinasso's summons for jury duty was faxed to him by his ex-wife.

Ironically, Guinasso had had his own domestic squabble with his ex-wife over a property issue in their divorce. His ex-wife of Sicilian descent had obtained a temporary restraining order against her Genovese spouse. What happened to him in this dispute, in which the authorities went "by the book," would play itself out in the Peterson trial, in which Guinasso became a referee of sorts. How he interpreted the courtroom rules would end up in the dismissal of three jurors, the first of whom was Justin Falconer. During deliberations, Guinasso volunteered to monitor the jury handbook, the rule book for the proceedings.

What is perhaps most surprising about Guinasso is that he sat dead center in the front of the jury box like a fullback with his arms folded over his stomach. He took few notes, but his recall of the events in the trial would be astonishing. By comparison, Greg Jackson, who was a doctor and a lawyer and who became the first foremen, filled 19 steno books. He wanted to go through his detailed notes; others would object, creating tension amongst the jurors.

Both sides hired gunslingers to help them through this process. Geragos turned to Pasadena-based Jo-Ellan Dimitrius, the glamorous blonde jury consultant who liked to wear striking St. John Knits suits in court. She helped Johnny Cochran win the O.J. Simpson case, the previous millennium's trial of the century.

The prosecution hired San Francisco-based Howard Varinsky, who had just helped federal prosecutors in New York convict Martha Stewart of lying to investigators about why she sold her ImClone stock holdings.

Both consultants would scrutinize the lineup of potential jurors, looking for little things that would be tip-offs to how a juror might vote. It was the nuances that counted, like a flash that Varinsky saw when Richelle Nice was in the jury box.

"I saw a true moment of rage when she was asked about her tattoos," said Varinsky, who had studied psychology. "It was very brief, a quick look, a blink. It's called a micro expression. She was being misjudged; it was in her eyes and she was insulted."

He wanted the Strawberry-haired single mother on the jury. "I knew from that moment that she would never vote to let Scott Peterson walk," he said. "She didn't want the world to know that she was the kind of person people thought she was."

Nice confirmed his suspicions during *voir dire*. "I know what it's like to be misjudged," she said. "How many times do you walk into a room where someone judges you as something totally different from what you really are?"

She became feisty. "Give me a good topic and I will debate you," she told the courtroom.

When Geragos asked her about judging someone who had cheated on his wife, which Peterson had done on more than one occasion, she said she would be open minded. "It does look bad," said Nice, who sat in the jury box wearing a pink tank top that revealed a fist-sized tattoo of an African mask with "Richelle" written below in an eerie script. "This case is out there; you have to be able to listen to anything. This is somebody's life."

After the jury voted to convict Peterson, it was puzzling why some of the jurors were ever picked for the panel. In Guinasso's case, on the surface he might appear sympathetic to Peterson because the law had treated him harshly during his divorce and yet the prosecution didn't veto him. It is doubtful that anyone ever imagined that his thirst for the letter of the law would have such an impact on the trial.

Varinsky never thought about the issue of the restraining order and the flap with the authorities "He was somebody who had the personal style and values I wanted," he said. "I never had a doubt about him. The restraining order was not part of his character. I knew he would vote the same way [as Nice]. I am interested in how a prospective juror will process his ultimate decision."

Another puzzling selection was a woman who accidentally ran over her young child, killing him. During *voir dire* she asked to discuss the matter in chambers. She told the judge she had killed a son, which is what Peterson was charged with doing.

Still other perplexing choices from a defense point of view were: a paramedic and fireman from Half Moon Bay whose job is to save people's lives; a PG&E engineer who coached youths in athletics; a woman who had been married to a man convicted of murder who was eventually murdered in San Quentin, where Peterson would be housed on California's Death Row.

"They picked the most dysfunctional jury," said Nice, who with her nine tattoos and bright red hair was easily the most recognizable juror.

Tom Marino, who thought his religious-based concerns about the death penalty might eliminate him, sees it differently. "I was amazed at the group that they came up with," said Marino, who was serving on his fifth jury. "The jury pickers did a good job. I was on other juries and there was always one, sometimes two, people who just won't cooperate. They already formed an opinion, which they are not supposed to do. When you deliberate, they'll just sit there and say when you all are finished discussing it, 'I'll let you know.'"

Nice's remark about a dysfunctional jury may have been right. After joining the deliberations, she complained about several jurors whom she considered whiners. Delucchi agreed with her and rebuked them for complaining about creature comforts and the trial's length.

"I remember calling two of the bailiffs and I was standing out in the hallway and I was just crying; these people were driving me fucking nuts," said Nice, whose oldest brother battled drug addiction and had served time in several California state prisons, including San Quentin. "'Do your job,' I thought. 'Do what you have to do. Quit being little sissies. Who cares if it takes us until Doomsday? This is what we signed up to do. Quit bitching.'"

And yet the panel did return a guilty verdict.

The first step in the jury selection process was getting past a 23-page jury questionnaire designed to help the attorneys weed out jurors who might be a threat to their case. Among the 116 written questions posed to prospective jurors were:

Do you have any knowledge of boats?

Do you have a bumper sticker on your car?

Do you currently own a gun?

What television and radio programs do you view or listen to on a regular basis?

Have you seen any movies in the last six months depicting the law or legal system, excluding this case?

Have you, any friends or relatives ever been involved in law enforcement (for example, FBI, DEA, Sheriff's Department, County Prosecutor's Office) or been employed by any such agency?

The questionnaire delved deeper:

Have you formed or expressed any opinions about the guilt or innocence of the defendant, Scott Peterson?

Has anyone expressed any opinion as to his guilt or innocence to you?

There were 18 questions about the personal lives of the men and women who would judge Peterson: What were their politics? What clubs and organizations had they joined?

Many of the questions focused on media outlets, especially cable news shows on Fox and CNN, where the Peterson case had become a staple. The questionnaire also looked for clues in what magazines these citizens of San Mateo County read, such as *Forbes*, *Martha Stewart* or *Cosmopolitan*. There were questions about recreational activities in an effort to learn if a juror was biased or sympathetic to Peterson, who was a golfer and who claimed to be a fisherman who was out on San Francisco Bay when his 27-year-old wife vanished. They were asked if they read *Golf Digest*, *American Angler*, *Field & Stream*, and *California Game and Fish*. Did they like to fish, boat, or golf? The questionnaire asked about pets. Laci was supposed to be walking McKenzie, the family's golden retriever, when she disappeared.

No one should ignore the impact of a successful TV show on our popular culture. There were *CSI*-type questions, possibly formulated because of the success of CBS' forensic crime drama that always got its killer by using high-tech forensics. Perhaps this popular show would affect the jury's perception of a circumstantial case in which there was a minuscule amount of DNA evidence. Did a potential juror trust DNA, fingerprints, hair and fiber analysis?

In Peterson's case, the clues were elusive. The case against the accused killer was entirely circumstantial, unlike a direct evidentiary case in which someone witnesses a murder, the body is found at the scene of the crime, and the killer is holding a gun or a knife or some instrument of death. Did a potential juror have "any attitudes or beliefs that would prevent you from relying on circumstantial evidence in a murder case?" the questionnaire asked.

It was not surprising that the questionnaire focused on pretrial publicity. There were 16 questions about the media. Did a potential juror "know, or have you read, seen, or heard anything about this case?" Did a prospective juror watch USA Network's TV movie *The Perfect Husband: The Laci Peterson Story*, whose star, Dean Cain, bore an eerie resemblance to the defendant? Was a potential juror in the case a Peterson junkie who obsessively followed the murder case in newspapers or online?

Another key question was about the consequence of a guilty verdict: "Do you have any moral, religious, or philosophical opposition to the death penalty so strong that you would be unable to impose the death penalty regardless of the facts?" Tom Marino, the devout Catholic who made the jury, had his concerns, which were assuaged by his parish priest.

A potential juror could get out of serving his or her civic duty due to financial hardships. The case was expected to last six months.

Some worked for companies that wouldn't pay them for that period. Others would be unable to pick up their children from daycare. "I don't expect you to go bankrupt serving on this case," Delucchi told the assembled jurors.

Despite the hurdles, Delucchi remained optimistic that he would get a jury. But a chorus of legal naysayers were worried. In the Peterson case, 940 were dismissed for cause—principally for financial or health reasons. Another 30 were dropped by peremptory challenges. Either side could terminate a potential juror for no reason at all. The "Big Spin," which would take place on May 27, would have 76 players, out of which 12 jurors and six alternates would be empanelled.

The process could be exhausting. Geragos employed investigators who were relentless in finding potential troublemakers. One woman had allegedly bragged on a bus trip to Reno, Nev., that the fertilizer salesman "was going to get what was due to him." Geragos labeled her a "stealth juror," which became one of his favorite terms. She was excluded. Geragos exposed a 33-year-old psychology student when he revealed in court that she told a chat room that she could beat the questionnaire. This "stealth juror" also failed to disclose that she had obtained a restraining order against her second husband because he had "threatened to murder her."

Telling the truth was a prerequisite. The potential juror who revealed she accidentally ran over her young son made the cut, but she might well have been excluded because attorneys on either side might think her family tragedy might cloud her judgment because a child, Conner, was also a victim in this case.

Julie Zanartu, who was selected for the panel, was surprised when she saw media cameras in front of the courtroom. "When we went in I recognized Mark Geragos right away because he's always on TV," she said. "I didn't know who the Modesto prosecutors were. Geragos makes sure that everyone sees him. I couldn't see Scott because I was in the back. When they all said 'good morning,' they had to make a big deal out of it. Then I saw Scott. I had been joking with people before I went. They said, 'I bet you'll be on that jury pool.' My husband even said, 'Be careful what you wish for.' Sure enough it was. I feel weird going to jury duty anyway. I get butterflies."

She filled out the questionnaire and revealed that her first husband had served time in San Quentin for murder and that he had been murdered in prison. It happened over 20 years ago when she was a teenager. When she came in for *voir dire*, the attorneys embarrassed her with questions about this part of her life. "They asked me in front of the media and I answered," she said. "Then the prosecution started asking more details. I said, 'I know the details but I'm not going to tell you.' The prosecution kept saying they have to know. I looked to the judge for some help. He said, 'How about going to chambers. I understand you wouldn't want to talk about this in a room full of media.' It hadn't dawned on me that there was a room full of media."

She was nervous and uncomfortable in the judge's chambers. "When we got back there they kept asking me questions," Zanartu said. "They asked me about other things too, like if I knew any police officers. I remember Mark Geragos had to sit right next to me. We were facing the judge. Scott was there too. Every single time we went in chambers Scott would be in there. He would stand behind. He didn't say anything."

The "Big Spin" at the end of May confirmed Delucchi's confidence in the process. Within a morning he had his jury of 12—six men and six women. On June 1, 12 original jurors took the box:

• Juror No. 1 was **Greg Beratlis**, a PG&E engineer from Belmont who coaches youth sports on weekends.

• Juror No. 2 was **Thomas Marino**, a retired postman from San Carlos. Like Peterson, he was a golfer.

• Juror No. 3 was **Lorena Gonzalez,** a social services worker from Redwood City and the only Hispanic on the jury.

• Juror No. 4 was **Michael Belmessieri,** a Marine Vietnam era veteran. He lives in South San Francisco and works as a project manager for a major manufacturer. He once served as a police officer in the Northern California city of Colma.

• Juror No. 5, the first of three who would sit in this seat, was **Justin Falconer,** a disabled airport security screener and also a single parent.

• Juror No. 6 was **Steve Cardosi,** a firefighter and paramedic who aspired to be a captain or chief in the seaside town of Half Moon Bay, Calif. He would eventually become the final foreman of the jury when the first foreman was dismissed.

• Juror No. 7 was **Frances Gorman,** a Filipina and the only Asian, who works for PG&E as an auditor and lives in Foster City.

• Juror No. 8 was **John Guinasso,** a Teamster who works as a supervisor and field auditor for San Francisco Parking Garage Inc. Guinasso, who lives in Pacifica, polices other employees, making sure they don't embezzle cash from parking lot revenues from Bay Area venues, including the lots near AT&T Park, the home of the San Francisco Giants.

• Juror No. 9 was **Julie Zanartu,** a clinical trial inspector at the biotech giant Genentech. She lives in South San Francisco. She has been happily married for over 16 years.

• Juror No. 10 was Pacifica homemaker **Mary Mylett.** During *voir dire,* she asked to speak to the judge in chambers about a family tragedy. This would eventually create some of the tensest moments of the deliberations when Mylett broke down in front of the jurors when she revealed what she had suffered.

• Juror No. 11 was **Fairy Sorrell,** the only African American juror, who works as an accountant and lives in Daly City.

• Juror No. 12 was **Kristy Lamore,** a former social worker from affluent Menlo Park who once handled child abuse cases and

CASE NO. SC 55500A

PEOPLE VS. SCOTT PETERSON

DATE TO RETURN:_____MAY 2 7 2004_____ TIME:___9:30___

OUTSIDE COURTROOM 2M (2ND FLOOR)
400 COUNTY CENTER
REDWOOD CITY, CA 94063

HON. ALFRED A DELUCCHI, DEPT. 42
650-363-4457

JUROR NO.____18106____

John Guinasso, Juror No. 8, was told to return on May 27 for the "Big Spin."

who was critical of the police who lacked a commitment to stop these crimes. She was also a golfer.

Usually, alternates are like a vice president of the United States. They sit and wait for a call that rarely comes. But as the trial unfolded, the six alternates—three men and three women—would become critical. Three of the alternates would replace dismissed jurors and decide Scott Peterson's fate. At the outset of the trial, the following six alternates took their seats in the box:

• Alternate No. 1 was **Greg Jackson**, who would replace Justin Falconer, the first Juror No. 5. Jackson, a doctor and a lawyer, was easily the best-educated member. He worked for a high-tech firm, Celera Genomics, in South San Francisco. The media nick-named him "Doctor-Lawyer" because of his dual career. Because of his legal training, he was selected as foreman, but he would eventually ask to be dismissed from the panel after a heated dispute with his colleagues.

• Alternate No. 2 was **Richelle Nice**, a single mother of four who lived in East Palo Alto. Flamboyant, vulnerable and weepy, she began corresponding with Peterson at San Quentin after the trial.

• Alternate No. 3 was **Dennis Lear**, a retired United Airlines mechanic whose son-in-law worked for Laci and Scott Peterson in the San Luis Obispo restaurant they owned called The Shack.

• Alternate No. 4 was **Debbie Germanis**, whose nickname was Shannon.

• Alternate No. 5, **Sharon McNeal**, took the nickname "Jazz." After the trial ended she was the only one who remained in the sheriff's van and didn't attend the jury press conference.

• Alternate No. 6 was **Michael Church**, a British-born San Mateo County employee.

Jury consultant Varinsky explained that long trials usually don't have as many highly educated jurors on a panel as shorter ones. "Their companies don't pay," he said. "The so-called doctor-lawyer is an exception to this."

Varinsky said there is a myth that nobody wants an attorney on a panel. The doctor-lawyer (Jackson) was a highly desirable juror for the prosecution. "He was upper middle class," he said. "There was a lot of discussion about DNA in the O.J. Simpson trial. He would keep it straight. Not putting a lawyer on a jury is a myth. If he was a criminal defense lawyer or a legal aid lawyer, that would have been different. He was an executive at a biotech firm and had a very nice house. People like that don't walk murderers."

He said the media, because of its inexperience in the jury selection process, often misjudges what they see on a panel. "The media see stereotypes," he said. "I don't see stereotypes. I burrow deeper and deeper. The prosecution can't make a mistake in a murder case like this one. You need it to be 12-zip. All the defense needs is one juror and it can hang the jury."

Varinsky was confident he would be on the winning side because of his "burrowing" tactics, in which he looked for the keys to how the jury would vote. "I was certain at the end of the trial it would be 12-zip," he said.

Scott Peterson lived in Modesto in the farm-rich San Joaquin Valley, where he sold his fertilizer. But San Mateo County residents inherited the Peterson case when Stanislaus County Judge Al Girolami ruled on Jan. 7, 2004, that the jury pool in Modesto was too tainted, and the fertilizer salesman could not get a fair trial there. There was the chance that some potential jurors might have been members of numerous search parties that combed the country-side for the missing mother-to-be or distributed missing persons posters throughout the Central Valley. The hunt for Laci over-whelmed the community that responded with an outpouring of emo-tion with candlelight vigils and even a trip to Los Angeles to search for Laci. Judge Delucchi knew they would have to see a lot of can-didates before seating the jury.

Varinsky said that a jury is rarely a cross-section of the com-munity. "That is the ideal," he said. But in some ways, the idiosyncratic jury may have been representative of the Bay Area, known to be more open and liberal than the rest of the nation. Nevertheless, many of the jurors still wonder why they were selected.

Marino thought the odds were against him serving. "There were two cases being selected at the same time," he said. "My first thought was one of hoping to get the Peterson trial because I knew or was told by someone that the Peterson jury pool would be so large that my chances of being picked were much less. I never thought in my wildest dreams I would end up serving on this trial. During *voir dire*, Geragos put him at ease when he sat in the jury box. "I felt very comfortable and found him very likable," he said. "He didn't make it seem like this case was a death murder trial, just like a run of the mill trial. No high pressure."

Dennis Lear didn't think he would make the final cut because his son-in-law had worked with Laci for about six weeks at the The Shack, the Petersons' San Luis Obispo, Calif., restaurant.

Laci trained him and he wound up buying the restaurant. "I thought, 'No way they could choose me as my future son-in-law knew the Petersons for a short while.' I had the easy out," he said. He didn't. "I calculated that no way Mr. G will let this ride. I wasn't real nervous when Mr. G started to question me, but as he continued to ask questions I could see my life for the next six months flying away," Lear said. "When he finished and walked over to Peterson and Harris and had a short meeting and I saw their heads agreeing, I was about to fall out of my chair. I'm thinking, 'no way.' All of a sudden Delucchi's saying, 'he's good,' It's like living in slow motion. This can't be happening!"

But it was, and he began to panic on his drive back to his home. "I'm thinking, 'If I can get to Mexico, they will never find me.' This was like going back to work for $15 dollars a day, and you got to buy your own lunch!"

* * *

Richelle Nice was sitting in the house in East Palo Alto that she shared with her mother, Rachel Cosio, when she got her summons. She, too, didn't think she would ever be a juror on the Peterson trial or any other.

Nice might have been able to avoid jury duty entirely because of financial hardship. She was living on a poverty income and her employer, the Stanford Credit Union, wasn't going to pay for jury duty. She probably would have gotten out of jury duty, if she asked to be dismissed.

"I didn't file for hardship because I really didn't think I would be picked," she said. "But I hadn't served on a jury before, so why not do my duty?"

Nice made it past the questionnaire and into *voir dire*. It was a curious process for her.

"I went to the bailiff at the door and said, 'Is this for Scott

Peterson?' He just looked at me and said, 'I don't know, just go have a seat.'"

When she entered the courtroom, her suspicions were confirmed. "The first person I saw was Mr. G," she said. "My heart fell to my feet. Then I saw Scott. 'Oh shit, this is it,' I thought. I had never been through this before, and this was my first case."

Nice was chewing gum when she entered the second-floor courtroom. "That's when I got labeled by the media as the gum chewing mother of four boys," she said.

Delucchi, the self-effacing judge who was revered by the jurors, told the potential panelists: "There are no right or wrong answers. I just need to ask to see if you would be a suitable juror."

Nice's mind was racing. "I thought Judge D was going to excuse me because my job wasn't going to pay me. Then Mr. G said he objected because I didn't file for a hardship so I shouldn't have to go through this. They went back and forth for a minute. Judge D asked me if my family would help me. I said they would have to, if I get picked."

A barrage of questions from Geragos and the prosecution followed. They asked about her brother who had been convicted on drug charges and sent to San Quentin. They also asked about her mother.

"Both sides seemed to focus on my mother being a drug counselor, and my brother being in the prison system," she said. "One of the questions was about whether or not we had said anything about the case."

Richelle and her mother had discussed the case. "I had said it didn't look good for him," she admitted. "They asked me about that, and I said it didn't look good because it didn't."

Nice figured she would be dropped. She had been chewing gum, which is often considered an insult to the judge. She was the sister of an ex-con and also a potential hardship case. "I figured I was out of there," she said. "But we were told to come back another day. This would be the day the jury and alternates get picked."

At the "Big Spin," she still thought it was unlikely she'd be picked, but her number was called.

"Holy shit, I'm an alternate," she said.

The excitement blurred her memory for a moment. Nice had to be back in court June 1, a date she wouldn't forget. It was her brother's birthday.

* * *

Like so many of the jurors, Greg Beratlis never even thought of the Peterson trial when he got his jury summons. He had been getting jury summonses routinely every few years. "I thought it was going to be a typical drunk driving trial," he said. But he began to get an idea of what was unfolding when he saw the media mob outside the courthouse. "It didn't click at first," he said.

When he went upstairs, he got his first clue. He saw Geragos and then Peterson in the courtroom. "I thought, 'oh my, this is the Scott Peterson case,'" the engineer said.

Beratlis, who had not followed the trial, didn't know the prosecution was from Modesto and had little impression about Geragos. Oddly, he felt a kinship to Peterson, whose confidence and bravado in the courtroom struck him profoundly. Under the wrong set of circumstances, "This could have been me," he said. "He was being tried by the media. That was unfair. He seemed to be saying, 'Hear me out before you judge me.'"

Looking back on the process, Beratlis thought some of the queries on the questionnaire were "strange," like did he have bumper stickers on his car or had he served in the military. Regarding questions about his family, his mother had been a victim of a crime the previous year and his stepfather had been attacked and beaten by two unknown male assailants. But his brother had been arrested for domestic violence and was convicted and served time for his behavior. Maybe this would be a red flag for the prosecution or the defense?

Dr. Joseph Rice, a jury consultant who helped pick the jury in the O.J. Simpson civil case for the estate of Nicole Brown Simpson, said Beratlis was more likely pro-prosecution. "Individuals who have had first-hand experience with violence or victimization tend to be more pro-prosecution," he said. Also, a football coach would tend to believe in rules and teamwork.

When he faced Geragos during *voir dire*, Beratlis was nervous. He thought it was like being in the NFL draft.

"It felt like I was on trial," Beratlis said.

The garrulous defense attorney began asking him questions like what if he didn't mount a defense after the prosecution rested its case? Could he find his client innocent?

Beratlis said he could. "Why would he have to defend anything because the defense doesn't have to prove anything," he recalled thinking.

Beratlis made it.

Judge Delucchi had his jury, or so he thought. Suddenly, the person sitting in the No. 9 seat announced that he had a letter stating that his employer wouldn't pay him. Delucchi dismissed the man and told the bailiffs to bring back the potential jurors who were already heading out the door. He told Julie Zanartu, Alternate No. 1, to take the No. 9 chair and chose a new alternate: Greg Jackson, who was heading out of the courtroom with a bunch of others who figured they had escaped service.

Jackson's presence on the jury would become one of the most divisive elements of the trial. His role as foreman would threaten the outcome of the trial and could become grounds in Peterson's appeal for a new trial.

For Zanartu, it was surreal. "The weird part was sitting down and they said they were satisfied with this jury," she said. "I thought, 'no, you can't be.'"

* * *

When Mike Belmessieri got his jury summons, his wife Annette immediately said, "It's probably about the Peterson trial." The Marine tanker laughed.

"There are lots of trials in San Mateo County, and even if it is that trial it is going to be a waste of my time," he said. "I've worked as a police officer and have a degree in criminal justice. There is no way that I'll end up sitting as a juror on any criminal trial."

He remained confident as *voir dire* started that he would be dropped. "I knew that I was going to be excused, so I felt comfortable in knowing that I would only be in the courtroom on this matter for a very brief time," he said. "I was relaxed and just taking in the moment. I was attempting to have some fun with a situation that I did not want to be in."

At the "Big Spin," as he took the seat for Juror No. 4, he still thought he would be exiting any minute. "When I did sit down I was still waiting to hear that I was being dismissed," he said. "When Judge Delucchi said that we were the jury I thought, 'What in the heck am I doing here? They've made a mistake.'"

Belmessieri didn't want the responsibility of serving as a juror in a double murder trial, but then his Marine Corps training struck him. "Once I accepted the fact that I wasn't going anywhere, and that I was a Peterson juror," he said, "I swore to God that I would do all I could to do my duty in a professional and honorable manner."

But the fate of Scott Peterson wasn't on him. It was on the prosecution. "The state would have to prove to me that Scott Peterson, a man whom I viewed as an innocent at that time, was guilty beyond any reasonable doubt of having murdered his wife Laci and unborn child Conner," he said.

* * *

Before he was selected, parking lot facility supervisor John Guinasso, who lives in Pacifica, was worried about finances and whether his Chevy Blazer would overheat during the drive to the courthouse. "I left there stunned wondering how I was going to balance work with jury duty, and how I could depend on my old truck making it there on time," he said.

Once he knew he was a juror he told his boss that he was on a six-month trial.

"He told me he knew I would be selected because of my honesty," he said. "He told me in no uncertain words that, 'John, you are too honest for your own good. Look back on the restraining order violation, you told the truth and it came back to haunt you.' I listened to him, and thought to myself that I have to live with me, and that I would do that without looking over my shoulder or carrying any false burdens."

SUPERIOR COURT OF CALIFORNIA
COUNTY OF SAN MATEO

To whom it may concern:

This will serve to certify that

Name:_____

Having been duly summoned to serve as a Trial Juror, appeared as ordered by the Superior court of the County of San Mateo on: MAY 2 7 2004 THROUGH OCTOBER / NOVEMBER 2004

monday - THURSday 9:00 am - 4:30 pm

_____
Jury Commissioner

On May 27 the jurors were told that their jury duty could extend until Oct. or Nov. 2004 every week from Monday through Thursday. However, they actually served until Dec. 13.

CHAPTER 3:
THE ALL-AMERICAN BOY

"I am not sure what a killer looks like, but I didn't think
he had the look. He was the All-American boy."
—Mike Belmessieri, Juror No. 4

On June 1, 2004, the first day of the Peterson trial, Greg
Beratlis walked into Judge Alfred Delucchi's second floor courtroom
and thought about the first time he saw Peterson in the courtroom
during jury selection.

"Scott looked at the crowd, and he was cool," Beratlis said.
"This is a trial about his life and this was a confident man who conveyed the message that he had done no wrong."

Despite believing that Peterson had already been convicted
in the press, Beratlis kept his mind open as he prepared to hear the
opening statements. "I thought, everybody wants to hang this guy,"
he said, "Well, prove it to me."

Beratlis is athletic, dark and handsome, like Peterson. But
there was something about Peterson's situation that hit Beratlis hard.
What if he had been wrongly accused? He would want to be judged
fairly. "That could be me on stand," he said. "Me."

What struck Beratlis the most about Peterson, however, was
that he didn't look like a criminal, let alone a killer. There were no
tattoos, no pock-marked face, no sloppy clothes or dirty nails. The
clean-cut Peterson just didn't look the part.

Looks didn't impress Tom Marino, the soft-spoken postman who had more experience on juries. A juror had to dig deeper for the truth. "I have seen that even if a guy is innocent but had tattoos and scraggly hair, people would jump up and say, 'Look at him, he did it,'" Marino said. "I sure would hate to be on trial and have a jury that just didn't like the way I looked say, 'Oh, look at him, he's smug, he's this, he's that, he's guilty.'"

Richelle Nice agreed that Peterson was a looker, not a villain. "Scott is a very handsome guy," she said. "He looked like a nice young man who had gotten himself into a mess; the boy next door, but not a killer."

But there was something troubling her. The others, too, would soon agree. "It's something about those eyes, those dark, deep eyes," she said. "It's scary, it's eerie. It's just emptiness all the way back, like there is nothing. Like it is just empty there; he's dead inside. Nothing."

Belmessieri, who commanded an M67 flame thrower tank and another one with a cannon, said Peterson didn't fit the mold of a man who would kill his wife and unborn son. "I am not sure what a killer looks like, but I didn't think he had the look," he said. "He was the All-American boy. I have a son and I thought about what it must be like for his parents to be going through these times. Scott was sitting there and he was smiling and seemed like a real personable kid."

But by the conclusion of the trial and after weighing all the evidence, Belmessieri had another impression of Peterson and it was chilling. "He was a killer," the Marine said. "You could look into those eyes and know he was evil."

"Usually when you see these kinds of things, it's some grubby looking guy who's been beating on his wife for the last three or four years," Dennis Lear said. "You think there's a good chance he's guilty. But Peterson, this was a young, good-looking kid. He had everything going for him. Why would he murder his wife? It didn't make sense."

Peterson's looks gave him an edge. "If anything maybe that puts that doubt in your mind," he said. "Laci was a good-looking girl and he's an All-American boy. So that maybe puts that doubt that maybe it was somebody from the outside, maybe she was thrown in the van. They had a baby on the way. This was a young, good-looking kid. It just didn't make a lot of sense."

John Guinasso's first impression of Peterson was positive. "As we sat there for a couple of minutes before Mr. Distaso was ready to give his opening statements, I thought, 'Why are you here?'" he said. "He was dressed dapperly in a suit and tie, and looked like he was dressed for work in the financial district. He was medium built with a little bit of color, with every strand of hair combed to perfection."

Anyone who plays golf long enough believes that you can tell more about the character of a man or a woman by playing a round than years of socializing at dinners and lunches. If true, Peterson's involvement in the disappearance of his pregnant wife Laci seems to be an anomaly. He was the quintessential boy next door who grew up in one of the most exclusive places in the United States, Rancho Santa Fe, Calif., in the cool and green mountains above San Diego. It was a rich kid's *Mayberry, RFD* with Scott playing Opie with a Ping putter.

The University of San Diego High School sits on a scenic bluff overlooking the Pacific Ocean and Mission Valley that rolls out to the sea. It's a school of privilege, a private co-ed Catholic institution just across the street from its big brother, the even more picturesque University of San Diego. There are about 1,400 students at the exclusive private school. Pretty, blonde coeds walk leisurely aside buffed athletes through a campus replete with spacious athletic fields and parking lots. It was during his four years here from 1986 to 1990 that Scott Peterson began to mature into manhood.

Peterson was a member of the school's powerful golf team that included such stars as PGA Tour star Phil Mickelson and Christy Erb, who went on to play on the LPGA tour. Peterson was selected as one of two alternates for the 1990 U.S. Junior Amateur Championships during the summer of his graduation and just before heading to Arizona State University (ASU) in Tempe.

Mickelson, one of the top players on the PGA tour who graduated two years ahead of Peterson at USDHS and was a teammate of his at Arizona State, has said that he could not recall much about Peterson.

As a student, Peterson was selected as a three-time member of the *San Diego Tribune's* All Academic Team for boy and girl golfers in 1988, 1989 and 1990. He was a solid B student. Smart, but not brilliant.

One woman who had a crush on him and even asked him out to the senior prom remembers him as the "preppy guy on campus. Probably the worst thing I could say about him is he knew he was good looking. He had a little bit of arrogance about him." Like the jurors, she noticed something strange about his eyes. "It's like he's looking through you instead of really connecting with you as a person. It's like I'm talking to you but I'm not interested. My mind is elsewhere."

"He was a gentleman," said one of his classmates, who graduated two years before Peterson and played on the golf team with him. "He didn't cheat; he walked around with a bit of confidence; he wasn't a recluse; he didn't seem down or shy. He seemed pretty normal."

And yet, the people who competed against Peterson say he remains a mystery. He was a man who seemed to have been bathed in beige. The only hint of life in the flash lane was his red Mazda Miata convertible. But he didn't floor it. "He drove fine," said a member of the golf team who carpooled with Peterson. "He didn't drive crazy."

Peterson fit in so well that nothing much stood out about him, besides his Miata. He was a young man who left a soft footprint in the sand. He would shoot in his high 30s or low 40s for the nine-hole game high school golfers played in competition. "He wasn't great, but it was okay," said a teammate who became a golf pro in the south. "He was a quiet guy. He kept to himself."

The pro said Peterson and his family lived the All-American life in Rancho Santa Fe. "He was wealthy or at least Rancho Santa Fe was a stereotypically wealthy town," the golf pro said. "He always had good equipment."

News that Peterson was embroiled in the disappearance of his pregnant wife stunned him. Just like the jurors said when they first saw the boy next door in court, it was a surprise. "I would have never imagined it, not at all," he said.

Peterson knew the etiquette of golf, his former teammates say. He didn't throw his clubs or make inappropriate comments on the links, something that might hint at more violent behavior. "He didn't have a temper or was weird," the student golfer said. "He was polite and friendly and not a cutup. He was just a kid."

Peterson's family was generous to their son's teammates. They took members of the team to play golf at their private course, the Rancho Santa Fe Country Club. At the end of one year, the Petersons held a team party at their home.

"He was a really nice guy," one former teammate said, "and he was a good player, but we had a great team with players like Phil Mickelson. He wasn't in that league."

Peterson went off to Arizona State where Mickelson was also attending. ASU's team was a national champion, but Peterson was not good enough to make the traveling team of five top players. "He was friendly, but not a jokester or a troublemaker," said an ASU teammate. "It was not in his personality to cheat. I am surprised about what happened to him. He was not that kind of kid; he wasn't weird or anti-social. He knew the rules, and he played by them."

A golf mom, who had a child play with Peterson in high school, recalled that he was especially polite for his age and not insecure. "He was very confident with himself," she said. "He was very respectful, but he didn't have a lot of personality."

As she observed, Peterson didn't belittle himself or others on the team if he or they flubbed a shot. "He was someone who could hold his temper and you only learn that in competition," she says. "He worked hard at his game and didn't cut up."

At ASU, Peterson abruptly left the golf team under a cloud and university officials won't discuss why. Following his departure from ASU in 1991, Peterson moved back to the Rancho Santa Fe area and lived at Reflections, a garden apartment complex on Capewood Lane, north of San Diego. Peterson lived in a two-bedroom unit that would cost about $1,500 today at the New England Village-style rental.

Not surprisingly, Peterson lived close to a golf course, Carmel Mountain Ranch Country Club, a semi-private golf club. In 1992 and 1993, Peterson attended Cuesta College in San Luis Obispo, where he played on the golf team. Once again, no one there recalls him. In 1994, Peterson was back in Rancho Santa Fe, living in a four-bedroom house, which cost his parents $550,000, according to real estate records. It, too, was a short drive to the Rancho Santa Fe Country Club. After taking some time off, he returned to college in the spring of 1994, attending Cal Polytechnic San Luis Obispo.

It was there he met Laci Rocha. They were an idyllic couple. While still attending college, they bought The Shack, a burger and bun sports bar that had become a student hangout. Ironically, Juror Dennis Lear's son-in-law, Fabrizio Paolozzi, bought the restaurant from Peterson (and some interim owners) and Laci trained him to cook hamburgers, a point Lear dutifully disclosed on his jury questionnaire. His son-in-law recalled Laci and Scott as "nice college kids."

Peterson was also a smooth operator when it came to women. When Laci's mother, Sharon, came to San Luis Obispo to meet him for the first time, Peterson began one of his smarmy seductions at the Pacific Café in Morro Bay, where he worked. He had already begun to pitch his fibs. "It's a pleasure to meet you Mrs. Rocha," he said, sounding like Eddie Haskell from *Leave It to Beaver*. "Ma'am, I have your favorite table waiting for you."

Waiting on the table were a dozen white roses for Sharon and a dozen red roses for Laci.

Scott and Laci soon became more serious. They moved into a one-bedroom and were married on Aug. 9, 1997, at the Sycamore Mineral Springs Resort in Avila Beach. There were 150 guests. They honeymooned in Tahiti. But the honeymoon would soon be over and foreshadow the double life that Peterson led.

Janet Ilse, a woman Peterson had been seeing for several months, made a surprise visit and upon seeing Scott in bed with his wife accused the rogue of cheating on her. Later that night at a dinner, Laci could be heard yelling at Peterson in the bathroom.

Just before graduating Cal Poly in 1998 with a degree in agribusiness, Scott met a woman named Katy Hansen in a class. At the graduation, she kissed him on his lips and put a Hawaiian lei around his neck, just before she saw he was with Laci. Hansen dropped him, only to get a dozen pink roses from Peterson and a note, according to media reports, which read, "No job, no home."

Upon his graduation, the Petersons remained in San Luis Obispo and ran The Shack. Laci later would take cooking classes in France. The couple sold The Shack on May 10, 2000, and moved to Modesto where they would briefly live with Laci's mother and her companion, Ron Grantski.

In Oct. 2000, Scott embarked on a career as a fertilizer salesman for Tradecorp, a subsidiary of a Spanish conglomerate. He began selling fertilizer in California and Arizona. Laci would take a job at Southern Wine & Spirits. They would buy their first and only ranch style home on Oct. 4, 2000, at 523 Covena Ave. in Modesto. It was a tidy home in a middle class residential neighborhood, not far from a park. The only drawback to the park was it was frequented by transients and drifters. But it was there that Scott and Laci began developing their life together, as an All-American couple.

Or were they? Richelle Nice became troubled as the image of Scott Peterson was shattered. "We all thought he was the perfect All-American family man," she said. "Now, we were faced with there is no All-American Family."

Mike Belmessieri recalls one of Peterson's fertilizer clients who testified during the penalty phase that Scott is "a heckuva nice guy."

But Belmessieri saw a troubling pattern emerge as the defense witness continued his remarks. "Scott Peterson is a wonderful guy," the client said. "He knows what he wants, puts the plan together and the key word, he executes it."

Belmessieri thought to himself, "That's the same Scott Peterson I know who had been sitting in this trial for six months. He knows what he wants, he puts a plan together, and he executes it."

CHAPTER 4:
THE GIRL NEXT DOOR

"What couldn't you like about Laci?
Great smile, attractive, vivacious, an outgoing person.
They looked like the perfect young couple."
—Julie Zanartu, Juror No. 9

"Look at that smile and how she just seems so full of life.
That's what brought people in—that smile, that look in her eyes."
—Richelle Nice, Juror No. 7

It was her smile.

There were just two color photos on Laci's missing persons poster. One was a close up of a beaming young woman with brown eyes and dark brown hair. The other showed Laci in a dark red maternity dress and wearing a chain necklace. She sat with her hands folded in a classic Madonna-like pose, and here, too, her smile beamed with joy.

This was a young woman who desperately wanted to be a mother and had difficulty getting pregnant. It should have been a time for happiness. But the words above the photos were chilling: "Missing, $500,000 Reward, Laci (Rocha) Peterson."

At the time Laci disappeared, she was 27 years old and only five-feet, one-inch high, the poster said. She was eight months pregnant and last seen on Dec. 24, 2002, at 9:30 a.m.

The smiles and her dimples and the sparkle in her eyes were filled with life. And they would become iconic, making this substitute teacher the Mona Lisa of Modesto, not merely in her hometown, but also across the country. She was the girl next door, the kind of hard working young woman parents would want their sons to marry. Strangers hunted for her; others showed up for candlelight vigils to pray for her return, and, by the time the trial ended, Modesto had become a shrine to her. Even today, her grave is frequently covered with flowers and little teddy bears for her dead son.

"What couldn't you like about Laci?" asked Julie Zanartu, Juror No. 9. "Great smile, attractive, vivacious, an outgoing person. They looked like the perfect young couple."

Laci became a pop cultural figure who connected with the jury and the public, too. There was a connection to her whether you lived in Modesto or Las Vegas or New York. She was likeable, and this magical quality would play a key role with the jurors as the trial progressed.

"Look at that smile and how she just seems so full of life," Richelle Nice said. "That's what brought people in—that smile, that look in her eyes. When she became missing, I didn't follow it too much but I remember seeing some of it and thinking, 'Where is her husband and why isn't he on TV begging for her to be brought home?' My heart just felt so sad for her and her family, Scott included."

But then the news surfaced that Peterson had cheated on his wife with Amber Frey.

"When Amber came out, I remember thinking this doesn't look good for him," Nice said. "Now, he has a girlfriend and he isn't anywhere asking for his wife's safe return, that didn't seem right. But being a cheater does not make you a killer! So maybe he had nothing to do with it. Could Amber have done it? Seeing her, I thought, no way she could have done that or had a part in it. I just think she is a dumb girl who wants so badly to have a man in her life, but at what cost?"

It was Scott who told authorities that he had last seen Laci on Christmas Eve at 9:30 a.m., getting ready to go out for a walk. She was wearing black pants and a white top, he said. The poster of the smiling substitute teacher haunted the nation.

"That smile was filled with life," said Mike Belmessieri. "Unbelievable. It was that emotional for me, I think for all of us. It was just so sad. You look at this woman and here's a beautiful young girl and the smile. There's life. There's greatness in this woman. There's a wonderful, warm, caring person. She had all the things people pay attention to."

Beratlis said Peterson's decision to kill his wife at Christmastime resonated with the jury and the people who searched for her. "A pregnant woman disappearing on Christmas Eve didn't help," he said. "Everybody poured their hearts into finding this woman. Later when people found that he had a mistress, or a girlfriend, or whatever Amber was, it was like a storybook. People were saying look at this drama. It had all the angles."

Scott oozed with smarmy charm, creating the perfect villain. "He's a pretty boy," Belmessieri said. "Charismatic, for the most part. Then he ends up having a girlfriend; he's carrying on a false image about how he's going to Europe and living his life. He's single; he's playing the role. And for Laci to be missing, it cut into everybody's heart. That's why it drew us in so much. You look at him and he wasn't the guy in the hooded jacket or sweatshirt in the dark. He wasn't Michael Jackson."

The saga of Laci and Scott had all the plot points of a film noir: a missing wife, a girlfriend, and the perfect villain. Each point pushed interest in the story and no one knew how it would end. "It had two things that Americans are most interested in," Belmessieri said, "mystery and sex."

Laci Rocha was born on May 4, 1975, at Doctors Medical Center, Modesto, to Sharon and Dennis Rocha, who owned a

365-acre dairy farm. Sharon and Dennis separated when she was two years old and she and her older brother Brent shuttled between their mother's home in Modesto and their dad's dairy farm.

When Laci was eight, one of her ovaries became infected and was removed, threatening her chances of bearing children. Having a child was something Scott had hoped would never occur. Witnesses testified during the trial that he was hoping the fertility treatments would fail. Gasps were heard in the courtroom when people heard the testimony.

Laci graduated Thomas Downey High School in 1993 and enrolled in California Polytechnic State University-San Luis Obispo, where she majored in ornamental horticulture. Her high school boyfriend, Kent Gain, followed her there, and went with her on her 19th birthday to get a sunflower tattoo on an ankle. But they would break up by July.

Within weeks after breaking up with Gain, Laci met Scott Peterson, who was also attending Cal Poly. She was so smitten that she heard wedding bells even before they started dating. "Mother, I have met the man I am going to marry," she declared.

"Have you dated yet?" Sharon asked.

"Not yet, but we will," her daughter responded.

Laci and Scott were married on Aug. 9, 1997, uniting the Rochas and the Petersons. But the two families were culturally different. The Petersons were country club golfers from affluent Rancho Santa Fe. In the early 1970s, Jackie bought The Put On, a dress shop in the chic seaside village of La Jolla. In 1975, Jackie and Lee formed San Diego Crating and Packing, which became a successful business. Throughout Scott and Laci's marriage, his parents would help their son out financially, even buying him a membership to Modesto's Del Rio Country Club. To pay Mark Geragos' legal fees of more than $1 million, the Peterson clan reportedly mortgaged homes and other properties.

Lee had three children from his first marriage to Mary Kamanski—Mark and Joe Peterson and Susan Peterson Caudillo.

Jackie Latham Peterson was a woman who had a string of relationships before she married Lee Peterson. She was the mother of Anne Bird and another child, both of whom she placed for adoption. Her third child born outside of marriage was later adopted by Lee Peterson. Scott is the only child born to Jackie and Lee.

Just sitting in the courtroom during the trial, the cultural clashes between the two families became more and more evident with each passing day. Lee Peterson sported golf shirts and sweaters as did other members of his family. Lee was a businessman and his family was fair skinned and light haired. The Rochas were darker and of Portuguese descent. They were dairy farmers and didn't mind having dirt under their nails, which became apparent to the jury as testimony progressed.

Belmessieri saw it and heard it in Dennis Rocha's testimony. "When Dennis came up and testified against Scott, he said, 'You always thought you were better and smarter than us.' It clicked to me. I now understood why Jackie had a problem with Laci."

The reason was simple for Belmessieri. "The Rochas are valley people and the Petersons are San Diego," he said. "It's like water and oil. One gets dirt on their hands and the other one might get a splinter. The Rochas are farm people. They are down to earth, out working the soil. Dennis Rocha, who we met later, is an average guy. He owns a water truck and a little ranch. He's a Marine Corps veteran."

Beratlis said that he and the other jurors were unaware of the class distinctions at the beginning of the trial. Despite the belief that jurors sneak peaks at the news or engage in conversations about the trial when they are out of the courthouse, it was only through their observations in court and testimony that they would learn of the clashes between the families.

"Geragos would take a piece of paper, showing it to the prosecutors and then pull it away as if teasing them with it," Beratlis said. "This would persist throughout the trial until Birgit Fladager took over for the prosecution and used the same tactic on Geragos."

The irony was that the Rochas were far more successful than the Petersons and had been so for generations. Laci and her stepsister Amy Rocha inherited thousands of dollars in jewelry from their paternal grandmother. Dennis Rocha had 600 Holsteins on his ranch. Had Laci lived, she and her siblings would have inherited several million dollars.

"As the trial unfolded I saw Laci as a woman who knew what she wanted," Beratlis said. "The pictures of the house were like making something nice and presentable, almost like out of a magazine. There were references to *Martha* [hosted by Martha Stewart] being her favorite show and the cooking books in the kitchen; the video of Laci and her friend during a pool party the summer before she died. It made you feel a little closer to what she was like. The photo that I had seen of her at the Christmas party made you wonder how Scott could be with Amber that same night. I mean, your wife is pregnant. This should be a time that you would want to be with Laci."

Beratlis had a visceral response to Peterson's wife. He could not understand how a man could destroy such a woman. "I kept saying to myself this is a pretty looking woman, there is no way Scott did this," he said. "No husband could hate his wife enough to take her and his future son's life. Just what did Laci do that was so wrong that she deserved to land up on a pile of rocks with her body eaten away? The photos of where Laci and Conner were found will be in my mind for the rest of my life."

Belmessieri was angered and haunted by the autopsy images of the headless and armless Laci Peterson and the eerie photos of the jelly-like body of Conner juxtaposed to her smiling poster and homey videos. "What went through my mind when I saw the photos of the remains of Laci and Conner?" he asked. "They were dumped in the bay as if they were garbage!"

Conner was especially troubling for Belmessieri, a father. "It is beyond my understanding why anyone would do such a thing to a defenseless gift from God," he said.

Laci looked more like a carcass than the smiling woman in her missing posters. Her ribs stuck out and the only organ remaining was her womb. Like a good mother who protects her baby while she is alive, in death Laci protected her son inside her womb from the bottom feeders of San Francisco Bay that devoured her body. "What a terrible waste," Belmessieri said. "My God, there is hardly anything left of her."

Then something hit the Vietnam era tank commander. It was like an aftershock to a man who never discusses his war experiences.

"For a brief second I felt a cold chill in my body, and I was reminded of another time I saw a human body in such a terrible state, not a photo, but the real thing," Belmessieri said. "Many years ago I saw a brother Marine killed by a fragmentation grenade. When the grenade blew up it was level and against his chest. Much like Laci there wasn't much left of that Marine. His head and arms, along with most of his body above his hips, were gone. We got a poncho and wrapped up what we could find of his remains to be later placed in a body bag. I put that vision away a long time ago. I hadn't even given the incident a thought in over 30 years. I have seen many photos of numerous murder crime scenes and suicides during my studies in homicide investigation, but I never got the feeling that I did when I saw the photo of Laci's remains."

He felt the horror of what it must have been like for the people who found the bodies of Laci and Conner. "I also looked in the direction of both the families, and Scott," he said. "I thought of how hard this must be on them. As I recall, none of them were looking at the photos. I think Jackie Peterson had her hand sort of covering her eyes."

Her son remained the iceman.

"Scott sat at the defense table, looking straight ahead, not looking at the photos," Belmessieri said. "That did not surprise me, but I was wondering what was going on in his head as the entire courtroom saw the remains of his wife and son. How could he just sit there and not completely lose it? There wasn't even what appeared to be a tear on his face. That observation had no impact on my decision of guilt, but at the time I wondered why I did not see some emotional reaction from Scott."

Life is all too often filled with the immeasurable. The jury had bonded with Laci Peterson. John Guinasso was yet another who was drawn to the murdered woman. "The Laci Peterson I envisioned during the trial was a bubbly, happy woman by all appearances," he said. "The photos we saw of her youth and adulthood all featured that beautiful smile. And during her pregnancy, she kept that inherited beauty as demonstrated by the photo of her in a red satin outfit sitting in a chair at a Christmas Party she attended without Scott."

The home video added even more. In the pictures that moved, she became real. "She liked cooking and entertaining," Guinasso said. "We saw a video of her in the kitchen with one of her girlfriends saying hi to Scott as he videotaped her while she was cooking. She was a very attractive young woman with plenty of life ahead of her. Unfortunately, her life was cut short by a monstrous act of the most intimate betrayal, murder by her husband, Scott Lee Peterson."

By comparison, the viewing of the autopsy photos had a devastating effect on Guinasso as they did for others. One moment, the courtroom was filled with visuals of Laci alive and loving and relatable. The next moment, she looked like a carcass devoured by jackals.

"Viewing the autopsy photos in the courtroom was one of mind shattering disgust," Guinasso said. "Laci, this beautiful woman, was reduced to a piece of floating debris that washes ashore in the East Bay. It was very difficult to look at. These pictures would scar my mind for eternity. I wanted to look away from the projection board, but I knew it was my civic duty to look and evaluate every piece of evidence in this trial. I had to be fair to the process."

Like the other members of the jury, Richelle Nice cracked emotionally when she saw the video. "The video just put a personality to the face we all saw and fell in love with," she said. "Seeing her alive had a great impact on me. My heart just sank into my stomach. I remember thinking how bad could it have been? It looks like a life I only dream of. How could this have happened? What happened? Who did this and why if it was Scott? You felt the love she had for him. It poured into that courtroom, with only pictures and statements."

The autopsy photos made the loss of the girl next door all too real for the jurors. Nice broke down crying as the photos were displayed on a giant screen in the courtroom. "Seeing how she was found broke my heart," she said. "I still see those photos in my head to this day. I just cried and cried when I saw them. How could any monster do this to such a beautiful person? Why? Because of an affair? I don't buy that one. She should not have been left for her mom to see her that way. None of her family, none of Scott's family, should be left with just this. It's hard to think and believe that such a beautiful woman could end up looking like that. That must have been a monster that did it, not even thinking about the outcome and what would be found."

CHAPTER 5:
THE PROSECUTION:
THE LITTLE ENGINE
THAT COULDN'T

"Ladies and gentleman, this is a common sense case."
—Senior Deputy DA Joseph 'Rick' Distaso

"Mr. Distaso's opening statement was as if he was reading out of a book."
—John Guinasso, Juror No. 8

On June 1, 2004, the San Mateo County Courthouse in Redwood City, which is normally a sleepy town in the San Francisco Bay area, came alive. Giant media trucks with their satellite dishes clogged the streets around the courthouse and a hastily built tent city arose in the cramped courtyard between the court and the other municipal buildings. Credentialed reporters and jurors passed through metal detectors along with members of the Peterson and Rocha families.

The inside of Judge Alfred Delucchi's courtroom was filled to capacity for the first day of the Peterson trial with as many as 150 people, some sitting in the aisles. Scott Peterson, in a neatly pressed beige suit, smiled at his mother Jackie and leaned over to talk to Geragos, who was sporting a grey business suit and a flashy designer tie. The prosecution was business like, quietly dressed for a Modesto workday. Sharon Rocha, Amy, Brent, and Ron Grantski took their seats on the other side. Neither side looked at each other.

Murder had divided the house of Peterson-Rocha. Every seat was filled with Modesto detectives, prosecutors, reporters, and a handful of spectators from nearby cities.

The jury of 12 and six alternates filed in for the first time at 9:15 a.m. Nine in the front row, nine in the back row.

On the first day of the trial, John Guinasso did what would become a metaphor for his role on the Peterson jury. He split away from the rest of the jurors, and instead of using the jury parking lot, he stashed his aging Blazer in a residential neighborhood and walked two and half blocks to the courthouse. It was a smart move for a loner who could make a quick getaway.

"Even though I was given a parking pass, I felt I would need to clear my mind of testimony before I ventured on with the rest of my day," he said. "I also did it to avoid any media attention being that the parking facility was very close to the courthouse."

Guinasso was nervous as the jurors and alternates met on the third floor before entering the courtroom. Jenne Carnevale, the bailiff who would become their minder throughout the trial, escorted the group down a back flight of stairs to a break room behind courtroom 2M. She asked the jurors to select an alias that they would be called during the trial. It would preserve their anonymity.

As part of the judicial process and throughout the entire trial, the jurors never knew each other's real names. It was for security. Even now, they call each other by their nicknames. As they would all learn, the trial of Scott Peterson would have a lasting impact on their lives.

Guinasso, financially strapped, thought about the monetary risks of serving on a jury, especially this one, which was expected to last about six months.

"I selected Bill, because the first thing that came to my mind was bills that would be piling up if we were ever sequestered," he said. "At this point in time, Judge Delucchi had mentioned that we would not be sequestered for this trial, but by the end, we were. I remember we all had fun selecting an alias."

They each chose a nickname on the spot:

• Greg Beratlis, Juror No. 1, took the nickname Zane.

• Tom Marino, Juror No. 2, became Mario.

• Lorena Gonzalez, Juror No. 3, selected Crystal.

• Mike Belmessieri , Juror No. 4, was Treadhead, a reference to his being a Marine tank commander.

• Justin Falconer, Juror No. 5, was Kekoa, a reference to his years of living in Hawaii.

• Steve Cardosi, Juror No. 6, chose Cap because of his career aspirations to become a fire captain.

• Frances Gorman, Juror No. 7, nicknamed herself Leilani.

• John Guinasso, Juror No. 8, was Bill.

• Julie Zanartu, Juror No. 9, was nicknamed Joe.

• Mary Mylett, Juror No. 10, picked Sean, the name of her deceased son.

• Fairy Sorrell, Juror No. 11, became Tracy.

• Kristy Lamore, Juror No. 12, had the nom de jury of Juliet.

"We had fifteen seconds to come up with a nickname that you could remember," said Dennis Lear, who would go from alternate to juror. "It was an interesting exercise with a group of strangers."

Not everybody chose a nickname on a whim or for fun. Zanartu chose her alias because of fear.

"I didn't want people to know who I was," she said. "I wanted to be invisible. I was afraid. The way people act, you don't know what they are going to do. They only gave us numbers. I didn't want anything they could even associate with me. Joe is non-gender."

The alternates also chose nicknames:

Greg Jackson, No. 1, called himself "D-Day" because he was reading a history of the Allied landings at Normandy on June 6, 1944.

Richelle Nice, No. 2, chose "Ricci," but the media called her Strawberry Shortcake, the crimson-haired cartoon character in the successful children's book series.

Dennis Lear, No. 3, chose Montara, which was the name of the town where he lived at the beginning of the trial.

Debbie Germanis, No. 4, picked Shannon.

Sharon McNeal, No. 5, who went to Costco to buy snacks for the jurors, chose Jazz.

Michael Church, No. 6, became Neo, the character from the movie, *The Matrix*.

Once Jenne Carnevale, the bailiff, had her listing of alias names, she led the group into the courtroom through the back door. They were cautioned about their conduct in the court. They would also find out that Jenne would scrutinize their every move, especially if anyone was falling asleep, which during early days of the prosecution's case would not be surprising.

Alt. # 1	Alt. # 2	Alt. # 3	# 1	# 2	# 3	# 4	# 5	# 6
D-day ↵5	Ricci	Montara	Zane	Callie Mario	Crystal	Treadhead	Kekoa	Cap
Alt. # 4	Alt. # 5	# 7	# 8	# 9	# 10	# 11	# 12	Alt. #
Shannon	Jazz	Leilani	Bill	Joe	Sean	Tracy	Juliet	Neo

The original seating chart for the jurors with the nicknames they chose for themselves.

"We were told not to make gestures or verbalize to any party in the courtroom," Guinasso said. "We could only gesture to Jenne, who would peer at us through a window situated next to Juror No. 6. She would have a pen and notepad and would chart any movements or demeanors of jurors that she thought would compromise their duty."

Guinasso would feel the long arm of the law touching him more than once during the trial. Jenne was a relentless watchdog.

"I was pulled out of line several times on the way back to the break room," he said. "The reasons were various, ranging from looking tired to being too animated with facial expressions while listening to testimony."

The burly juror was sometimes getting only a few hours sleep at night because of the graveyard shifts he worked with the parking company.

"As we entered the courtroom in single file as we did throughout the trial, I made a habit from day one to enter and turn my head immediately left and not to look at the defendant or any of the attorneys and to proceed to my chair," Guinasso said. "Each chair had a number on it corresponding to your juror number. I sat in my chair in the front row and remembered thinking that I must stick out like a sore thumb as I was wedged between two ladies. Matter of fact, I was the only male juror in the front row."

Guinasso, finally seated, began looking around the jammed courtroom. To accommodate the crowd, the court had extra chairs placed in the aisles along the walls. He glanced at the media and at the spectators who had stood in line in the early hours of the morning to get to see the trial. He then turned to the families of the Peterson and the Rocha clan and finally focused on the prosecution table and the defense table. A stack of thick binders were piled side by side and against the wall that separated the gallery from the attorneys.

And then he looked at Peterson who already had begun trying his manipulations.

"I remember Scott surveying the jury box with a smile, but noticeably, the smiles were directed more towards the women jurors," he said. "My angle of perception was very clear. I was situated with a perfect view of Scott at all times, and was only about 10 feet from him. At times I could [almost] hear dialogue between him and Mr. Geragos or Mr. Harris."

The first days of the trial were filled with opening statements in which both parties laid out their case, which was entirely circumstantial. Although such cases can often be as powerful as direct evidence cases, in the case against Peterson, there was no motive, aside from his being an adulterer and that didn't mean he was a killer. The DA didn't have a murder weapon and there was no DNA of significance. Unlike TV's *CSI*, there was no smoking gun. Moreover, Peterson had a spotless criminal record. He was the All-American boy, cold but clean.

The two men trying this case—Rick Distaso and Mark Geragos—were opposites in their professional and personal styles. Geragos is flamboyant, a bon vivant who seeks the spotlight, while Distaso is low-keyed and avoids the limelight. The defense lawyer is flash in his designer suits and ties, while the prosecutor is off the rack. During the trial, Geragos was a man about town, who was seen in the bars and cigar stores in Redwood City. At Vino Santo, the bartender at the local media hangout, recalled that the L.A. lawyer finished a bottle of single malt scotch that cost $20 a shot. At night, the mustachioed Geragos could be seen engaged in animated conversations with reporters at his hotel, the San Mateo Marriott. During breaks and lunch, he always had his cell phone clasped to his ear. He didn't walk, he swaggered to the right as if he was imitating John Wayne. The jurors often mimicked his stroll during their breaks.

By contrast, Distaso and his team avoided the prying eye of the media. They returned each night to the Marriott Towne Place Suites, a corporate hotel in Redwood City that had its own kitchen and free breakfasts. The only glimpse of the prosecution and the detectives who worked on the case was in the late afternoon when they all assembled in a guest room that had been converted to a war room to go over their case. There were no nights on the town.

Geragos was the Zephyr, and Distaso was the Little Engine That Could. The jury was not impressed as the ascetic DA unveiled his case, starting with his opening day remarks. On paper, the prosecution's case was compelling, but when it was delivered in the courtroom, it bombed. It was emotionless, as Guinasso said. It was as if Distaso and the prosecutors from Modesto had fired a shotgun at the jury, scattering ideas and theories all over the place. The impact of the DA's pitch and subsequent witnesses called to the stand not only puzzled the cackling legal analysts that covered the trial but also the jury.

"I just looked at it like this big Hollywood attorney versus these little Modesto country bumpkins," said Richelle Nice. "I'm not trying to talk bad. You've got this big LA lawyer and then these other guys."

Guinasso was typically blunt, starting with the clothes Distaso and his colleagues wore. If clothes did make the man in a world where nuances and non-verbal communication are ever so important, the DA and his team looked like losers.

"From day one, the prosecution was overmatched in several ways," Guinasso said. "First off, the prosecution's attire appeared from a catalog compared to the tailored suits that Mr. Geragos wore. The prosecution's haircuts appeared to be from a local barber shop compared to the hair dresser that was used by Mr. Geragos. The prosecution's demeanor seemed one of an intern trying to learn the ropes of the judicial process."

While some members of the jury may have considered the prosecution's opening statements humdrum, under the law prosecutors are subject to legal restrictions in their remarks. Prosecutors are not permitted to present argument when they open. They are only permitted to give a recitation of the facts that are expected to be produced at trial. They can't explain what the evidence means, how it relates to other evidence, and how it demonstrates guilt. That is only allowed in closing argument.

But the story of this trial is how the puffing Little Engine found enough steam to roll over the mountain to zoom past the city slick Zephyr and his handsome client.

Like all murder trials, the case against Scott Peterson began with an arrest. Typical of Peterson and his upscale lifestyle, the handcuffs were slapped on his wrists at one of the finest public golf courses in Southern California, maybe in all of the state. At 11:10 a.m. on April 18, 2003, Peterson was arrested at Torrey Pines. For days, Peterson had been taunting the authorities who were shadowing him, but when Peterson was apprehended, he had nearly $15,000 in cash, camping equipment, and a newly bought used Mercedes, registered to his mother. He also had the address of where Amber Frey worked.

Running is never a good sign for a defendant. California Attorney General Bill Lockyer boasted, "This is a compellingly strong case. I would call the odds slam-dunk that he is going to be convicted."

"Slam Dunk?" The top law enforcement officer in California later tried to soften his stance but his words put pressure on the prosecutors. Would the authorities in Modesto be up to the task? Or would they be trounced by media smooth Geragos?

Following the disappearance of Laci Peterson in Dec. 2002, the Modesto Police Department performed an exhaustive investigation. More than 100 cops were involved in the searches and tracked down thousands of clues. But it wasn't until March 2003 that they declared the obvious: someone murdered Laci and her unborn son. The investigation included the use of wiretaps, Global Positioning

Satellites, cadaver dogs and forensic computer technicians. But the detectives, led by Craig Grogan, Jon Buehler and Al Brocchini, felt they didn't have enough to arrest Peterson until the bodies washed up on the rocky shores of the Bay on April 13 and April 14, not far from where Peterson contended he had gone fishing on the day his wife disappeared.

The Stanislaus County prosecution was led by District Attorney James Brazelton, a tall man with his salt and pepper goatee and a steel gaze. He looked like a Civil War era officer. Attorneys in Redwood City, many of whom had been prosecutors in San Mateo County, had little regard for the Little Engine. Stanislaus County was farm country and these were farm lawyers, they believed, no match for them or the express train from Los Angeles.

From the earliest days of Laci's disappearance, Brazelton chose two senior deputies to handle the case—Distaso and Dave Harris as co-counsel. Distaso was in charge of the opening and closing for the guilt phase, and Harris would handle the penalty phase. The rail-thin Distaso had the ascetic look of an Italian Renaissance cleric. The reddish blond Harris was tweedy and ruddy with the look of a Mr. Chips. At one point in the case, Harris dipped into an evidence bag and withdrew a homemade cement anchor that Peterson had made. Harris couldn't contain his yuck factor when dust collected on his hands. The two senior deputies defined methodical, as the jurors would soon learn, so much so that some had difficulty keeping awake as the case plodded along.

Like Geragos, Distaso was graduated from Loyola Law School in Los Angeles in 1992, a decade after his principal opponent. He began his career as a lawyer in the Judge Advocate General corps of the Army. By 1996, he joined the Stanislaus County DA's office. He gained a reputation as an honest and straightforward prosecutor. He had won two murder convictions by the time he got the Peterson case in Dec. 2002. It is doubtful that either prosecutor ever envisioned the confluence of events that would turn this case into the first major trial of the new millennium.

Dave Harris, who graduated from California Western School of Law in San Diego, spent four years in San Diego and Kings countries in California before joining the Stanislaus DA's office in 1991. He handled a variety of criminal cases over the years and one capital case, in which a jury convicted the defendant but gave him life without the possibility of parole.

For most of the trial he handled his witnesses in an unassuming fashion until his talents emerged during the cross-examination of one of Geragos' chief medical witnesses, Dr. Charles March, who imploded on the stand.

When Distaso began his opening statements, he made it very clear to the jury what he would try to prove. Peterson was a premeditated killer who methodically planned the death of his wife and unborn son. He conjured his plan soon after he met Amber Frey, a blonde masseuse from Fresno whom he bedded the first night they met. The so-called fishing expedition to San Francisco was nothing more than his attempt to give himself an alibi on the day his wife mysteriously disappeared. The trip also afforded him a way to dispose of her body and that of his unborn son in the steel blue waters of the Bay.

Distaso relentlessly attacked Peterson's character. While his pregnant wife sat alone at a formal Christmas party in Modesto, Peterson was wooing Frey at another party. He told Frey, the single mother, that he didn't care if he had children and her daughter was "enough" for him. He was even considering a vasectomy. It was a portrait of a womanizer. Peterson was a bum, morally. He told Amber Frey countless lies, many of which she secretly recorded for the Modesto police. Peterson said he was duck hunting in Maine when he called Frey; another time he was in Brussels for his job as a fertilizer salesman for a Spanish holding company. All the while, he was in Modesto. Distaso's trump card was playing the secret tape recordings in the courtroom.

Distaso painted Peterson as a smarmy operator and manipulator of women. Just days after his wife vanished, the fertilizer salesman read Amber Frey a poem called "Hops" by Nobel Prize laureate Boris Pasternak, the Russian author who had risen to international fame with the publication of his novel, *Dr. Zhivago*. The poem's first stanza contained the lines:

> *Beneath the willow wound round with ivy,*
> *we take cover from the worst*
> *of the storm, with a greatcoat round*
> *our shoulders and my hands around your waist.*

Distaso relentlessly revealed more dirt about the defendant. Peterson originally told the police that he was not having an extramarital romance, but he would be caught in a lie when Diane Sawyer interviewed him on her ABC News magazine, an excerpt of which was shown to the jury. Then came the autopsy photos of the shocking remains of Laci and the unborn Conner. Laci had no head, gone too were most of her arms and legs, only her womb remained, and it had protected the eerie-looking fetus from the bottom feeders of the Bay.

A picture may be worth a thousand words, but even when police confronted Peterson in yet another lie—a snapshot of him and Amber from a Christmas party—and showed him the photograph, he replied in yet another manipulation, "Is that supposed to be me?"

Peterson didn't just lie to Amber, Distaso said. He offered two versions of his whereabouts on Dec. 24. In one version, he told people he was golfing. In the other, he said he had gone fishing in San Francisco Bay.

Distaso told the jury that within three weeks of beginning his affair with Frey, he began his plan to kill Laci and Conner. The plan began when he bought a 14-foot aluminum fishing boat to toss his dead wife's pregnant body in San Francisco Bay. Ever the planner, Peterson researched tidal flows and wind conditions in the area and then dumped the body of his pregnant wife into the Bay, hoping that it would never surface. But, Distaso said, on April 13 and April 14, 2003, passersby discovered the two bodies washed ashore not far from where Peterson claimed he fished. It was as if Laci and Conner had come back from the sea to get their killer.

Distaso further revealed that Peterson approached two real estate agents about selling his one-story home in Modesto about six weeks after his wife disappeared.

Soon after the remains of Laci and Conner washed ashore, the authorities intensified their scrutiny of Peterson, who by mid-April was in San Diego County where his parents lived. The momma's boy went back to momma. When the authorities arrested him, Peterson had grown a goatee and dyed his hair and eyebrows blonde, saying the chlorine in a friend's pool had bleached his hair. In addition to camping supplies, clothing and other items, Peterson had four cell phones, missing posters of Laci, and a picture of him and his wife. He also had a letter from Frey dated Feb. 16, 2003, Distaso pointedly noted. Scott Lee Peterson was about to go on the lam.

"Ladies and gentlemen, this is a common-sense case," Distaso told the jury as he wrapped up his almost four-hour opening statement. "I'm going to ask you to find him guilty of murdering his wife, Laci, and his unborn son."

The jurors missed nothing. Greg Beratlis noticed how stressed both Geragos and Distaso were on day one.

"During opening statements, Geragos was sweating so badly that sweat was dripping from his ears," he said. "After the trial I watched him on *Larry King Live* and he was doing the exact same thing. He was talking about some other case. I thought, 'Man, it's just pouring off his ears.' Distaso was the total opposite, just big red splotches on his neck, like roseola. You could tell this was really wearing on them."

Guinasso remained unimpressed with the prosecution's front man after his flat and dispassionate opener.

"Mr. Distaso's opening statement was as if he was reading out of a book," he said. "As a juror there was no expression of conviction from him. You could tell Mr. Distaso was nervous because he had this red rash on the back of his neck that would become darker when he became more nervous."

Guinasso even caught Distaso in a mistake. What else might be wrong in the prosecution's case?

"He mentioned that the bodies of Laci and Conner were found near the San Mateo racetrack, Bay Meadows, as he pointed to a satellite photo of Golden Gate Fields," he said. "I knew that it was an error, but did the rest of the jurors? Did they think the bodies washed up in San Mateo? This was never corrected, but luckily it did not affect the outcome, as testimony of witnesses cleared the way for an accurate portrayal of events. Mr. Distaso's opening was very long, and at times abstract. As a juror, you had to listen carefully and extract the facts from his hazy portrayal of events during the opening statement."

Julie Zanartu looked past the prosecution's presentation. Like Sgt. Joe Friday's droning calling card on Dragnet, she wanted the facts, just the facts.

"Distaso didn't seem as polished as Geragos," Zanartu said. "It wasn't as interesting when he talked. He wasn't confident. It didn't matter. The facts were what were effective. It could have been the most entertaining thing in the world, but it doesn't matter. Facts were facts."

Beratlis carefully watched Distaso's performance. The stress of his opening remarks took a physical toll on him, even at the very beginning of the trial.

"Distaso seemed to stumble over his words. He was not the polished lawyer that you see on TV shows like 'Perry Mason' or 'Law & Order.' Distaso opened up with how Scott Peterson was and is the only person that could have committed this murder. Not following the case I did not know what to make of any of this. I didn't know what kind of person Scott was, and just because he didn't respond the way the police thought he should did not make him guilty."

Having observed Geragos during *voir dire*, Beratlis was more impressed with the defense attorney.

"He was confident; he had a swagger," he said.

CHAPTER 6:
STONE COLD STUPID

"You have to be careful with attorneys.
Sometimes they present facts and sometimes they present smoke and mirrors."
—Mike Belmessieri, Juror No. 4

"I remember the choice of words: stone cold innocent.
We had just listened to the prosecution portraying Scott as cold.
I thought stone cold was an odd choice of words before the word innocent."
—Julie Zanartu, Juror No. 9

If Scott Peterson was the All-American boy, Mark Geragos moved quickly to dispel that notion in his opening statement. It was no longer a secret that the polo shirt wearing fertilizer salesman had been having an affair with Amber Frey, a Fresno massage therapist and a single mother with a daughter. This was no boy next door. He was a cheat and a sneak and, as the jurors would soon discover, an extraordinarily skillful liar. Geragos' gambit to disclose the shady side of Peterson was to confront the issue of adultery quickly. He was attempting to show that Peterson, like other men, may have had an illicit romance, but that didn't make him a murderer, only an adulterer.

Maybe he was exhibiting boorish behavior in that he cheated on his wife, Geragos bellowed, suggesting that the jury may "want to call him a cad," but there was no evidence that Peterson was a killer.

"What I am holding in my hand are [California] Department of Justice reports for all of those searches," Geragos thundered,

71

dropping the thick cache of reports onto the defense table with a thud as if he were a made-for-television lawyer like Perry Mason. "What they got with all of those tests was zip, nada, not a thing."

He added that the Modesto cops, the FBI and the California Department of Justice had scrutinized all the evidence—the Peterson house, his new boat, and the warehouse where he worked—and came up with nothing, or as the flamboyant attorney liked to repeat, "zip, nada, not a thing."

Geragos was trying to defuse the prosecution's opening arguments on June 1 that not only was Peterson "a liar and a cheat who read romantic poetry to his secret lover—even as hundreds of volunteers scoured the Central Valley looking for his missing wife," but also guilty of double murder.

Geragos' counterattack was much more dramatic and perhaps reflective of living in the show-business climate of Los Angeles. Unlike Distaso, who took all day to methodically unveil his circumstantial case, Geragos made his tight presentation in a morning.

"The evidence will show that not only is Scott Peterson not guilty, but Scott Peterson is stone cold innocent," Geragos said, concluding his opening statement.

Powerful words—"Stone Cold Innocent."

These three-words would hang over the defense case throughout the trial. It was the prosecution that had to prove the Modesto fertilizer salesman was, to recast Geragos' boast, "stone cold guilty." The defense had "nada" to prove. Geragos didn't even have to mount a defense case. And if Judge Delucchi believed that the prosecution failed to make its case, he would toss the case out of the second floor window of his courtroom. The phrase "stone cold innocent" would become the albatross around Geragos' neck. As the defense case evolved, the jury began awaiting his Hollywood surprise ending, even to the final days of the trial. It was as if Geragos, a veteran defense attorney, suddenly became stone cold stupid.

"This is an argument Mark and I have had," said Stan Goldman, a Loyola Law School professor who taught an evidence class to both Geragos and Distaso. "His theory is to get to the jury early and overcome the negative evidence. He seems to think of opening statements as a wish list of what he hoped he would prove. I have always been more circumspect in what you claim you will show and what you say you will prove. He doesn't think that way. I don't think it played out for him in the Peterson case."

What happens, said Goldman, who attended the trial as a legal analyst for Fox News, is that the jury loses confidence in such remarks and the entire defense case.

"The jurors think you lied to them," he said. "The prosecution has to prove its case, but now the jury is waiting for you to prove it."

Although Geragos did not specifically say he would prove Peterson "stone cold innocent," juries interpret such boasts as a promise of proof.

"What he is saying is that when he finishes his cross examination you will see this guy is stone cold innocent and that is what any normal person would interpret from these remarks," Goldman said. "Mark is a very good lawyer, but he didn't have an overriding theory of his case. He believed that if he took care of each prosecution witness, the case would fall. In this situation, there was no over-all theory to save Scott Petertson's life."

"Stone cold innocent?" said Belmessieri. "He didn't have to prove to me that he was innocent. The prosecution had to prove to me that Peterson was guilty. By saying this, Geragos seemed to suggest that even though he didn't have to, he would prove his client was innocent. It just hung over the trial, and by the end of the defense case, I thought, good try Mark. You said that you would show us he was innocent. All you did was prove to me he was guilty."

Zanartu was not impressed by Geragos' showmanship during his opening statement or his remarks about his client's innocence.

"I remember the choice of words: stone cold innocent," she said. "We had just listened to the prosecution portraying Scott as cold. I thought stone cold was an odd choice of words before the word innocent. Then to bang everything onto the table to make sure we were paying attention. I thought it was theatrics."

Not every juror found fault with Geragos' remarks at the start of the trial. Geragos' thumping theatrics and the boast that Peterson was "stone cold innocent" impressed Guinasso, who the defense attorney ironically would repeatedly call a "stealth juror" who was secretly waiting to convict his client.

"The opening statement of Mr. Geragos was one of confidence," said Guinasso. "He spoke in such a way that it was easy to follow. He spoke with great conviction and was animated to a point that if you were on the edge of being bored, the theatrics of Mr. Geragos would take you off that edge."

What Geragos didn't know, however, was that Guinasso paid strict attention to what was being said not only during opening statements, but also throughout the trial. "The statement that caught my attention was that he was going to show that Laci was alive on Dec. 24, 2002," he said. "I thought that was very powerful, because if he could do this, I would have to acquit Scott."

He also liked the defense attorney's Hollywood stunts.

"He ended his opening statement masterfully, when he pointed to the binders against the wall filled with court documents, and then held one up over his desk and let it fall a couple of feet which made a loud noise and said, 'There is no evidence in this or any of these binders that my client, Scott Peterson, murdered his wife Laci. My client is stone cold innocent.'"

CHAPTER 7:
JUSTIN FALCONER:
THE BIRDMAN CRASHES

"Justin Falconer seemed to be a nice guy, but I felt he was somewhat immature, and I knew that he couldn't keep his mouth shut."
—Mike Belmessieri, Juror No. 4

Mark Geragos has a big mouth, and he uses it.

On June 2, 2004, following his thudding opening statement, the L.A. defense attorney strode into Judge Delucchi's courtroom. He and Peterson were the beige brothers, both decked out in varying tones of tan. They looked sleek.

The balding and well-polished Geragos quickly established that he had the gravitas and the prosecution didn't, for the moment. Geragos looked like an all-pro middle linebacker ready to run over his opponents if they dropped the ball and his courtroom opponents obliged, a lot, soon after Distaso began calling his first witnesses.

During the next day and a half, Distaso called seven witnesses, including Amy Rocha, Laci's sister who had cut Scott's hair at Salon Salon the night before Laci disappeared. The prosecution was relentlessly methodical, like its carefully laid out opening statement. They were putting the pieces of their case together, but watching them was like looking at a retiree assembling a jigsaw puzzle in an old-age home. To those in the jury box and to legal analysts and members of the media inside the courtroom, the prosecutors had quickly bogged down in minutiae. It was looking like a rout for the defense.

"Geragos controlled the courtroom," said Juror No. 8, John Guinasso. "He was dominating."

Distaso looked more like a sandlot footballer next to the brawling Geragos. Guinasso quickly became puzzled at what was unfolding, starting with the DA's first witness, Margarita Nava, the Peterson's housekeeper, who testified with the help of an interpreter. In this game of life and death, Geragos was ahead.

"The prosecution's demeanor seemed one of an intern trying to learn the ropes of the judicial process," Guinasso said. "Mr. Distaso's nervous approach was one of disarray compared to the theatrical and smooth performance of Mr. Geragos. Judge Delucchi even had more respect for Mr. Geragos early on in the trial when he addressed Geragos as Mr. Geragos and Rick Distaso as just Distaso."

The common belief amongst trial experts is that you open your case with powerful witnesses who draw the attention of the jury. Conventional legal wisdom suggested that the prosecution in the Peterson case might have opened with testimony from Laci's mother Sharon Rocha who in all likelihood would have broken down in the witness box, possibly shrieking at her former son-in-law, much in the way she would do so effectively at the end of the trial. Why not open with Amber Frey, who helped the police catch her lover in a web of lies by recording her conversations with him? Or why not open with testimony about the remains of Laci and her unborn son that were found on a rocky shore not far from where Peterson said he went fishing? They were so horrifying that even today many of the jurors are haunted by what they saw. Distaso might have called Amy Rocha, Laci's half sister who was the last person, other than the killer, to see her alive.

Instead, the prosecution chose Nava, followed by a succession of five lesser witnesses. It was as if they were following a rigid, emotionless game plan and Geragos was that looming linebacker racing to pounce on any fumble.

"The jurors remember what they heard first and what they heard recently," said Prof. George Bisharat, who teaches criminal procedure at University of California's Hastings College of the Law in San Francisco.

Jim Hammer, a former San Francisco prosecutor and Fox News analyst, echoed Bisharat after the prosecution presented a manager from a Trader Joe's outlet as one of its first witnesses who testified about what Laci Peterson bought to prepare for a Christmas brunch.

"Every law student is taught that the two things the human mind remembers are the first and the last piece of information it hears," Hammer told the *San Francisco Chronicle*. "A Trader Joe's receipt is not the most powerful thing they have.... The prosecution should never present its case like a mystery. The point isn't to intrigue the jury, but to convince them."

But Distaso and Harris had their game plan. With Nava, the prosecution tried to establish what Laci was wearing the day before she went missing and that she was so physically fatigued as she approached the birth of her son, that it was doubtful that she would have walked her golden retriever, McKenzie, in the nearby park. The defense maintained that this made her vulnerable for kidnapping by transients who camped in the park. They were good points, but not especially powerful for an opening witness. Geragos was ahead of the prosecution.

"Geragos owned the courtroom," Belmessieri said.

Distaso had already made errors in his opening statement, which Guinasso, Juror No. 8, quickly noted during the DA's discussion of the location where the remains of Laci and Conner were found. There were others. Distaso claimed that Peterson lied when he told detectives that Laci was watching a segment from Martha Stewart's syndicated homemaking show that featured a report on how to make meringue. The prosecutor charged that the episode on Dec.

24, 2002, never mentioned meringue. But the next day, Geragos, in his opening statement, played the segment from Dec. 24, not once but twice, in which Stewart mentions meringue. The prosecutors were looking like incompetents and worse, perhaps, fabricators.

It got worse.

On June 14, the DA and his police investigators looked shady when Modesto Police Officer Matthew Spurlock revealed that he failed to disclose previously that the usually unflappable defendant cursed and threw a flashlight to the ground, potentially disputing his stone cold demeanor.

"It sounded like the word fuck," said Spurlock who arrived at Peterson's home on Christmas Eve. "It sounded like gritted teeth."

Geragos shouted out his objection in front of the jury and asked for a mistrial, accusing Distaso of popping unexpected testimony and never before revealed facts without warning.

"It's nothing but a cheap shot," Geragos said loudly.

What was important about this issue was twofold. A prosecution is supposed to reveal, by law, any exculpatory evidence that could undermine the case against the defendant. The result here was damaging to the prosecution's integrity. What else had the prosecution hidden that could help Peterson's case? Secondly, the hidden information, in this instance, undermined the prosecution's contention that Peterson was unemotional and uncaring at the time his wife disappeared.

The jury never heard how the flap was settled. They were excused and Geragos demanded Judge Delucchi declare a mistrial because Distaso failed to mention this incident during discovery. Delucchi denied the defense motions and the case resumed with Geragos, the judge said, getting his chance to refute Spurlock's remarks, which in all likelihood would have varying interpretations anyway.

Although the jury was unaware of what transpired in the courtroom, at night legal pundits on TV railed against the prosecution, which the jurors were not allowed to watch. Their deafness to this news aside, Distaso's slip would only add power to the growing drum roll of attacks on the prosecution for incompetence.

"The news crews would get up at 1 or 2 a.m. for the first guest at 4 a.m., which would be 7 a.m. in New York for the morning shows," said Peter Shaplen, the media pool coordinator for the Peterson trial, "and then it would go through the day with the morning drive shock jocks on radio. The coverage would peak starting at 5 p.m., Pacific Time with Dan Abrams on MSNBC, Greta Van Susteren on Fox News and Larry King on CNN and Rita Cosby, who was with Fox at the time, and Nancy Grace on Court TV."

Each show, the former ABC News producer said, would have its agenda, but the thrust of all of them was to get the most noise out of the day's events of the Peterson trial. Scott Peterson, unbeknownst to the jurors, had become the dark side of fame.

"It was almost as if each show tried to out-hyperbole the others," he said. "It became evident that the greater the hyperbole, the better the show was. There was no interest in nuance. It was all black and white and they were all looking for the talking head that could deliver the death blow to the other side. It would be like slamming an ace in tennis."

Although the jurors would often walk past TV news crews covering the trial, they were unaware of their reporting, every juror for this book said. Little did they know there was also a lineup of attorneys who had become talking heads. Many of these were relentless in their attempts to get on the air. Daniel Horowitz, a Bay area defense attorney, showed up with his resumé and passed it to news producers. He got on the air. Anne Bremner, who had worked in the U.S. Attorney's office in the Seattle area and later as a defense lawyer, also became a regular. They weren't narcissists; getting on TV news shows meant money. Bremner said her appearances on television brought millions of dollars in business to her firm.

The talking head corps would move from show to show, and although they were rarely paid, they would be ready at all hours of the day and night for their commentary. Some dreamed of quitting their law practice and getting permanent posts as legal correspondents. Being on TV was intoxicating. During the upcoming Michael Jackson trial one lawyer quit her job in Connecticut and left her husband and young adopted daughters to hitch a ride on the fame train. Other reporters, mostly print, called her "the runaway mom." Needless to say, she got a part-time post on MSNBC.

The legal chorus at the Peterson trial during the dark days for the prosecution had only one message, Shaplen recalled, and it wasn't good for the prosecution.

"The only message," Shaplen said, "was the game was over for the prosecution. They lose. The prosecution had failed to prove its case and their witnesses were collapsing under Geragos' cross examinations."

One attorney did stand up for the prosecution: Gloria Allred, whose client Amber Frey, Peterson's sometime girlfriend, was expected to be one of the major witnesses for the prosecution.

"Gloria was omnipresent at the podium [outside the court where legal analysts offered their comments on the progress of the trial]," Shaplen said. "Her mission for the media was to tell them how well the prosecution was doing and how her client had a pivotal role in the murder case."

Allred was a counterpoint to the pro-defense attorneys, such as Michael Cardoza, a former Alameda County prosecutor, who, it would be later learned, had conducted a mock cross-examination of Peterson, perhaps in a successful effort to persuade the cocky defendant that he never should step into the witness box in his own defense.

Early on, Geragos showed his startling knack for turning prosecution witnesses into his own such as when he asked Modesto Police Officer Derrick Letsinger about a crumpled rug that was found on the floor that appeared in a videotaped tour through the Peterson house. The cop thought the area rug looked suspicious.

"The crumpled rug?" Geragos asked Letsinger. "That's what you found suspicious?"

"Yes," the police investigator said.

"Did anyone take the rug into evidence?" the defense attorney asked.

"No," the cop said.

The answer raised the issue of incompetence once again.

Almost mockingly, Geragos asked if a hair curling iron in the bathroom looked suspicious, too.

Again, the cop said no.

Further adding to a sense of ineptness, Geragos got Letsinger to admit that investigators did not collect the glasses on the kitchen counter, which suggested one more time that the cops had already singled out Peterson as the killer in a rush to judgment.

Another mishap occurred during the testimony of Laci's yoga instructor, Debra Wolski, who said she told investigators that Laci was so weak and her feet so swollen that she needed help getting to her car. Under Geragos' cross-examination she revealed that she hadn't told that to the cops. This testimony suggested that the prosecution hadn't completely debriefed its witness, not to mention raising the issue of inventing evidence.

When the prosecution tried to show that Peterson tried to pawn Laci's Croton watch, which she inherited from her grandmother's estate, Geragos scored a blow when he showed that whoever the person hocking the watch was, it wasn't his client. Someone else's fingerprints were on the state-required pawnshop form.

Outside the courtroom, the jury never heard the responses from media and legal analysts who attacked the prosecution on nightly cable news talk shows.

"The DA's case, the analysts once again said, was so disjointed that Geragos might not even have to put on a defense and would ask for a summary judgment," Shaplen said, echoing media speculation.

On June 17, 2004, the trial took another dramatic turn and one that would have a devastating impact on the fate of Scott Peterson. It started innocently when Justin Falconer, Juror No. 5, was caught on a media pool camera, stopping at the court's metal detector where he began chatting with Brent Rocha, Laci Peterson's brother.

Jurors are forbidden to discuss the trial with anyone. Falconer reportedly said "you lose today" to Rocha, who only smiled back in response.

Judge Delucchi subpoenaed the videotape from KTVU, the Oakland station that was acting as the pool camera at the entrance of the courthouse. On June 21, Delucchi ruled that the talkative Falconer hadn't done anything wrong and the media had misreported the incident and his comments. He actually said something closer to: "I'm ruining all your [TV] shots, I guess you're not going to be on the news today."

But Falconer had stepped into a vortex of events. On June 23, Delucchi dismissed Falconer for talking to other jurors about the case and also to his girlfriend about it. Juror No. 5 was a loose lipster who could sink this trial by continuing to break the rules of silence. The juror who played the key role in removing Falconer was Guinasso.

On the morning of June 23, Guinasso, six days after the Rocha incident, wrote a note to Judge Delucchi. It was succinct, and it was powerful. It left the judge little wiggle room to keep Falconer on the panel. Guinasso had assumed the unofficial role of sergeant at arms, policing the conduct of colleagues, and he wasn't afraid to speak. If others on the jury didn't like him, so be it. He was the loner.

"Your honor," Guinasso wrote to Delucchi, "Juror No. 5 constantly speaks about the facts of this case. The following examples are as follows:

1. Modesto Police reports being inaccurate. He spoke about his S.F.O. screening experience regarding reports and they were inaccurate.

2. The weight of Laci during her pregnancy. The various weights were compared on her medical charts that were provided by her medical doctor.

3. The anchor that was discussed on 6-22-04.

4. The questions he had about Det. Brocchini's testimony on 6-22-04."

The parking lot facility supervisor added, "I have asked him repeatedly not to discuss this case, but he continues anyway. Juror No. 2 and Juror No. 3 have also asked him not to discuss this case."

Guinasso also wrote that Falconer talked about chatting about the trial to his "girlfriend," who said that a Court TV anchor [Nancy Grace] called her boyfriend "a loose cannon" and "gregarious."

Such conversations between Falconer and his girlfriend and his discussion about it to the other jurors broke the juror rules against discussing the murder trial outside the courthouse.

"He claims he takes pride in being a 'loose cannon' and being gregarious," Guinasso added in his note.

Guinasso told the judge that he now worried about the fate of the trial with the loose-lipped Falconer's inability to refrain from making comments.

"My concern is that he may prejudice himself and some of the jurors from providing a fair trial," he wrote. "He constantly speaks about the prosecution not hammering home any points, and the wonderful job Geragos is doing."

It was signed, "Concerned Juror, No. 8."

After reading the notes, Delucchi removed the 28-year-old Falconer because he had become a distraction. Not surprisingly, Falconer could not stop talking about the trial once he was kicked off the jury.

"I see no reason whatsoever to find Scott Peterson guilty," he told a gaggle of reporters outside the courthouse. He continued to attack the prosecution during other interviews and for a few weeks became the darling of the TV talk circuit.

The departure of Falconer was a blow to the defense. Jim Hammer, a former San Francisco prosecutor, told the *San Francisco Chronicle* that the defense had lost its "surest bet of at least a hung jury."

From the start of the trial, Falconer was the loose cannon that Nancy Grace had observed. Guinasso recalled meeting Falconer when the trial opened on June 1, 2004. They were both on the third floor of the courthouse. Even then, Falconer's mouth was open and his lips were moving.

"I noticed a husky blonde-haired young man with a crew cut that was talking to one of the other male jurors (Steve "Cap" Cardosi, Juror No. 6)," he said. "It seemed they bonded immediately as they appeared to be two of the youngest jurors. I stood there observing the others until the bailiff corralled the six alternates and 12 jurors including myself. We were directed down a back staircase and into a break room located behind courtroom 2M. This was the day Jenne, the bailiff, had us select an alias that would be used for the duration of the trial. Justin selected a Hawaiian alias, Kekoa. I believe it meant 'warrior' in Hawaiian."

On the second day of the trial, Falconer's lips started moving in violation of Delucchi's orders against discussing the murder trial.

"As we were waiting, Justin starts speaking about the presentation of the prosecution and the defense," Guinasso said. "I stood there listening as he was speaking to Cap (Juror. No. 6) about the obvious disarray of the prosecution's opening statement and the graceful presentation by Mr. Geragos. He then included detailed information as to the inaccurate reporting of facts by the Modesto Police Department regarding the date of the Martha Stewart video pertaining to meringue cookies. I thought at this point he was crossing the line. I did not confront him at this point, hoping he would obey the court's admonishment after hearing it a few more times from Judge Delucchi. This would never happen."

As the trial progressed, Falconer kept talking about whatever came into his mind.

"I noticed one thing about Justin. He seemed to want to be the center of attention," Guinasso said. "He would tell stories about himself, some of which seemed to me to be incredible.... He was like a defiant child. It continued to be all about Justin."

As the testimony in the courtroom continued, Falconer would continue to ignore the court admonishment about speaking about the trial.

"It got to a point where other jurors and I would mention to him that he should not be speaking about the case," Guinasso said. "It would shut him up briefly, but not to the point of obeying the Court."

On June 22, Guinasso decided to do something as he sat at his desk during a graveyard shift at the parking lot company in San Francisco. He was going to write a letter to Judge Delucchi about Falconer.

"My conscience wavered back and forth on this delicate decision," he said. "I did not want to cause friction between any of the jurors, but for the judicial process to be fair."

He summarized his concerns in the note and the facts in the case that Falconer discussed, like Laci's weight in her last trimester: 153 pounds; the cement anchor in the 14-foot boat not being heavy enough to anchor the vessel in San Francisco Bay; the inaccurate reports of the Modesto Police Department.

Guinasso added that Falconer talked about the trial with his girlfriend and how he enjoyed one of the news reports terming him a "loose cannon."

What irked Guinasso the most was that under Falconer's growing barrage of remarks against the prosecution's case, the jurors with weaker minds might be prejudiced over a period of time.

With his message ready to go, Guinasso faced another issue.

"How was I going to get it to Judge Delucchi without any of the jurors and alternates knowing?" he thought. "I decided the best way was to walk in last into the break room and hand it to Jenne in an envelope addressed to Judge Delucchi."

But the impact of implementing his plan hit him eventually.

"I had a hard time finishing my shift that morning due to the built up anxiety over this matter," he said. "Six a.m. did not come soon enough, as I punched out and got into my old truck to take the 34-mile journey to the courthouse. I turned the radio channel to a sports talk show just to remove any of my thoughts of what was going to transpire later."

As usual, Guinasso parked his truck after the 45-minute drive in a residential area two-and-a-half blocks from the courthouse. Guinasso had little sleep.

"Once I parked, I normally took a nap in my truck until about eight o'clock, but on this day, I could not sleep," he said. "I opened the squeaking door to my truck to a calming floral scent that accompanied the air as I walked towards the courthouse."

He passed through the metal detectors at the front entrance of the courthouse and headed downstairs to the cafeteria and had breakfast. Life was suddenly in slow motion.

"I looked at the clock in the cafeteria and it appeared to be stuck on seven thirty, but it was all my imagination," he said. "It just seemed that long. It took forever to get to 9 a.m. The tension was building."

Guinasso climbed the staircase to the third floor of the courthouse and sat in a rickety chair aligned against the wall. "I sat there waiting for Jenne to escort us down into the break room," he said. "As we walked, I nervously grasped the letter I wrote and handed it to Jenne behind the door as I was closing it to the break room. I sat in my chair and waited."

He now faced a Chinese water torture.

"Fifteen minutes go by, then twenty, then a knock sounded at the door upon Jenne's entrance," he said. "Her first words from her mouth were 'Juror No. 5, come with me.' At this point I knew that Judge Delucchi took my letter seriously. Justin got up with the words, 'What did I do now?' As the door closed behind Justin, the rest of the jurors looked at one another with complexity. I was the only one that knew. It was very uncomfortable."

Twenty minutes later, Falconer returned to the jury break room and he was shaking his head. Another juror was then escorted into Delucchi's chambers. One by one each juror and alternate was escorted down the hallway into the judge's chambers.

"I waited nervously with great anticipation for my turn," Guinasso said.

It came.

"I walked down the hallway to a door that had a glass window with the name Quentin Kopp affixed to it," he said. "Jenne opened the door, and the first thing I noticed was Judge Delucchi behind a large desk, with a court reporter sitting in a chair left of him. I quickly took the oath before taking a quick glimpse around the room as I was curious to its setting."

Peterson was there.

"I remember seeing Scott in a blue suit positioned against the wall closest to the door entrance," he said. "I noticed two bailiffs guarding him. As I sat down, I was sandwiched between Mr. Geragos to my left and Pat Harris to his left. I looked right and saw Mr. Distaso and to his right was Dave Harris. I became suddenly nauseous. This room they called the Chambers was overwhelming to me. It was not anything I had imagined."

Suddenly, Delucchi started talking to him.

"Juror no. 8, this is your letter?" he asked. "I replied yes."

The judge asked Guinasso to explain what he had written. "I started by saying that Justin is speaking about how well Mr. Geragos presented his opening statement and how awful the prosecution had performed theirs," Guinasso said. "I then paused and asked the judge that as a juror, this case is not judged on one's presentation, but the evidence itself, isn't it? This immediately provoked a smile from Mr. Geragos."

Guinasso became pro-active in the conversation with the judge. "I followed up by stating that, 'If this was a baseball game, we were probably only in the bottom of the third, isn't that true, your honor?' He replied yes," the juror said.

Guinasso outlined Falconer's ramblings. Judge Delucchi followed up by asking if any juror had asked him to be quiet. He replied yes, but it has not done any good. The judge excused him and he returned to the jury break room.

Guinasso knew the stakes had become high. He also knew that Distaso and his colleague Dave Harris were now aware that their case was in trouble. At least one of the jurors, Justin Falconer, would have voted thumbs up for Peterson if the case ended that day.

"This would be a pivotal point in the trial and unforeseen by the media due to the private nature of the judge's chamber," he said. "Mr. Distaso and Dave Harris have now heard for the first time from an actual juror how bad they were doing after three weeks, and how well Mr. Geragos and his defense team were performing."

Inside the jury room, there was trouble unfolding and Guinasso was ready for the storm.

"Upon entering the break room, I noticed Justin, Cap, and Ricci talking to one another," he said. "I took a chair and sat down. It was no longer than a minute when Cap, Juror No. 6, Cardosi, said, 'We have a rat in here.'"

Richelle Nice backed Cardosi.

"She piped in stating that if anyone has any problems with anyone in here, he or she should address that person," Guinasso said. "I replied that we are all adults, and that everyone is responsible for their own actions."

The three jurors glared at Guinasso, suggesting their own code of silence.

"At this point," Guinasso said, "I was not liked by Justin, Cap or Ricci. I remember Cap stating to me that I looked tired and I should remove myself from the trial. This comment would be one that persisted during the first three months of the trial. My reply was that Judge Delucchi knows that I work a graveyard shift, and that I come to jury duty when I finish work."

Guinasso fired back again to the other jurors. "The judge would have removed me if he thought it would be detrimental to the process," he said. "Since I am here, it is not your worry, but the court's." This was Guinasso's way of saying mind your own business.

More jurors paraded through the judge's chambers, some spent more time than others. Guinasso assumed that they were offering factual information to the judge. Guinasso ran a scenario of options through his mind.

"I knew one of two things would happen," he thought. "Justin would remain as a juror or be dismissed from the trial."

Jenne knocked on the door and asked Falconer to follow her down the hall into Delucchi's chambers. The others looked concerned. Time ticked away.

"Fifteen minutes elapsed before the next knock on the door from Jenne," Guinasso said. "Upon her entrance were the words, 'We are going to the courtroom.' We all walked in and were stunned to notice an empty No. 5 chair. I became very nervous as I sat there awaiting Judge Delucchi's announcement."

He didn't delay the process.

"Alternate Juror No. 1, please take juror chair No. 5," Delucchi said.

An angry Geragos asked for a new trial and Delucchi responded with one word, "No!"

The decision to replace Falconer with the first alternate, Greg Jackson, or D-Day as he was known to the other jurors, would also have an enormous impact on the future of the trial and the fate of Scott Peterson.

When Greg Beratlis, Juror No. 1, first met Justin Falconer in the hallway outside the courtroom, he wasn't impressed.

"I remember thinking how young this guy was," the football coach said. "He seemed like he was nervous, the way he was kind of joking around with Cap [Steve Cardosi]. Those two seemed to hit it off. Justin had told me that he was a security guard or something like that at San Francisco Airport and that he was on disability. We were all trying to get along, so most of the first few weeks were about idle chit-chat."

When Beratlis arrived at the courthouse on Monday, June 23, he knew something was wrong.

"Everybody was just kind of staring into space as if somebody had died," he said. "Then Justin walked in and stated that he thought he was in trouble for saying hi to Laci's brother Brent Rocha. That's when John said that anybody in the room should know better than to talk to anybody involved with the trial. Everybody knew then that Justin must have done something wrong. We were all escorted into the judge's chambers one at a time and asked if Justin had said anything to us to have influenced our minds. I explained to the judge that I wasn't sure what had happened, only that Justin had said that he ran into Brent Rocha at the entrance."

Beratlis would have had to agree with Falconer's assessment of the trial at that point.

"The prosecution was not providing enough evidence or a thorough enough investigation to make Scott the murderer of his wife," he said. "There were too many holes in the testimonies. One was the Martha Stewart meringue reference that was supposedly not in the 24th of December show. Another was the fact that not all the 290s [convicted sex offenders] in the area had been interviewed, including a person from Monterey, who was in the park at the time of Laci's disappearance."

Modesto cops seemed to want a quick resolution of the case. The easiest person to focus on was Laci's husband.

"It just seemed that the prosecution wanted a nice clean murder trial and that Scott Peterson was going to be the fall guy," Beratlis said. "Scott Peterson was going to go through this ordeal for just being the husband, I thought, and it was bad luck. I remember thinking this trial was a waste of money and time."

Like the others, Mike Belmessieri, Juror No. 4, was not impressed by Falconer, whom he thought was immature and couldn't play by the rules.

"I knew that he couldn't keep his mouth shut," he said. "I got the feeling that he was toying with the media. Days prior to his dismissal he made mention on at least one occasion that when he was returning from having lunch, he ruined a media photo opportunity with one of the families."

Belmissieri rarely spoke to Falconer. He also recalls Falconer trying to discuss the trial. "Richelle, Fairy, Steve, and some of us were walking to a restaurant to have lunch and he said something to me about inspector Al Brocchini's testimony. He was questioning the legality of the search when the officer found the gun in Scott's truck. I terminated the conversation by saying that we should not be talking about anything to do with the trial."

But Falconer couldn't stop.

"I believe it was later on at lunch that day Justin said that he thought that Bill (John) was sleeping while in the juror's box," Belmessieri said. "I told him that I thought he should talk to one of the bailiffs or someone else about that issue."

The motor mouth kept on talking whenever he had a listener.

"I suppose the proverbial icing on the cake was the morning when he came into the room we were using as a jury assembly and announced that his girlfriend was 'pissed off and wanted to kick some ass' because some blonde woman on television was talking about him," Belmessieri said. "I later found out that he was talking about a woman named Nancy Grace [a Court TV anchor at the time] and someone I knew nothing about. He said something about Nancy Grace saying that he [Justin] made some gesture to Scott Peterson and said something. I did not know anything about the television person that he was speaking about so I asked him if the blonde woman was attractive, and he replied 'yes.'"

Fed up, Belmiesseri turned the tables on Falconer.

"I told him that he should relax and that if I were he, I'd probably feel pretty good if I had a young attractive blonde woman paying any attention to me," he said.

Belmiesseri disputed the belief that Falconer would have voted to free Peterson had he not been dismissed.

"I do not think that he is without intelligence," he said. "If Justin had the opportunity to have gone through the deliberation process, as we the jury did, he would have agreed that Scott Peterson was guilty. Anyone who sat in those deliberations would have to be completely brain dead to not have arrived at that conclusion."

The sudden dismissal of Falconer cast a shadow over the remaining jurors, who did not know why he was removed from the panel.

"I didn't know if they just threw him in an alligator pit," said Julie Zanartu, Juror No. 9. "I kind of got paranoid. It was like I'd better not say anything. By the questions they were asking me, 'Did I ever hear him say this or that?' I got the gist that people were complaining that he was talking. Then I realized you can't say anything. You could say something and people would misconstrue it. It made you pay attention. When I would see Brent or anyone else I wouldn't even look at them. Then it was like I couldn't even make eye contact with people. I was so afraid. What are people saying or thinking about us?"

Even after Falconer was dismissed, the prosecution didn't change its tactics even though it had first hand knowledge that their case was in trouble. Throughout July, the prosecution kept making mistakes. Geragos kept pounding their witnesses. One of the lead detectives, Al Brocchini, admitted that he had "excised" potentially exculpatory evidence—that witnesses had seen Laci at Scott's warehouse and that she would have been in a position to see his boat. Brocchini recovered a bit on re-direct, saying that the information was contained in another officer's report.

It wasn't until Aug. that the prosecution began to make its case with Amber Frey, Peterson's sometime girlfriend.

CHAPTER 8:
LIAR, LIAR PANTS
ON FIRE: AMBER FREY
EXPOSES
SCOTT PETERSON

"These tapes were the sole factor, in my opinion,
in putting Scott Peterson to death."
—John Guinasso, Juror No. 8

"Yes, I am an asshole."—Scott Peterson,
overheard by John Guinasso, Juror No. 8,
during the playing of the Amber tapes

On Aug. 10, 2004, a nervous Amber Frey, who has become the best known massage therapist in the history of Fresno, showed up at the Redwood City Courthouse in a black pants suit and matching high heels. Her flowing blonde hair was a striking contrast to her dark business attire. Around her swan-like neck was a thin gold crucifix.

The outfit was also a stunning contrast to the casual clothes she wore at a Jan. 2003 press conference in Modesto 19 months before when she revealed that she had been romantically involved with Scott Peterson. She went from looking like a femme fatale to a class act. In all likelihood Frey's clothes and her lightened blonde hair were suggested by her attorney, Gloria Allred, who for years had demonstrated how important striking outfits were in public and before the camera.

"She was flanked by two deputies on the way to the witness stand," said John Guinasso, Juror No. 8. "This was the first time during the trial that there was so much security for a witness that was taking the stand. I asked myself why? Her blonde hair draped her shoulders as she sat in the witness box. I was literally five feet from her, as the jury box was to her left. She seemed very nervous."

She was.

"Her eyes darted around the courtroom and they stopped at the defense table and Scott Peterson," the observant Guinasso said.

Allred and her partners at their Los Angeles-based law firm of Allred, Maroko & Goldberg, which was representing Frey, had also carefully prepped their client for what was about to happen to her on the witness stand, especially the much-anticipated cross-examination by Geragos.

As heroines go, Amber Frey is a shy one, but she would play a decisive role in the demise of Peterson's defense. The jurors have had mixed feelings about just how important her presence and testimony were in his conviction and sentencing. Some said she was the turning point. Others were unimpressed by her testimony, but were impressed by her courageous decision to help capture Peterson in a web of lies that she caught on a series of audiotapes she secretly recorded for the Modesto police. She became the prosecution's star witness and the beginning of the end for Scott Peterson. Frey and her tapes added a voice to the smirking defendant, who would not take the stand, and Geragos couldn't save him with a blustery cross-examination.

"She was the turning point in the case," said Anne Bremner, a former Seattle prosecutor who was a TV legal analyst at the trial. "The tapes showed what a complete liar he was. It was devastating to the defense. They showed how glib he was and that he could lie about everything, even to his mother. He was a smoothie and he conned her, but not the jury. Once you undermined his credibility, it is over. He was not only a liar and a cad but a bad person."

And that laid the groundwork for a conviction. "Once the jury saw that he was such a liar," Bremner said, "it was no longer a quantum leap to finding that he murdered Laci, and the jury came to believe that he did."

Cross-examining Amber Frey, Bremner said, was yet another blunder on the part of Geragos, especially when he started off his rebuttal of Frey with a quip, "I have no questions."

"What?" uttered a stunned and angered Judge Delucchi.

With the adroit timing of a standup comic, Geragos added, "Just kidding."

Bremner, too, was shocked.

"These tapes were so incriminating and then to get up and make light of them was an insult to the jury and to Laci's family," she said.

By now, Greg Beratlis, Juror No. 1, had become fed up with the quip-meister.

"The swagger didn't hurt him, the humor did," said Beratlis. "There were jokes, even in the interviews with the witnesses when he was working them. They would say something and he would come up with a funny line. It was almost like he would try to put us at ease."

It didn't work. "This is not a funny time," he said. "It's really serious. Maybe, if we were in a bar together, this might be a time to joke around with your friends. But you've got the Rocha family sitting right there and you have Peterson fighting for his life and he is making jokes?"

Peter Shaplen, the media coordinator who observed the remark and Amber's ensuing testimony, said Geragos should have taken his own advice and never brought Frey to the stand.

"He never laid a glove on her," he said. "She was totally pre-pared and she was prepared by pros. She went toe to toe with him and didn't slip."

Those pros were Allred's team.

"What could she say that was going to help the defense," Shaplen said. "Every time she opened her mouth, Peterson came out looking like a liar and a philanderer. The whole case changed after Amber's testimony and it was a massive change."

Julie Zanartu said until Amber's appearance on the stand and the playing of her tapes, she thought Peterson might be innocent.

"It just made me start to think that it was possible that he could kill Laci," she said. "Before, it was like it could be a coinci-dence that he had a boat. He could have been looking for a place to fish on his computer. I was willing to give him the benefit of the doubt in all of this. Amber was bringing everything together, maybe a motive, possibly."

Zanartu said she didn't know what to expect from Frey's tes-timony and the massage therapist didn't miss a beat on the stand. She answered all the questions thrown at her by Geragos.

"She was very credible," she said. "I figured Geragos would be really tough on her, but he wasn't. She was very clear and well coached, but it didn't come across that they were trying to make it look like she was hiding information or had something to do with the murders."

If Frey was touted as the prosecution's leading witness, she delivered.

"She pretty much was the star of the trial because her tapes exposed Scott so badly," she said. "There was no way of getting around that he was carrying on with her while his wife was missing. It was so strange. There were all his stories that he was in France. The whole time she knew exactly where he was. I was embarrassed for him because he was so busted."

Zanartu didn't think Peterson was in love with Frey. She was just his prey.

"I don't know if he was ever in love with her," she said. "I don't think he was. When she took the stand, I think she was still in love with him."

Belmessieri, the Marine tanker, was blunter.

"I don't think Scott was ever in love with Amber; he just used her to live this dream world he felt he deserved," he said. "The tapes really verified that the kid was a pathological liar. He might have walked if there were no tapes."

Zanartu thought the tapes showed how callous Peterson was to the disappearance of his wife and how much he wanted to pursue Frey. Peterson's own words were dooming him.

"You would think he would stop everything and say my wife's missing, plus he was lying to her that he wasn't married for a long time and when he did confess, he lied again," she said.

The jurors didn't just listen to the tapes, they also watched Peterson to see his reaction to his damning conversations. Frey hardly looked at her ex-lover at the defense table and she avoided looking at the jury, but Peterson's gaze at her was eerie.

"He was looking right through her with this weird stare," Zanartu said, "not at her but through her. It was strange. He didn't look at other witnesses like that. It wasn't an angry look, but a dismissive one, like you are nothing, like you don't matter."

Frey kept her composure during Geragos' cross-examination. "She had it all together," Zanartu said. "As far as winning, I don't know. He really didn't go after her. I was expecting this fancy lawyer, you know, to do what you see on TV and go after these witnesses and turn them into big liars, but he didn't. As far as winning, she told the truth."

The impact of the tapes on the fate of Peterson took a surprising twist. The tapes played less of a role in his conviction than they did when it was time to send Peterson to death. His well-documented lies derailed the testimony of defense witnesses who tried to mitigate the prosecution's argument that the fertilizer salesman had no redeeming qualities and deserved death.

In another twist, Geragos' opening remarks also didn't help Peterson when he called his client a "cad." The tapes underscored the dark side of Peterson to the jury and the fate he deserved.

"The whole time Mark Geragos was saying he's an asshole; he's a cad, but he's not a murderer," Zanartu said. "Then toward the end, we found out he is a murderer and he's also an asshole. The tapes exposed him for what a liar he was. He lost all credibility. If he was going to lie about one thing, he is going to lie about everything and he did."

Frey wasn't the reason why the jury found Peterson guilty, she was just another part of the equation.

"She was just part of it," Zanartu said. "She pretty much exposed him for being a liar."

Frey's testimony and her bag of tapes affected Dennis Lear in the same way, but more importantly the legal team from Modesto finally was pulling its case together.

"The Amber thing was a big deal," he said. "Some people have liaisons or whatever you want to call them so to me that didn't mean that he was automatically guilty. But I think once you've realized how he lied over the month or two that he was dating her, it helped the prosecution's case. But it took three or four months before I started feeling that way."

Surprisingly, as critical as these tapes were, listening to them day after day after more than three months in court began to take its toll on the jury.

"Bored ain't the word," Lear said. "I was angry because I thought the prosecution was overplaying it, at least at the time."

Frey wasn't on the stand that long.

"All she did was get up there and say that she and Peterson had a conversation, and then they would go let her feed her baby and we had to sit there for another hour and a half, maybe three hours listening to these tapes," Lear said. "We never got to see much interaction with her."

Lear became withered by listening to the tapes.

"It was good evidence from the prosecution, obviously," he said. "But we were all sitting there and we were ready to die. You heard six or eight of those tapes and it was like 15-year-olds in high school. In hindsight, you say, oh well, okay, this certainly helped the prosecution's case. It made it viable, but Jesus, we had to listen to those things."

As crucial as the tapes were, Zanartu also found listening to them trying, especially when the couple would hang up their phones.

"It kind of sounded like teenagers with silly talk," she said. "They didn't need to play all of the tapes, but apparently the prosecution had a reason for it."

Tom Marino also thought the prosecution should have edited the tapes, but he was surprised at what they contained. The prosecution's opening statements didn't foreshadow the explosiveness of the information, especially Peterson's callousness.

"He seemed not to be concerned about his missing wife and as though he thought he could get away with it," he said. "It was the prosecutor's way of getting Scott to testify without having him on the stand. But had the tapes not been made, there was more than enough evidence to prove his guilt."

Guinasso was less impressed by Frey. The tapes, however, ruled out any possibility for him that Frey might have been involved in the murder or disappearance of Laci. But he didn't like what he heard about Frey's character, like her leaving her daughter with Shawn Sibley so she could embark on a sexual relationship with Peterson in his hotel room on their first date.

"She lived for the moment," he said. "She was romanced; she lives in a fantasyland at times. She proved over and over that she makes the same mistakes."

Despite the frustration of listening to all of the tapes, Guinasso said the recordings showed how Peterson premeditated the murder of his wife and unborn son. It started when Shawn Sibley told him that she was going to tell Amber that Scott was married.

"Scott says let me tell her," he said. "It was then he starts his plan and gets the boat and looks up the current charts in San Francisco Bay. Then he tells Amber that this is the first holidays that he will spend without his wife."

Guinasso did not factor Frey's testimony into his equation for guilt because Scott never confessed on the tapes.

"Geragos said it in his closing," he said. "Scott was a cad, a 14-karat asshole, but you know what? The prosecution never proved that he did the murder when you listened to these tapes. We used them mostly during the penalty phase because each of us could give their own weight on the witnesses. I gave her a zero."

Yet many members of the media and TV legal analysts called Amber a hero. The media always looks for heroes who can be reduced to easy sound bites. What is so amazing about the Peterson trial is that the jurors, even now, don't always agree on the pieces of the puzzle that they assembled to convict and sentence Peterson to death. Guinasso didn't think much of Frey as a heroine. "The only way in my mind that Amber is a hero is that she had him put to death," Guinasso said.

But Marino does. "Indeed, she was a heroine," he said. "After all, knowing what she knew about the situation, she still worked with the police and was able to convincingly ask Scott these questions that showed he was seemingly unconcerned about his missing wife. Yes, she was the star witness. Asking those questions might put her in danger. Would he come after her? Would he hire someone to hurt her and her family? I am sure she asked herself all of these questions, but she did whatever the police asked of her."

As the tapes would suggest, the willowy Frey is a needy woman and Scott Peterson was yet another example of her bad luck with men. At the time she began her brief romance with Scott Peterson, she had one child outside of marriage and by the time his trial ended, she had a second love child in what would become a doomed relationship with a Fresno chiropractor. In 2006, she married for the first time. Her husband works in law enforcement.

Frey's relationship with Peterson began in a foolhardy way. He seduced her, beginning with his slipping strawberries into a glass of champagne at his Fresno hotel room on Nov. 20, 2002, shortly after they met at the Elephant Bar. It was their first date. Dinner followed at a Japanese restaurant, then dancing at a Karaoke bar and finally sex without a condom.

"She doesn't have the best judgment," Zanartu said. "That was dumb."

Frey's testimony would reveal how accomplished Peterson was as a lothario. "She'd been used to being burned by men, but this guy was completely different," said Greg Beratlis. "She'd been taken advantage of and then she finds her knight in shining armor. He'd given her more than probably anybody had given her—champagne and strawberries. She had probably only seen a six-pack of Coors Light prior to that."

Guinasso was struck by how surreal the ensuing story was, especially Amber's testimony about the early days of her relationship with Peterson.

"This paralleled any soap opera on a weekday afternoon, but amazingly to me, it was real life," he said. "I sat there asking myself was Scott that good of a manipulator or was Amber that gullible? My questions would be answered by the taped conversations between them."

Frey's cooperation with the Modesto police began five days after Laci Peterson disappeared on Christmas Eve. On Dec. 29, Frey learned from a Fresno cop who was a massage client of hers that the missing pregnant woman in Modesto was Peterson's wife. For days, Peterson dodged TV camera crews in Modesto and at the Red Lion Inn, hoping to avoid being captured on tape.

His mantra was always the same, "It's not about me; it's about Laci." Hear it once, you buy it; hear it 10 times, something is wrong. It was during these early days of Laci's disappearance that Peterson's arrogance surfaced during his interactions with the media. One can only imagine what the outcome of this saga might have been had Peterson used his charm and manipulative skills on members of the media.

In retrospect, Peterson's camera shyness can now be understood. He didn't want Amber or anyone who knew her to see his face. She hadn't or if she had, nothing clicked that her lover was the husband of the missing Modesto mother-to-be.

But Frey did have her suspicions about her elusive lover and had begun making inquiries about him and even had her friend, the Fresno cop, check into him. When the cop called back with the bad news, she acted. On Dec. 30, 2002, six days after Laci disappeared, Frey called a Modesto police hotline to report what she learned and met with investigators. The next day, Frey was taping their conversations on a cheap portable recorder the cops supplied her.

In court, Frey's recordings were expected to show that the Modesto fertilizer salesman repeatedly pitched her a load of manure on the phone and probably more when they met in person. Peterson, who was in Modesto during his phone chats, said that he was in Paris and Brussels for business.

"Everyone's in the bar now, so I came out in an alley, a quiet alley, isn't that nice?" said Peterson in a faux Parisian call to Frey on New Year's Eve, hours before he would appear at a vigil for his wife. "It's pretty awesome, fireworks there at the Eiffel Tower, a mass of people, all playing American pop songs."

During his calls, he also told Frey he had been in Maine for a family vacation during the Christmas holidays, which gave him another excuse for not spending the holidays with her.

When he felt Frey might get suspicious about his relationship to Laci, he hoped she would swallow another line, maybe even feel sorry for him when he revealed on Jan. 6, 2003, that he was the husband of the missing pregnant woman and had never been in Europe during the holidays. This revelation was forced on him by his growing notoriety in the media, which he believed would get back to Frey and so he acted first. Working for the cops, Frey asked him if he had killed his wife, but he denied it and tried to manipulate his lover in a Jan. 6, 2003, call.

Amber: "I deserve an explanation of why you told me you lost your wife, and this was the first holidays you'd spend without her. That was Dec. 9, when you told me this, and all of a sudden your wife's missing? Are you kidding me? Did you hear me?"

Peterson: "I did. I, I, I don't know what to say to you."

Maintaining his innocence, the stammering spin doctor hoped to twist the situation into sympathy for himself. He was like the kid who murders his parents and hopes for pity because he is an orphan.

Peterson: "Sweetie, you think I had something to do with her disappearance? Amber, do you believe that?"

Amber: "Let's see, how can I believe that? How could I believe anything?"

Peterson: "I am not evil like that. It hurts me that you believe that I could have something to do with her disappearance."

Later, Peterson told Amber that he was faithful to her.

Peterson: "I never cheated on you."

Amber: "You're married. How do you figure you never cheated on me? Explain that one to me."

Peterson: "I want to explain that to you, Amber. Honey, I can't."

Zanartu's eyes were opened by such exchanges. "He lied about everything on the tapes," she said. "Of course, he is going to lie about not killing his wife."

Beratlis said he initially wasn't impressed with Frey, but the tapes were compelling.

"I didn't think Amber Frey was that big a deal; at first," he said, "but after the trial I looked back and it was really one of the turning points. You suddenly realized that Scott Peterson could turn off and on this other personality, this charm. He always controlled the situation through his lies."

Frey proved to be a skillful cross-examiner. At one point, she got her lover to reveal that his favorite movie was *The Shining*, a 1980 horror movie about a maniacal killer played by Jack Nicholson who unsuccessfully tried to kill his wife and son. The disclosure suggests his state of mind.

"It's the best movie ever made; it scares the hell out of me," Peterson told Frey.

On listening to the tapes and the lies, Belmessieri concluded that Peterson "was a chameleon and a sociopath."

Beratlis understood why Frey fell victim to Scott's charm. The PG&E engineer said he kept hearing Peterson use the word "amazing" over and over again in his taped conversations. After the trial, Beratlis tried the seduction technique himself, to see its "amazing" effects.

"It works great," he said. "It is not awesome; it's not 'you are great.' It's one of those words that is complimentary. It is easy to accept. I went to dinner and had a waiter serving me and said, 'You know, you are doing an amazing job.' After that the stuff was coming. There was no waiting. The waiter kept asking, 'Can I help you?'"

Frey's tapes and testimony took place over a two-week period. Guinasso was so close to Peterson that he could see him mumbling and muttering to himself. At one point while listening to the tapes, Guinasso studied Peterson's reactions to his recorded words.

"I sat there listening and focusing on Scott at the defense table," Guinasso said. "Scott sat there, rarely looking up and thumbing through a binder of information and muttering at times."

Suddenly, Peterson stunned him with a remark.

"'Yes, I am an asshole,'" Guinasso heard Peterson say. "This was audible from where I was seated. I chuckled with agreement as I witnessed it."

Guinasso thought Frey—who only spent one day being questioned by prosecutors and the next several days off the stand after she authenticated the tapes—was getting special treatment not given other witnesses. Not surprisingly, while the tapes were being played, Frey was given a seat in the gallery where the Rocha family sat.

"We as jurors were amazed that a witness had left the stand and was allowed back into the gallery," he said. "It didn't seem right to me. It seemed like special treatment. Amber should have been treated like any other witness, except for her nursing breaks."

One day during Amber's stint in the courtroom, Guinasso feared that a brawl might break out, which is why there were so many armed sheriff's deputies in and around the courtroom.

"Dennis Rocha was seated in the front row of the gallery and had positioned himself in a direct line of Scott Peterson," Guinasso said. "He was listening to the tape in which Scott states to Amber that he was in Paris on New Year's Eve while he is actually at a vigil for his murdered wife. Dennis Rocha directed his laughter towards Scott in such a manner. I thought his next move was to perform bodily harm on Scott. It was hard for Dennis to control his emotions after hearing the constant lies of Scott, knowing that this was his son-in-law."

Amber, Guinasso believed, was not without her own character defects.

"I found Amber to be equally at fault for being part of this relationship," he said. "I think there were enough clues in the Amber tapes that should have rung a bell in her head that he was married. I think she denied the obvious to pursue this lustful relationship."

Guinasso had scant praise for Frey's parenting skills. "I did not find Amber a very responsible parent. She appeared to forget about picking up her child after spending the night with Scott Peterson, and on one occasion she had a man she had just met pick up her daughter at school," he said.

But Guinasso did not believe the recordings were the smoking gun that exposed Peterson as a murderer.

"These tapes only demonstrated that Scott was a great manipulator, liar, user and fabricator," he said. "He was imaginative for the sole purpose of achieving his goal, sex. He targeted the weaknesses of Amber and pursued them until he accomplished his goal, which he did, lustful sex with the 'other woman.' These tapes played no part in determining Scott's guilt during deliberations."

But when it came to the penalty phase of the trial, the recordings had a decisive impact. Not surprisingly, Guinasso was blunt.

"Isn't it ironic that through these tapes Scott puts himself to death?" Guinasso said. "By the overwhelming accumulation of aggravating factors of evidence regarding his character, it superseded the sparse amount of mitigating factors that were presented by the 39 defense witnesses during the penalty phase of the trial."

In short, Peterson was caught by his lies, which could not overcome all the character witnesses Geragos presented during the guilt phase.

"Amber Frey was not the star witness in the guilt phase, but her tapes were the sole factor in my opinion for why Scott was condemned to death," he said. "The star witness for the guilt phase was Angelo Cuanang. He was the expert fisherman from South San Francisco who was asked the question by Pat Harris of the defense team, 'If you caught a 153-pound sturgeon, and attached four

10- pound weights, could you pick it up and toss it overboard from a fourteen foot aluminum boat without having it capsize?'"

Without hesitation, Angelo Cuanang replied, confidently, "Yes."

"As a juror, it told me that Scott could have performed the act of disposing of Laci in the Bay without having his 14-foot aluminum boat capsize," Guinasso said. "Remember, the prosecution or defense did not present a boat test during the trial. Angelo Cuanang's testimony carried that much more weight in the deliberation room during the guilt phase."

Two years after they recommended the death penalty for Scott Peterson, the seven jurors remain united by an experience only they can fully understand. Left (front to back): Richelle Nice, Dennis Lear, Tom Marino. Right (front to back): Greg Beratlis, Julie Zanartu, John Guinasso, Mike Belmessieri.

The Little Engine That Could. The prosecution's winning team. Front: Craig Grogan, lead investigator for Modesto Police Dept. Back from left to right: Kevin Bertalotto, Criminal Investigator from the DA's Office; Rick Distaso, Deputy District Attorney; Birgit Fladager, Chief Deputy District Attorney; Dave Harris, Deputy District Attorney.

The morning after the verdicts, residents continue to leave flowers for Laci and toys for Conner and hate signs for Scott Peterson.

At the time of the trial, a TV crew discovers Laci's unmarked grave.

Residents of Modesto express their disgust for Peterson outside his house with hate signs hours after the guilty verdicts.

Amber Frey and her attorney Gloria Allred.

Defense attorney Mark Geragos typically checks in during his lunch break in Redwood City.

Richelle Nice, a.k.a. Strawberry Shortcake.

Mike Belmessieri as a young Colma, Calif., policeman, taken in 1972.

Photograph Copyright by Julie Zanartu.

Julie Zanartu and Greg Beratlis at the Radisson Inn, Brisbane, while taping the *American Justice* episode.

Photograph Copyright by Julie Zanartu.

Left: Tom Marino, Juror No. 2, and right: Richelle Nice, Juror No. 7, relax during the tense days of deliberations.

John Guinasso, Juror No. 8.

Tom Marino and Julie Zanartu.

Left: Dennis Lear, Juror No. 5, Mike Belmessieri and right: Tom Marino.

Greg Beratlis, Juror No. 1, samples the Crowne Plaza cuisine.

Richelle Nice and Tom Marino at the jurors' reunion BBQ held at Tom's house in August 2005, eight months after the verdict was decided.

Dennis Lear and Julie Zanartu.

Dennis Lear and Mike Belmessieri.

Julie Zanartu and John Guinasso.

The local newspaper issued its headline on the day of Scott Peterson's death penalty verdict.

CHAPTER 9: BIRGIT FLADAGER: THE STEEL FIST IN A VELVET GLOVE

"I think when Birgit came into the prosecution's case
was when it really came together"
—Mike Belmessieri, Juror No. 4

Amber Frey and her secret tapes finally gave the prosecution's case a boost, but would the DAs from Modesto stumble once again as the trial progressed or pick up the kind of momentum that the Little Engine That Could needed to get over the hill for a guilty verdict?

It was then that Birgit Fladager, the chief deputy district attorney who quietly had been supervising Distaso and Dave Harris, stepped forward. The jurors nicknamed the conservatively dressed former Navy JAG attorney "Dorothy Hamill" for her bobbed blonde hairstyle and wholesome looks. It was now her turn on the ice.

"She was the savior just when the prosecution needed it most," said Anne Bremner, the former Seattle prosecutor turned defense attorney. "She refocused the case and was the best lawyer in the courtroom."

Bremner said Fladager's job was to protect what Frey had established and drive home a guilty verdict and secure the death penalty in the double murder case. "She had to make sure the prosecution met the burden of proof for guilt and not merely skate over it, and that is what she did," said Bremner, who was a veteran at trying capital cases. "She gave the jury what it needed to come back with a conviction."

But Fladager had help. Before her appearance, Distaso and Harris laid the groundwork for what would follow. They revealed that in early 2003, only weeks after Laci's disappearance, Scott Peterson began making a series of trips to the Bay where police divers were searching the cold waters for the remains of his wife and unborn son. Peterson, however, would stay only a few minutes in the area after driving 90 miles from Modesto. To the prosecutors and, perhaps to the jury, the trips had all the appearances of his retuning to the scene of the crime.

Distaso and Harris also laid out other pieces of their case against Peterson, further adding to the power of Frey's appearances. Four days after Laci's disappearance, a police tracking dog named Trimble had picked up Laci's scent at the Berkeley marina where Peterson launched his fishing boat, which he had bought for $1,400 in cash, and followed it out to the end of a dock, where it looked out over the water and gave an "end of trail indication."

Fladager's colleagues documented that Peterson had made a cell phone call that placed him near his home at 10:08 a.m. on Dec. 24, 2002, even though he said he had left at 9:30 a.m. This established a time line by which Laci, who was nearly full term in her pregnancy, would have had only 10 minutes to prepare herself, go for a walk in the park with their golden retriever, McKenzie, and get kidnapped. At 10:18 a.m., Karen Servas, a neighbor, found McKenzie standing in the middle of the street in front of the Peterson home.

After narrowing the time line about Laci's so-called walk in the park, which by now seemed a remote possibility, Distaso and Harris also showed that there were other pregnant women who were walking their dogs in the Modesto neighborhood where the

Petersons lived, defusing the defense argument that Laci was seen walking McKenzie that Dec. morning.

One of the most important points established came from Laci's obstetrician, Dr. Esther Tow-Der, when she testified about the examination of Conner on Dec. 23, his mother's last appointment. The unborn child was in excellent condition and was due on Feb. 16, 2003.

If Amber Frey's testimony appealed to the heart, then the testimony of Dr. Brian Peterson, a forensic pathologist from Contra Costa County, touched the souls of the jury when he detailed what had happened to the remains of Laci and Conner, which Dave Harris brought out during his Sept. 15, 2004, direct examination. Sharon Rocha and other members of her family stayed away from court during the graphic presentation. But the jurors had to look; it was their duty and it struck deep. Dr. Peterson's testimony was so powerful and horrifying that even after two years, what they saw in the courtroom still haunts them.

Laci's skeletal remains looked like the carcass of a devoured animal. "There were a lot of parts missing," Peterson said. "The head, the neck, the forearms, the lower leg. There was no brain to examine because there was no head. No heart or lungs to examine because the chest was empty. There was no liver or kidneys because the abdomen was empty."

The only organ that did remain was the uterus of the eight-month pregnant woman. The most important part of his testimony was that the unborn Conner could not have been born by Caesarean section or in any natural way. Peterson, who is not related to Scott Peterson, testified that Conner died in utero and was finally expelled from Laci's uterus when gases built up in what is called a "coffin birth."

Peterson continued his slide show the following day, when he presented autopsy photos of the eerie remains of Conner, whose translucent body and hooded eye sockets made him look like E.T. What saved him from being devoured was a mother's womb. "If he had spent substantial time in the water like Laci did, he would have been eaten," the pathologist said. "My conclusion was that [Conner] had been protected by the uterus."

Whether Conner was born alive or died in his mother's uterus was one of the most important elements in the case against Peterson. Geragos and his team insisted that both bodies were dumped into San Francisco Bay to frame his client. Laci's abdomen had been cut open to get her baby out of her womb, he suggested. But Dr. Peterson's testimony, in which he pointed out that there was a hole in the top of Laci's uterus, destroyed the defense theory, particularly since the baby's umbilical cord appeared to be torn, not cut.

These photos quickly left their mark on the jurors, several of whom cried openly in the jury box. Peterson never looked up from the defense table. Scott's mother, Jackie, held a notebook in front of her face to avoid looking at Laci and what would have been her grandson.

It was at that point that Fladager, who had been sitting in the first row behind the prosecution table, moved to the forefront and put the lead detective in the investigation, Craig Grogan, on the stand. The stocky cop, who had been on the case from the beginning, came up with 41 reasons in Jan. 2003 for why Laci and her unborn son had been dumped in San Francisco Bay, which is exactly where Peterson said he had gone fishing.

"Obviously the question for the police was did he actually go to the Bay and is that where he left [Laci]?" Fladager said after the trial. "Or is that an alibi and did he leave them someplace else and is he trying to throw them off so they're looking in the Bay and not where he really put her? They needed to weigh that out."

Peterson's remarks and the spot near where their remains were found in April 2003 would inextricably link Peterson to the crime.

Working together, Fladager and Grogan packaged the evidence in easily understood terms that made the circumstantial case against Peterson even more compelling.

"I personally thought of Detective Grogan's 41 reasons as the Cliff Notes to a real life drama," Guinasso said. "As a juror, it was easy to follow. It kept one's attention. If it didn't keep a juror's attention, then the 6.0 earthquake that happened toward the end of Grogan's direct would awaken anyone from boredom. I sat there thinking to myself what else is going to happen in this trial?"

A partial listing of the 41 reasons included:

• Cement debris on the flatbed trailer in Peterson's warehouse.

• The secretly bought fishing boat found in the warehouse.

• The parking stub from the Berkeley Marina, dated Dec. 24.

• Cell phone data that he made phone calls near the San Francisco Bay.

• Dog scent of Laci detected at the Berkeley Marina.

• Scott Peterson said he was at the marina.

• He had a two-day fishing license bought on Dec. 20 and filled out for Dec. 23 and Dec. 24.

• Fresh water fishing tackle found in the boat but not used.

• A Jan. 11, 2003, wiretap in which Peterson whistled with relief after hearing a phone message from Sharon Rocha that searchers in the Bay had only found an anchor and not a body.

• He made three trips to Berkeley Marina after Dec. 24, which directed the investigators back to the Bay.

• Witnesses said Peterson initially used an alibi that he was golfing and not fishing.

• There were umbrellas in the back of his pickup truck wrapped in a tarp and they were the same size as Laci, creating an excuse for being seen loading something into his truck.

• The police and searchers combed local lakes but didn't find Laci's body.

• Police tested water in Peterson's boat and it was salt water, not fresh water.

• The authorities discovered that Peterson had been searching the Internet for fishing sites and places to launch boats throughout California.

• The usually meticulous Peterson left a mess of concrete debris at his warehouse, creating the suspicion that he never thought anyone would return to search the facility for the fishing boat.

• Records showed little activity on his cell phone on Dec. 24 until after 2 p.m. when he began leaving messages to Laci that he would be late, in a possible attempt to create an alibi.

• He stopped to buy gas on his return from the Bay, but only $13 worth.

• A probe of his computer searches on the Internet showed that Peterson was looking for areas in the Bay with deep water currents.

• He paid cash for his fishing boat and did not register it.

Authorities discovered that the fishing boat's cover was in Peterson's pickup truck on the night of Dec. 24, raising questions about why it was there and not on the boat in the warehouse.

• During a search of the Peterson house on Dec. 26 and 27, the police rediscovered the boat cover in the shed with a leaf blower leaking gas onto it.

• During the search, the cops found that the meticulous Peterson had stored the boat cover sloppily and not neatly folded.

There was other compelling testimony Grogan unleashed against Peterson. Peterson was the last person to see his wife alive and the one who called Sharon Rocha and told her that her daughter was missing soon after he arrived at his house. The cops found only one cement anchor in the fishing boat, but the mess in his warehouse suggested that he had made several others, which could have been used to weigh down Laci's body. Cement rings left on a flatbed trailer suggested the spot where Peterson poured the cement for the anchors into buckets.

"It seemed like a tremendous mess from making one eight-pound anchor," Grogan said.

Grogan, who would spend eight days on the stand, underscored what Frey previously established: Peterson was a liar, further undermining his credibility. Initially, Peterson denied that he had a lover, but when the investigator produced a photo of him and Frey at a Dec. 14 Christmas party, the fertilizer salesman looked at it for several moments.

"Is that supposed to be me?" he asked.

Fladager brought something else to the trial her male colleagues couldn't—a woman's touch, which was a counterpoint to the testosterone-injected Geragos. Fladager also brought Laci back to life with home videos and a blouse that the jurors touched.

"Up until then all we had were scary skeletons and a still photograph of Laci," Bay area defense attorney Daniel Horowitz said. "She wasn't really a person in this process. Amber Frey was a person, Scott was a person. The most important person, Laci, had been reduced to an autopsy photo. It was almost eerie and strange. When Birgit took over, all of a sudden we saw videotapes of Laci as an alive, warm, caring human being. We could feel her loss as a human being."

When Fladager brought Laci's blouse into the courtroom it was as if she had handed the jurors a holy relic. It was last seen on the night before she vanished at Salon Salon by her sister Amy.

"The jurors handled it like it was something precious almost as if they were touching Laci, as if they loved her," Horowitz said. "Juror No. 6, [Steve Cardosi] after he handled the blouse looked right at the Rocha family and made eye contact."

Like Geragos, Fladager had pizzazz.

"That's the kind of gamesmanship that was going on," Beratlis said. "She played the same game that Mark Geragos and Pat Harris played."

Belmessieri felt Fladager's impact as well.

"I think when Birgit came into the case for the prosecution was when it really came together," Belmessieri said.

Media Coordinator Peter Shaplen began noticing the courtroom drama heightening with the arrival of Fladager.

"Before Fladager arrived, Geragos had been much the master of the courtroom," he said. "Distaso got confused and flustered. Geragos owned it. What she did was throw Geragos off his game. Distaso rarely took the podium and never seemed to move. Geragos was always moving around and it was as if he was toying with Distaso. But she played Geragos' game by asserting her physical presence in the courtroom."

That was done, he said, by placing herself in front to the jury, which helped obscure Geragos at the defense table. She was comfortable moving into the middle. "When Geragos objected, she gave him a look as if he was a naughty child and then paused to look at him as if she was saying, 'Are you done, yet?'" Shaplen said. "It was like a parent looking at an unruly child."

It's no surprise that Fladager could dance so nimbly with Geragos in the courtroom. At a high school in Keflavik, Iceland, where her dad was doing some Defense Department work, she took ballet lessons and practiced with the Icelandic National Ballet School.

She was the youngest child born to Myles and Phyllis Fladager. Her father was a Navy aviator who later became a lawyer. She graduated St. Olaf College in Northfield, Minn., and spent a semester in France. She went on to McGeorge School of Law in Sacramento, which had been started with the help of Raymond Burr,

TV's Perry Mason. She graduated in 1986. Like Distaso, she went into the military and served in the Navy's JAG program stationed in San Diego. She joined the Stanislaus County DA's office in 1990 and was promoted to Chief Deputy in 1999. In 2006, she was elected district attorney. "Even though she is very soft spoken," said her father, Myles, "it's sort of like a steel fist in a velvet glove. She's very bright, organized, and does her homework. She gets everybody's attention."

Before Peterson she was no stranger to circumstantial cases. She was co-counsel, with Distaso, in a case involving the murder of 14-year-old Genna Lynn Gamble, who was strangled in Oct. 1995. There was no blood, fingerprints, hair, or DNA evidence. Two years later, Gamble's stepfather, Douglas Mouser, a computer expert at Lawrence Livermore Laboratories, was charged with the murder. Despite the dearth of evidence, Fladager and Distaso pieced the case together and Mouser was convicted of second-degree murder in 1999.

"She doesn't have to throw her arms around to get the jury's attention," said Richard Herman, who defended Mouser. "She has a great deal of personal pizzazz. She has that which is very important to any trial attorney, which is believability. If she says something, the jury will listen."

With Birgit controlling the train, the prosecution began to make its slow and steady climb to the top of the hill, but what she did was create a team effort by all members of the prosecution. In the middle of Grogan's testimony, she turned the case over to Dave Harris who began questioning Dr. Greggory DeVore, a witness called out of order.

DeVore, a high-risk obstetrician who had conducted more than 75,000 ultrasounds, concluded that Conner Peterson died on Dec. 23, hours after Laci's visit to the obstetrician and a day before Scott reported that his wife was missing. He estimated that the gestation period for the boy was 33-weeks and one day. He based his findings on the size of the child's femur after his death with ultrasounds taken during the first trimester, which, as he said in court during Geragos' cross-examination, was "the gold standard."

Losing this point, Geragos would later introduce his own medical expert, Dr. Charles March, a fertility specialist, during the defense's case in what would become one of the biggest blunders of the trial.

"Dr. DeVore's testimony washed Dr. March right out of the building as far as I am concerned," Belmisseri said. "He was direct, to the point, indisputable. He spoke as an expert in the field."

Nice concurred.

"Cut and dried, there was no disputing it," she said. "I loved that guy. He did his research, all the way down to the bone."

What DeVore's testimony did was cripple the defense argument that Laci had been kidnapped and murdered by her abductors. DeVore's testimony, once again, pointed the finger at Peterson. A compelling circumstantial case continued to build for the prosecutors and then Grogan took the stand again.

Fladager, unlike her opponent Geragos, was quiet and did not hover over Distaso and Harris. Instead, she would sit in the front row of the gallery next to the Rocha family. She took notes and would at times get up and whisper advice to her colleagues. She made her move, kept the prosecution team from derailment, stabilized the case and then stepped out of the limelight. Grogan was her principal witness of the 174 called by the prosecution. Distaso and Harris would resume handling the trial and rest on Oct. 5, two court days later.

"It was very noticeable to all the jurors what was happening," Guinasso said. "The prosecution team was now being sparked by Birgit Fladager. It was amazing to see the shift of momentum in the trial."

CHAPTER 10:
A STONE COLD DEFENSE

"We gave Scott the fairest trial he could have had.
He was innocent in all our eyes until the evidence
proved him to be stone cold guilty."
—Richelle Nice, Juror No. 7

Mark Geragos was sauntering through the hallways of the Redwood City Courthouse, when a reporter asked if he was going to put on a defense after the prosecution rested its case. Fond of recalling some advice his father, a former Los Angeles County deputy district attorney, liked to give him, he quipped, "Rarely does the defense case get better after the prosecution rests."

He should have taken pop's advice.

But it was too late. Geragos already promised the jury during his opening statements that he would show that his client Scott Peterson was "stone cold innocent," and after nearly five months, the jury awaited his defense of a man whom he called "a cad," but not a murderer.

If someone wanted to rope an albatross around the neck of the jurors, Geragos could not have picked a better gambit than one in which he promised to prove Peterson didn't kill his wife.

"Stone cold innocent. Well, I had a feeling that Mr. G was going to show us that Scott did not have anything to do with the murders," Richelle Nice said. "He really made me think okay, good, we will find out that someone else did it."

Geragos, who had pounded away at prosecution witnesses, made a lot of other promises to the jurors during his opening remarks. He said he would show that Peterson's wife, Laci, was kidnapped and kept alive until Conner was born and then killed by her abductors, who, it was suggested, might be Satanists. He promised the jury he would present eyewitnesses who would say they saw Laci alive on the day she was supposed to have been murdered.

The jury waited to see Geragos pull his rabbits out of his fedora. And wait they did as the defense attorney began calling his witnesses to bolster his promises.

"I just kept waiting all the way to closing statements," Nice said. "Okay, here it comes. He just ended up giving me pieces of the puzzle that didn't fit right into place. We gave Scott the fairest trial he could have had. He was innocent in all our eyes, until the evidence proved him to be stone cold guilty."

How did this happen? Geragos could do nothing wrong in the opening months of the trial during which he shredded prosecution witnesses and turned them into his witnesses. His sheer presence had kept visitors in the gallery from dozing off during the prosecution's case. But after Amber Frey and Det. Craig Grogan and his 41 Reasons, the prosecution had steadied its case and chugged forward.

Some legal analysts believe that despite Geragos' optimistic opening statement, he should have rested his case and offered no defense at all, announcing that the prosecution from Modesto had failed to meet the burden of proof for a murder conviction. For months, Geragos skirted the issue of putting Peterson on the stand.

"They would have been nuts to put him on the stand," said Stan Goldman, Geragos' old law professor at Loyola. "O. Henry, Faulkner, Hemingway couldn't answer the problems with his story in any plausible way. Putting Scott on the stand would have been so incredibly dangerous given the things he said on tape to Amber.

Even in the hands of an average prosecutor he could look like an absolute lying psychopath."

Compared to the prosecution calling 147 witnesses, Geragos seemed to have mounted a lightweight defense, calling just 14 witnesses, two of whom were Peterson's parents, Lee and Jackie Peterson. After only six days of testimony, Geragos abruptly rested his case to a surprised courtroom. After making so many empty promises in his fairy tale opening statement, Geragos' promises were now stone cold.

"Those were false promises," Greg Beratlis said. "I was always looking for his smoking gun to take the case in another direction to show that Scott is not the only person who could have killed Laci, but his remarks were never proven. There was supposed to be a van with dark-skinned individuals who kidnapped her, but that never panned out. Or, he said, she had been dragged away by bikers or homeless people who were stealing the child, but that wasn't proven. There was no reasonable doubt about why she was abducted. Was she a burr in the side of somebody in the society of homeless people who lived near her house?"

Peterson's parents, who had an obvious agenda of saving their son, tried to explain why Peterson had been carrying $15,000 in cash in his car when he was arrested in San Diego County, presumably on his way to Mexico in a newly bought, used Mercedes. They also tried to explain why he was carrying his brother's driver's license, suggesting he was trying to get a discount at the Torrey Pines municipal golf course, even though he did not have a reservation to play.

Among the other witnesses Geragos called was an animal trainer who testified that his tracking dog did not pick up Laci's scent at the Berkeley Marina where Peterson launched his boat on Christmas Eve.

But the fate of Peterson would rest on the silvery tongue of Dr. Charles March, a former USC medical professor and expert on fertility but not the gestation period of a fetus, unlike the prosecution's expert, Dr. DeVore.

March's testimony was the heart of the defense case. If his expertise showed that Conner Peterson was born after his mother died, then his father could not have killed his son or his mother. Someone else did and kept the baby boy alive after his mother died and then murdered him. Such testimony would raise doubt about Peterson's guilt.

On the morning of Oct. 21, 2004, March's testimony could not have gone better for Geragos. Based on a pregnancy test in June and an ultrasound in Sept., the doctor concluded that "her son did not die on Dec. 23 but six days later on Dec. 29."

This testimony played directly into the defense theory. March, however, did concede that attaching a time of conception is not an exact science and there is no way to completely guarantee the age of a fetus at death.

"It is less than a non-science," he said. "It's a 100 percent impossibility to narrow something down."

The words would haunt him hours later.

During the afternoon break, Henry Talbot, a law professor at the University of San Francisco, said that although the arrogant March could not establish 100 percent the date of death, "all of the data indicates Dec. 29." It looked like Scott Peterson would soon be a free man.

But, Talbot said, "the jury has to be really confident in what he believes in."

During the afternoon session, Dave Harris faced the cocky March who in a matter of minutes would admit that he made a mistake in picking Dec. 29. Unnerved, his face began to twitch; he touched his hair and his face. The arrogance and confidence that he exuded before the lunch break left him a beggar.

"I am sorry," he said.

"Cut me some slack," he pleaded.

Former San Francisco prosecutor James Hammer would later ask, "How many times have you ever seen a defense expert beg the prosecution to cut him some slack?"

The gynecologist and man of science testified that one of his key calculations was news from a baby shower that Laci was pregnant on June 9 when she tested positive to a home pregnancy test. March said that Laci, who had difficulty conceiving, would not have told her friends that she was pregnant on June 9, if her condition was not true.

Harris moved in for the kill. "Where in the medical records does it talk about Laci Peterson using a pregnancy test on June 9?" he asked.

"Nowhere," March admitted, starting to perspire.

Harris closed in on the witness.

"So you're making an assumption to form a medical opinion, isn't that correct?" Harris said.

"Based on 30 years of being a doctor...that's a pretty good assumption," March said.

Harris bored in on his shaky prey which stunned the courtroom when he admitted that he was merely a fertility expert and the prosecution witnesses were more experienced than he was at forensic pathology and forensic anthropology. They were better experts than he was at picking a date of death for Conner. One of the prosecution's witnesses was a colleague of March's at USC.

"Dr. DeVore is absolutely excellent," March said.

"Do you think he knows how to read an ultrasound?" Harris asked.

"Yes," March said.

March shockingly admitted that he had done no testing himself, but relied upon the testimony of the prosecution witnesses and their tests.

"I took it all in," he said.

He also admitted that he could not be certain about the exact day of conception, despite the news that Laci Peterson told friends that she was pregnant at the June 9, 2002, shower. But the waffling doctor said Laci might have been pregnant before that date.

"Bad information is crucial to your opinion," Harris said.

"It is one of many pieces of information," March said, who added, "I am sorry; I made an error; I made a mistake."

As March continued to fall apart, Guinasso, Juror No. 8, began looking up at the ceiling of the San Mateo County Courtroom with a smile on his face.

"Yes, I was 100 percent totally wrong," March said about picking the Dec. 29 date.

After the recess, March continued his implosion.

"Is Dr. DeVore in a far better position to measure bone?" Harris asked.

"Yes," March said.

"Are you in a better position to give an opinion [on bone growth]?" Harris asked.

"No," March admitted.

Harris said March's opinion was not based on any expertise in forensic anthropology or forensic pathology.

"You are an expert in fertility," he said.

"Yes," March said.

Talbot, the USF law professor, said he was stunned by March's testimony.

"This is the heart of the defense case," he said. "This was a handpicked expert. How can he base a scientific medical opinion on something that came up in conversation without anything to back it up?"

The defense was wounded.

"Their credibility went right out the window," said Greg Beratlis. "Everything now pointed to guilt when he said he 'made a mistake' and 'cut me some slack.'"

Beratlis began to rethink other parts of the defense's case, such as Geragos attempting to cast doubt on the thoroughness of the Modesto police's investigation, in particular the failure to interview all sex offenders in the area where the Petersons lived. On his initial hearing of Geragos' argument, this sounded plausible, but when it was revealed that some of these sex offenders were in their seventies and unlikely to have been predators any longer, he had second thoughts about Geragos.

"Trying to put out such doubts was hypocritical," he said.

Belmessieri dismissed the defense's medical expert. The prosecution's medical experts, who pointed to Peterson's guilt, had more of an impact on him.

"Let's get this straight, the only thing that March was good for was telling me how to get my wife pregnant and I already figured that one out," he said.

Marino, too, had no faith in March's testimony.

"I am not a doctor, I am not a scientist," he said. "But the common person could see that these times and dates for the baby being born could not have fit for the defense."

Zanartu was blunter in her assessment of March's testimony.

"He didn't know what he was talking about," she said. "He was going to show that the baby was born alive. It would have been a big deal; that would have been it. There is no way Peterson could have done it. He just was not credible at all, and I don't know why Geragos put him there in the first place. Didn't he talk to his witness first? 'Cut me some slack' was ridiculous."

March's squirming was almost comic to her.

"He was the most uncomfortable thing," she said. "But

watching Dave Harris was so funny because he was letting Dr. March hang himself."

After March's meltdown, Prof. Goldman was asked what he thought of the medical expert's testimony.

"Does the world Chernobyl ring a bell?" he said.

*　　*　　*

Former San Francisco District Attorney Terry Hallinan, who had observed several days of the Peterson trial, stepped out of the courtroom and was asked what advice he would give Distaso to win a circumstantial evidence case like the Peterson trial.

Hallinan paused for a moment. "It all comes down to the summation," he said.

Geragos, who had just come out of the courtroom, heard the remark and nodded in agreement. But it would be Distaso, not Geragos, who was expected to have the final words during closing arguments and as it turned out, the mild-mannered prosecutor, who rarely became emotional during this lengthy trial, would astound the courtroom and his detractors.

Distaso was ready. On Monday, Nov. 1, 2004, he astonished the courtroom with an impassioned closing argument. No more the ascetic, methodical DA, he passionately attacked Peterson and, at times, flashed his anger at the fertilizer salesman who cold bloodedly calculated the death of his wife and child.

"She probably had no idea what was coming," said Distaso, who showed photos of the smiling expectant mother on a large split screen in front of the jury box. Opposite Laci in life was Laci in death, a headless carcass whose flesh had been eaten by bottom feeders and predators in the dark waters in San Francisco Bay.

The show-and-tell presentation visibly moved members of the jury. Laci's mother, Sharon Rocha, who had previously avoided these slide shows in the past, lowered her head. Laci's brother, Brent, looked away.

Distaso had long maintained the case against Peterson was "common sense" and he repeatedly exploited the simplicity of this argument during his closer.

"It's a simple case, where a man murdered his wife," he told the jury.

In many ways, it was. Peterson admitted that he went fishing in San Francisco Bay on the day his wife vanished. Her haunting remains and those of her eerie looking unborn son washed up on the shore of the Bay, two miles away from where Peterson said he fished. It was time and place, said Distaso, showing the jury an aerial photo of the Bay.

"The only person that we know without any doubt who was there in the exact location where Laci and Conner Peterson's bodies washed ashore at the exact time they went missing is sitting right there," Distaso told the jury, pointing at the defendant. "That alone is proof beyond reasonable doubt."

He added, "You can take that fact to the bank, and you can convict this man of murder."

Distaso would go on to dismiss the defense's contention that transients or homeless people snatched Laci and killed her and later her son. Surprisingly, the prosecutor tossed out the notion that Peterson murdered his family to be with Amber Frey. She was merely a symbol that the footloose Peterson didn't want to abandon his bachelor lifestyle and be a father.

"Amber represented his freedom," the prosecutor said. "Freedom is what he wanted."

Distaso admitted that he did not know how Peterson murdered his wife, but in all likelihood she was strangled or suffocated at their home and he drove her body to Berkeley Marina and dumped it in the Bay. The DA turned to ABC News anchor Diane

Sawyer for more common sense and showed her interview with the formerly camera shy philanderer. He told Sawyer that he had told his wife that he had been having an affair with Frey and that was okay with her.

"Do you really expect people to believe that an eight-and-a-half-month pregnant woman learns her husband has an affair and is saintly and casual about it?" Sawyer asked.

Stammering for a moment, Peterson responded, "Well, yeah, you know, no one knows our relationship but us."

Distaso once again exposed Peterson's narcissism.

"I don't think there is a single person in this court who believes that," Distaso said, mimicking the defendant. "Well, yeah, I expect people to believe me. I am Scott Peterson."

The following day, Geragos, ever the showman, started his sound bite summation in his attempt to save his client's life. He once again played the sex card and told the jurors that his client might be a liar and a cheat, but he was not a killer. There was nothing in the fertilizer salesman's past to suggest he was a man of violence. But he was sleazy.

"I don't think he's the kind of person, one with absolutely no history of domestic violence, who just snaps and one day murders his wife," Geragos said. "What the stark reality is, is this guy got caught with his pants down."

Further embellishing on Peterson's life as a sinner, Geragos walked over to the defense table where his client sat and asked, "Do you hate him?"

The jury stayed mute.

Geragos continued the character assassination of his client.

"This guy is the biggest jerk who ever walked the planet; he cheated on his wife and he felt like a 14-karat asshole for doing it."

But, of course, Scott Peterson wasn't a murderer.

Geragos went on to tick off a list of reasons why Peterson wasn't guilty of the double murder of his wife and his unborn son. No matter what police investigators did or where they searched, whether it was the couple's home in Modesto or in the Berkeley Marina, nothing was ever found linking his client to the murders.

"There is no evidence of her dying in that house or of a struggle in that house," he said. "That's because she wasn't killed in that house. Clearly, she was alive when Scott Peterson left to go to the Berkeley Marina that morning."

Even Distaso agreed that Amber Frey, his star witness, wasn't a motive in the killings, Geragos said. The theory that Scott wanted his freedom was nothing more than a theory, proving nothing.

The defense lawyer further argued that Laci was alive on the morning of Christmas Eve, 2002. Geragos once again maintained that homeless people or transients kidnapped and murdered Laci and the authorities raced to focus on Peterson within an hour of his wife's disappearance. His client was a victim of a rush to judgment. He was innocent beyond a reasonable doubt.

"There is no way you can say that there is clear and convincing evidence this morning," Geragos told the jury.

Distaso made a brief rebuttal, showing how Laci's struggle for survival may have caused the cuts on Scott's hands.

"I thought Distaso was brilliant," said Guinasso. "He made a 360 from his opening statement to his ending. Maybe he learned from G. He was more theatrical; there was more emphasis in his voice. He didn't use a monotone. There was no reasonable doubt in his mind when he was talking. He raised his voice. I thought he did a great job."

Once gain, Guinasso thought Geragos blundered in his glib character assassination of his client.

"He referred to Scott as a 14-karat asshole," the Teamster said. "It's like lighting a firecracker and it doesn't go off. That was

Mr. G He had all these lines at the beginning, even though he didn't have to prove anything. There were no scientific experts who could back his arguments. I knew the prosecution had the momentum after June. It snowballed at the end. G was being steamrolled by the snowball. As a juror, I wondered, maybe he ran out of money for the case."

By the end of Geragos' close, Richelle Nice was no longer impressed with the defense case. Too many empty promises had done their damage.

"We were on edge waiting for this big defense lawyer to show us who kidnapped Laci and people who saw her alive on the morning she vanished and being pulled into a van. But there was nothing," she said.

The implosion of Dr. March was the final blow to Geragos' case.

"When March spiraled downward, G's whole case was gone," she said. "It was almost comical. I looked over at the defense table and it looked as if they felt, shit, we fucked up."

Nice called Geragos' closing argument "anti-climactic" after March and found his defense case empty.

"He put on 14 witnesses versus 147 by the prosecution," she said. "He didn't put up a defense at all. He didn't even try. He comes out in these nice suits and his big dream team and his swagger into the courtroom and his cell phones and they produced nothing. It all looked like an act."

Nice said if Geragos had taken the advice of his father and not presented a defense, it would not have mattered.

"It would not have gotten a different verdict," she said, "but he might have had a lot more respect. The penalty phase might have gone differently, but who knows? He did not do his clients right."

Nice said she and the other jurors hoped that Peterson would testify, even though they knew that he had a right to remain silent.

"I wanted to hear what he had to say and not just sit there looking so arrogant," she said.

Had Peterson showed a human side, it might have touched some of the jurors during the penalty phase of the trial where the fertilizer salesman's life was at stake.

"It might have made a difference," she said.

CHAPTER 11:
DELIBERATIONS (GUILT)

"When we walked into the deliberations there was no book for how to do it.
Here it is, show time, game day. And all I could think of were
those pictures of Laci and the baby."
—Greg Beratlis, Juror No. 1

When John Guinasso entered the cramped deliberations room at the Redwood City Courthouse, he could feel a sense of relief. The trial, which had consumed five and a half months of his life and had strained him emotionally, was almost over. Almost. Little did he know that the process of deliberations would plunge the jurors into an even more stressful period.

After months of sitting and observing the trial unfold and avoiding any discussions of the case with friends, family, or even other jurors, he could finally talk about what had transpired. So could the others who were gathered around the glass-covered maple table surrounded by 12 wooden chairs.

The second-floor room, located directly behind Delucchi's courtroom, normally served as a break area for county personnel. At one point during the trial, the jurors surprised a worker who was changing her clothes. There was no specific conference room designated for jury deliberations. Like a lot of what transpired at the courthouse, everything was done on the fly. Understandably so. Redwood City never had a case like this. Few cities ever do.

"The first thing I heard when we went into the room was a big sigh," Guinasso said. "We saw the light at the end of the tunnel. Now, we had this heavy burden of interpreting the facts."

Before they did anything, they just talked. And it was silly stuff, like Mark Geragos' high-styled wardrobe and Peterson's designer outfits. They compared the defense's slick uniforms to Rick Distaso's subdued outfits. Distaso's garb was dismissed by one juror as "Sears, & Roebuck," which was not a law firm.

But looming over them was the verdict—guilty, not guilty, or a hung jury. Most had no idea what would happen next. It was as if these 12 people were playing sandlot football and began drawing their next play in the dirt with their fingers. But this was the Super Bowl.

"When we walked into the deliberations there was no book for how to do it," Greg Beratlis, the football coach, said. "Here it is, show time, game day. And all I could think of were those pictures of Laci and the baby. You go through those kinds of emotions. The baby was milky when it was found by a dog on the beach. Is that any way to treat your wife? What did she do wrong other than that she was pregnant. She was bubbly. She was life."

As the tension over the trial momentarily eased, Kristy Lamore, the blonde-haired Juror No. 12 nicknamed Juliet, nominated an obvious choice for foreperson, Juror No. 5 Greg Jackson. His medical and legal background seemed to make him a perfect choice. Jackson, however, was not a courtroom lawyer or a practicing physician, but rather an attorney and biologist for a Bay Area high-tech medical/pharmaceutical company.

Jackson accepted the role but would soon be embroiled in a series of disputes that would threaten the outcome of the trial. From the start, Jackson, who spent the first three weeks as an alternate, was the odd man out, preferring to isolate himself from the others, which was most noticeably seen in the way he dressed. While the others were casual in appearance, he wore business attire, as if he would be more comfortable sitting at the defense table.

The reed-thin, fair-skinned Jackson was always busy during testimony, jotting down notes in a growing stack of steno books, filling both sides. While the others jotted down a few notes, he seemed to be auditioning for the job of court stenographer. Such jurors who take voluminous notes are sometimes referred to as "scorekeepers."

In the early days of the deliberations, the jurors observed his changing wardrobe. Gone was the business attire, replaced by tattered blue jeans, faded t-shirts and a worn San Francisco Giants baseball cap with a 'G' on it.

Beratlis wondered about a change in the doctor-lawyer's attire as soon as they went into deliberations. "He shows up in Levis, t-shirts and a baseball cap," he said. "Suddenly he's breaking loose."

The jurors soon became frustrated by their foreman, particularly one of his quirks by which he would delineate his role as either a juror or the foreman. It was like a game of hat tricks.

"He did this thing for a while with his hat," Julie Zanartu said. "He'd say, 'Okay, now I'm in the jury,' and he would put the hat on. Then he would say, 'Okay, I have to say something as the foreman.' And he would take the hat off."

To Zanartu it was just a crummy old baseball cap. "It didn't say 'honorary foreman' or anything," she said.

The foreman's sartorial quirks were a metaphor for the frustrations of his fellow deliberators. "As a foreman, he would never offer his opinion about the evidence," Tom Marino said. "The one part that didn't go well with a lot of jurors was when D-Day, as foreman, would go through a subject and everybody was clear on it. But he never gave his opinion. We would ask him, 'What do you think? You're not just the foreman. You're also a juror.'"

But the juror-foreman said he needed to go through his pile of notebooks before he could come up with a simple decision on a

particular piece of evidence or testimony. The others had been refer-
ring to their notes but were doing it in the deliberation room, which
was too crowded for Jackson to spread out all of his steno books. "We
weren't allowed to take those books home," Marino said. "We weren't
allowed to look at those during breaks or any time. They kept the
books overnight."

They asked for the courtroom because there was more space
for D-Day to spread out his steno books. To help their frustrating colleague, the group asked for some down time and, according to
Marino, told Jackson: "You could take your notebooks into the courtroom and read all you want, and then come back and let us know,
you know, your opinion."

In yet another unusual quirk, Jackson asserted his authority
as foreman by sitting atop the back part of his wooden chair with his
feet planted on the seat, as if he were on a throne.

Although some of them had previously served on juries, especially Marino, most of them looked to the highly educated doctor-
lawyer to guide them through the labyrinthine process of deciding
Peterson's fate. Still, there was an undertone of panic as the panel
got down to the business.

"It was almost like being in a car wreck," said Beratlis.
"What do I do now? It's like all the blood rushes out of you. All of
this burden. Where do you start? You don't want to make a mistake."

The female jurors began setting the structure. They decided
that each juror had two minutes to talk at a time. Juror No. 3,
Lorena Gonzalez, a.k.a. Crystal, kept the list of speakers and kept
time with her watch. Lamore, who had the most legible handwriting, delineated the list of items to be discussed on a white board.
They also created an area near the door that they labeled, "Parking
Lot," on a sheet of butcher-block paper that warehoused subjects for
later discussion.

The process by which the jurors deliberated was simple. "If
you had a question or if you had some concern about some piece of

evidence or something that happened, you'd put it up on the white board," Zanartu said. "And then it would go around the table. And then say what do you feel about this? And everyone would discuss it for their allotted period of time. Is this a big thing or is this hardly anything, like what kind of pizza was Scott eating on Christmas Eve? It really didn't matter. That's not going to convict him."

Guinasso volunteered to monitor the jury rulebook, which made him the second most powerful figure in the room. One of the most important elements of this guide was that the jurors could only discuss evidence entered into the trial and not outside issues or thoughts. Guinasso was a strict interpreter of this dictum. It would immediately place the blue-collar Guinasso in conflict with the white-collar attorney and physician.

Once the housekeeping duties were established, the jurors adjourned for the first day.

As the 12 jurors and five remaining alternates boarded a hotel bus to the Crowne Plaza in Foster City, they entered a world in which they, too, would become prisoners of the criminal justice system. At the hotel, the prison-like atmosphere for the jurors quickly set in. The rule of silence once again settled over the pack. It was okay to talk about the trial during deliberations but not outside the cramped room. At the hotel, everything was regimented. The group could only watch four TV stations programmed into the rooms: HBO, The History Channel, The Cartoon Network and the Weather Channel. Any television that played in the jury common room was a plus, but that programming was carefully monitored by one of the 21 sheriff's deputies sworn in to protect these inmates.

Not surprisingly, the food too was institutional-like.

"I washed up and proceeded to the common room where I sat at a table by myself," Guinasso said. "I ate dinner, salmon over rice with vegetables. Salmon seemed to be on every dinner menu, and the joke among the jurors was that they were expecting it on the breakfast menu, too."

Life at this Bastille was anything but five-star. The meals were buffet style. "We weren't living the life of luxury," Beratlis said.

At 6 a.m. the jurors received a wake up knock on the door from a sheriff's deputy. The second day of deliberations began at 9 a.m., just like a regular day in court.

Inside the drab white jury room equipped with a microwave and a coffee/hot water dispenser, jurors began suggesting areas for deliberation, coming up with a list of 25 items that Lamore wrote on the white board.

Zanartu suggested that they view the taped interview Det. Al Brocchini conducted with Peterson. The jurors saw that when Peterson answered his cell phone call from his sister-in-law, Amy Rocha, instead of acting concerned or even in torment about the disappearance of his wife, he blithely answered the phone.

"The thing that drove it home for all of us is when he was sitting there with Brocchini and his wife is just missing, he focused on, 'Hello,'" said Mike Belmessieri.

Peterson's remarks meant nothing to Beratlis at the beginning of the trial. But by the end, it clicked.

"Little things started coming together," Beratlis said. "When I first saw that Brocchini interview during the opening statements, I didn't know who Amy was. Scott picks up the phone in the middle of the conversation and just says, 'Hi Amy, what's going on? What are you doing?'

"Wait a minute, I'm going to be sitting in a chair with both my hands in my pockets. My phone rings and I'm thinking to myself, it's my sister-in-law. If my sister-in-law is calling me at 12:30 in the morning and my wife is missing, I'm thinking she's got some information. It wouldn't be, 'Hey, how's it going?'"

Beratlis said Peterson further damned himself when he asked about grief counseling.

"The detective says it's only been six hours that his wife has been missing, and it's Christmas Eve, and it's going to be hard to find someone right now and Laci might turn up," Beratlis said. "But Peterson told Brocchini, 'We're going to need it.'"

Why would Peterson need grief counseling?

"If she shows up, everybody's going to be joyous," Beratlis said. "They're going to go, 'Yeah, we're happy.' But he's telling them we're going to need it."

Lamore wanted to discuss why the defense didn't conduct a boat test to see if Peterson could throw Laci's 153-pound body overboard without capsizing the 14-foot boat. Guinasso, the keeper of the rulebook, quickly objected because jurors are not allowed to deliberate on matters not introduced as evidence. Foreman Jackson adamantly objected.

"I raised my voice and gestured to the binder that we were only to discuss the facts of the case," Guinasso said. "D-Day's face became red as he glared at me, and then a sudden burst followed with the words, 'I want off this trial because of the hostility in the room.' At that moment, I turned to Treadhead [Belmessieri] and said, jokingly, 'He has never been at a union meeting.' Treadhead laughed."

The war between the two men had begun. Not accustomed to becoming a joke, the foreman halted the proceeding, scribbled a note, and then knocked on the door for Jenne, the bailiff. She returned and escorted D-Day to the judge's chambers. She told the jurors to stop deliberations.

"We all sat there looking at one another with blank looks on our faces," Guinasso said. "We were once again sitting there looking at the time go by. I could not help thinking that if D-Day were to remain on the trial, why would I want him as the foreperson, if he was willing to quit on us?"

After 15 minutes, the foreman returned and deliberations resumed without any discussion about what had transpired in the judge's chambers.

The battle between Guinasso and D-Day quickly resumed when the foreman approached the white board and drew a triangle, which Jackson said was a symbol for the defense.

Guinasso snapped. "Can you please lead this process with common terms or at a level where all of us can relate to you?" he said.

This remark drew a demonstrative expression from the foreman. The doctor-lawyer wrote three words on the white board—"acquittal, guilty, and hung"—and said the trial would conclude with one of those three terms.

"You can erase acquittal from the board," Guinasso said.

"This drew another expression of frustration," the Teamster said. "Even though we had not deliberated much, I sat in the courtroom five-and-a-half months listening to testimony and weighing the evidence. The binder, which contained the law about deliberations, stated that it is not helpful to state your decision at an early stage, but it didn't say you could not."

The heat between the two men rose when the foreman chose the next topic: Dr. Charles March, Geragos' beleaguered medical expert. "This witness could exonerate Peterson," the doctor-lawyer said.

Jackson's interpretation and lecture about Dr. March's testimony puzzled the others, especially for a witness many laughed at as he imploded on the stand. Jackson seemed to be using his medical background to lecture the others and, perhaps, even go beyond March's testimony. The foreman annoyed the others by bending the two-minute rule when discussing his points, sometimes going on for 10 to 15 minutes.

By now, Guinasso had become "an unofficial type of leader," Belmessieri said.

Beratlis thought the doctor-lawyer would keep them focused but he quickly strayed and began handling the case as if he were talking at a medical convention.

"That's when John called him on it," Beratlis said. "John always called it straight up. He set the tone. We wanted to vent. It was, 'no, we've got to come back to not just putting in our own emotions but the facts.' That's what John was saying. You can't bring your doctor background into this because that wasn't brought up in the case. You're not another witness."

Just as with Justin Falconer, Guinasso wasn't concerned about being liked. He wanted to maintain the integrity of the judicial process, which he believed, if not followed, would result in a mistrial. In the twilight of this long trial, he was once again holding to the letter of the law.

"John rubbed everyone the wrong way for the first couple of months because he was really outspoken," Beratlis said. "When Justin Falconer got kicked off, he said, 'Hey, shut your mouth and don't talk to anybody. If you're in a walkway and you see anybody you have the duty to follow the rules, which is no contact.'"

"John is a tough cookie," Belmessieri added. "He was there many times reminding us we had to follow the rules.

The conflict between the foreman and the jury parliamentarian centered on Jackson's loose interpretation of the rules of engagement. He was, in essence, playing by his own rules because of his education and training. Refusing to be patronized, Guinasso wouldn't budge.

"What really shook Greg Jackson up was when we got into the testimony of Dr. March," Belmessieri said. "I think that D-Day, because of his medical profession, thought he was going to teach us things. He kept going into things that weren't even there and disputing things that were. I think Greg had maybe 19 notebooks. He didn't know a damn thing they said. He had no clue. What John said was, 'wait a minute, deal with what March said not what your opinion is of what he said.'"

Jackson couldn't take the heat.

"When he was confronted, he got his feathers ruffled a bit," Belmessieri said. "He was talking like everything that March said was gospel."

Beratlis worried that Jackson might want to rehash the entire trial through his notebooks.

"Instead of having an opinion, he wanted to go through all the books," Beratlis said. "John even asked him about that, saying, 'What are we going to do? Spend six more months going through your notebooks because you wrote instead of listened?' John only wrote two books. This guy was writing so much that he wasn't listening."

On Friday, Nov. 5, the jurors concluded the week with a request to see Peterson's fishing boat. The jurors wanted to see for themselves whether Peterson could use the boat to dump his wife into the Bay without flipping it. It was granted for the following Monday.

* * *

Facing their first weekend sequestered in the Crowne Plaza, the group decided to throw a party to dissipate the stress from the deliberations. Guinasso worried about the impact of the trial on his finances.

"This Friday would be memorable; the jurors felt some sort of relief because they had two days off before they had to go back to deliberations," he said. "I felt myself bored, frustrated, and thinking about the income I was losing from work. I was hoping we could deliberate on a Saturday but the county never scheduled a day of deliberations."

By the time Guinasso stepped into the common room for dinner, the party was in progress. Like on so many other occasions, a woman took charge. Zanartu became the social director. She brought a boom box to crank up the music, which featured AC/DC, soul music, hip-hop and hits from the '70s and '80s.

"We were doing the bump at one point," she said. "And you know, just messing around."

Doctor-lawyer became a party animal, bumping and shimmying to the music, his baseball cap turned sideways as if he were a gangsta rapper. Richelle Nice took snapshots of the occasion and Jackson.

"He begged me not to show them to anyone," she said.

Beratlis noticed as the button-down foreperson got down. "He's shaking with everybody else. Prior to that he was a loner. But I took him for what he was. He was aloof."

"There was beer and wine being consumed," said Guinasso, who chose to sit the dancing out with Belmessieri. Guinasso drank beer and the Marine sipped Johnny Walker Black and puffed on a cigar.

"Everyone could really put it away," Nice said.

"As we sat there, I looked at Treadhead and said that I hope some of these jurors don't become accustomed to this, or we will have to start calling this place Club Med," Guinasso said.

Guinasso wasn't kidding. He was concerned the deliberations might drag on because some of his colleagues were having such a good time. Although the curfew for the revelers was extended to midnight on the weekend, they had to be in their rooms by themselves, alone. Family members could not visit the jurors but could leave clothes and amenities with the sheriff's deputies.

On Friday night, Guinasso couldn't sleep. He turned to the Cartoon Network and watched Tom & Jerry. Ever the worrywart, he became fearful the following day when he saw Zanartu's exercise equipment delivered.

"I thought, oh no, she's making it her home," he said. "I thought to myself, that if a moving van pulls up Sunday, I was jumping out the second story window. I could not take it any more."

Beratlis hardly saw life at the hotel as a fraternity party. "It wasn't fun and games," the football coach said. "I equated it to being in an old folks home. Meals were at certain times of the day, and all we could watch was the Weather Channel, Cartoon Network, A&E, and ESPN."

The movie selection was like the pabulum fed to the codgers in a senior care center: *Shrek, Antoine Fisher,* among others. No news and no Spice Channel, which was what Peterson ordered within weeks of his wife's disappearance. For sports fans there were the Raiders and 49ers games. "If you wanted to get exercise, you did whatever you could," Beratlis said.

The toll, however, was affecting Beratlis emotionally and physically. "Once you were sequestered, you missed your kids and your wife," he said.

"I was drinking vodka to get to sleep."

During the deliberations, Beratlis was in such agony from back pain that he had to lay flat on the floor with a lumbar pillow placed under his back, which he had strained while remodeling his house. The stress began to affect his body as well. "I had chest pains and I went to see a doctor afterwards," he said.

Mary Mylett, Juror No. 10, known as "Sean," had been secretly battling her own emotions during the trial. She had accidentally killed her 22-month-old son when she didn't see him walk in front of her Dodge van 18 years earlier. She had disclosed this in the judge's chambers during *voir dire* but not to the other jurors.

Then at lunch one day during deliberations, "she unloads a bombshell," Beratlis said. The jurors had no idea about the accident involving her son, whose name was Sean.

"I think the hardest part for me was to find out that her son's name was Sean, and we were calling her Sean," Beratlis said. "She's reliving the accident over and over during the trial."

It was another disruption in a deliberation that was filled with controversy.

"I know what it's like to lose a life," Mylett told the *Modesto Bee* after the trial, "and I know what it's like to take one."

* * *

Once again the jurors were treated like prisoners when they arrived at the courthouse on Monday morning, Nov. 8. They were lined up and electronically searched with a wand and metal detectors before they entered the deliberations room. The battle between the foreman and Guinasso would resume. The first subject on the agenda, however, was the 14-foot aluminum boat in which Peterson allegedly transported the body of his wife to its watery grave. But before they could see the boat, the blunt-talking Guinasso asked that Jackson be removed as foreman. The group agreed to vote and Jackson won a 7-5 majority. D-Day retained his throne.

Jenne, the bailiff, knocked on the door and led the jurors through a passageway to an underground garage, where the boat was stored as evidence. Surprisingly, Judge Delucchi wore a suit and not his black robes.

The prosecution and defense were ready for the jurors. Sheriff's deputies were guarding Peterson, who was typically dressed in a suit but not shackled. "We were allowed to touch and look inside the boat," said Guinasso. "Inside the boat numbered areas were marked where pieces of evidence were found. As I walked around the boat, I stood about five feet from Judge Delucchi when Juror No. 1, Greg Beratlis, asked if he could get inside the boat."

The judge agreed but noted that it was on a trailer and not on San Francisco Bay. "We never got close to the boat prior to that," Beratlis said. "There was some question about the size of the boat and could a body be put in there and why wouldn't it be sticking out? And how could a person stand up, grab a body, and throw it over the side? We were talking about the stability. Would it tip over?"

Beratlis and the foreman got into the small boat. Once again, the judge reminded them that the aluminum craft was not on water. As they moved around in the boat, Guinasso shot a glance at Peterson. "I watched Scott's chin drop to his chest as he watched the jurors in the boat," he said. "This was the first time I noticed any animation from Scott. It appeared he let his guard down to this unusual setting."

Some of the jurors also noticed Peterson's reaction. They told Beratlis that he turned ashen.

But there were other things that Beratlis observed by being inside the boat. "The boat was beautiful," Beratlis said. "It was a deal. And to realize the way it was maintained. And now, there was a pair of pliers inside and they were rusting. And there was water left in it. Scott Peterson was the kind of guy who put coasters under everything. Everything had its place from what I picked up at the trial. Now I look at the boat and he's abusing the boat. It just didn't fit."

Geragos, furious, protested that they were experimenting.

* * *

The first topic when they returned to the deliberations room was the boat evidence: the day Peterson bought the small craft, who knew about the boat, the searches on his home computer for different marinas to launch the craft.

Suddenly, Fran Gorman, Juror No. 7, a.k.a. Leilani, raised her hand in what would become yet another controversy amongst the jurors. Gorman, a Filipina who worked as an auditor for PG&E, disclosed that during the trial she went home and used a home computer to investigate the fishing website that Peterson searched in Dec. 2002. "All the jurors told her to stop, but she couldn't," Guinasso said. "She was like a child that could not hold a secret. She disregarded our pleas about what she had done.

"She wanted to tell everybody her findings. We did get her to stop before she told us her findings. Amazingly, D-Day, the foreperson, was the only juror who did not plead for her to stop."

What Gorman had done was a direct violation of the judge's warning not to conduct independent investigations. Such probes could cause a juror to be dismissed.

Jackson, however, did not raise this issue to the other jurors or to the judge. Instead he resumed deliberations that touched upon two critical wiretaps. In one, Peterson whistled at the news from Sharon Rocha that divers had discovered an anchor in the Bay and not the body of Laci.

The foreman was the only juror who believed the whistle meant that Peterson was hopeful that his wife was still alive. "Everybody else had the view that it was a sigh of relief that they hadn't found his wife because it would have put Scott in the place of the crime the day he went fishing on Christmas Eve," Guinasso said.

The other wiretap centered on a message from Scott's mother about a Laci sighting in Longview, Wash. "As Scott is listening to it, he laughs villainously, knowing that his wife is never coming back," Guinasso said. "D-Day's perception was that the laughter by Scott was one of happiness and giddiness knowing that his wife and unborn child are still alive."

Belmessieri, the tank commander, disagreed with D-Day. "If it was my wife, even my ex-wife and I don't even like her, I'd be on a plane immediately and fly over to Longview," he said.

The knock on the door by Jenne, the bailiff, ended the fourth day of deliberations. Guinasso was troubled about Gorman's disclosure that she had done her own investigation. More importantly, he was concerned that the foreman had not reported the matter to the judge.

"In my mind, this would be a great cause for a mistrial," he said. "I left there hoping that this would have concerned at least one other juror, as I did not want to be the one who would write another note to Judge Delucchi."

Guinasso had already been called a "rat" during the dismissal of Falconer. He didn't want to be placed in the position of undermining another juror. "This was the day I hoped somebody would speak about Fran's investigation at home," he said. "As we were taking our seats Fran sat down first. Then I did. As the others were being seated, I slid the black jury binder across to Fran and pointed to the page where it stated that outside investigations were not permitted.

"She gave me a look of concern, followed by anxiety and tearing. I sat there knowing she knew what was going to transpire next."

The other jurors were unaware of what would unfold. Guinasso wrote a letter to Delucchi about Gorman's investigation. "I knew this would only be used if no one else expressed concern about the matter," he said.

To Guinasso's surprise, Juror No. 3, Lorena Gonzalez, conveyed her concerns about Gorman's probe to the foreman. Others indicated that they were concerned about a mistrial and the judge should decide Gorman's fate.

"I was so relieved that the majority supported my thoughts about Fran," he said.

The foreman wrote a note to the judge and called in Jenne, who returned and asked the group to stop deliberating and for Gorman to accompany her to Delucchi's chambers.

Guinasso felt as if he had stepped into a nightmare. "I sat there asking myself if this process would ever have a conclusion because each day we would start the morning off delaying the deliberation process," he said. "I was also becoming more frustrated with the idle time and the lost wages from work."

Gorman returned and sat across from Guinasso and looked nervous. The bailiff asked Beratlis, Juror No. 1, to the judge's chambers. Others would follow, just as they had done when Falconer was dismissed. Guinasso's turn came.

"The only difference this time is that I would be positioned between Mr. Geragos and Birgit Fladager," he said. "I was asked by Judge Delucchi what I thought of Juror No. 7 [Gorman]. I told the judge that if Juror No. 7 were to remain on the jury, it would taint the judicial process. I told him I did not want to be part of it if she remained."

Delucchi sent him back to the deliberations room.

"As I was walking towards the door, Scott was standing against the wall and gave me a slight nod, meaning to me one of thanks," Guinasso said.

Gorman was asked to return to the judge's chamber, but this time she never returned. The bailiff returned to the deliberations room and asked for Gorman's notebooks. The jurors knew what that meant.

Beratlis said Gorman's disclosure put the foreman in the spotlight.

"Greg Jackson felt the screws were put to him," he said. "Guinasso said this is a mistrial if we allow this. Jackson said, 'well not necessarily.' John said, 'what the hell kind of lawyer are you? You're our foreperson, and you're going to tell me if we allow this and keep this a secret this is not grounds for a mistrial?' That set off Greg."

Belmessieri agreed with the decision that Gorman had to leave because of the threat of a mistrial. "It's not right for Laci and her unborn child to do anything but give them a fair trial, and it's not fair to Scott," he said. "We reminded ourselves many times to do that. We commended ourselves many times in doing that."

Nice concurred. "That's why I get so upset when people say we rushed the decision," she said. "We gave Scott a very fair trial. If we didn't give him a fair trial, Fran would have been left on."

Gorman said that the controversy started during the testimony of the prosecution's computer expert, Lydell Wall, who was discussing Peterson's activities on eBay. Wall testified that he did not know that much about eBay, she said, but continued to offer his interpretation.

"I found it strange that a computer expert would be unfamiliar with eBay, so I listened skeptically to anything else he said about the web," she said.

She was troubled by what she believed was an inconsistency in the evidence over the date when Peterson surfed the Internet for fishing sites, which might have helped the defense establish that he began combing the Internet before Shawn Sibley, Amber Frey's friend, confronted him on whether he was married. If true, it would undermine the prosecution's charge that Peterson had begun planning the murders on Dec. 6, 2002, on the day of the confrontation and had in fact actually planned the trip as a Christmas break, not as part of his murderous scheme.

"Was it possible that Scott had planned to go fishing all along?" Gorman wondered. "At the time I felt the question needed to be resolved."

On Aug. 27, she looked into the matter on her own.

"I pulled up the www.usafishing.com site and viewed the date of the published report," she said. "I saw that it was dated Aug. 25. Reports for other waterways were even older. I checked again on a later date. Again, I found a report from a previous date, confirming that www.usafishing.com doesn't update its content daily. I thereby concluded that a fishing report dated Dec. 5 didn't necessarily establish that Peterson was planning to go fishing before being confronted by Sibley. In fact, there now was no evidence of interest in fishing that pre-dated the confrontation."

She said that the only time she discussed the issue was when the jurors were deliberating about the "fishing trip" and that the topic never came up again. A few days later, two jurors objected to her activities. The doctor-lawyer was forced to write a note to the judge. Inside the chambers, she admitted what she had done. After some questions by the judge she realized, "I had to go."

Belmessieri respected Gorman for acknowledging her indiscretion. "She said, 'This is what I did. I don't know if it was the right thing to do. I think I may have violated the rules. I need to tell you about this before we go any further.'"

The jury soon returned to the courtroom, but before Guinasso entered, he pointed to Richelle Nice and whispered that she would become a juror. "She suddenly expressed a vivid nervousness," he said. "We took our respective seats in the courtroom. Judge Delucchi asked Alternate No. 2, Richelle Nice, to become Juror No. 7."

Up until then, Nice had been out of the loop with the four other alternates in a first floor room in the courthouse. She and the others were given laptops so that they could write their feelings down and watch a selected group of DVDs. Through a window she noticed the media scurrying outside, signaling that something big was happening.

Guinasso's nightmare of a never-ending deliberation resurfaced. Judge Delucchi told the new jury to start the deliberation process over. But he said they could select another foreman. "Our first order of business when we returned was to select a foreperson, who could be a facilitator and move the process along," he said, nominating Juror No. 6, Steve Cardosi, the fireman-paramedic from Half Moon Bay.

Guinasso, in nominating Cardosi, oddly enough, thought he was doing Jackson a favor by removing the burden of being the CEO of the deliberations. "This would allow D-Day to read his notes and deliberate from them without having the extra burden of being a foreperson," he said. "D-Day sat with a yellow highlighter as he read the front and back of each notebook. Mind you there were 19. All I could think of was he would slow the process down with meticulous detailing of the evidence."

With a new foreman in place, the jurors erased the white board, took down the notes that had been posted around the room, and any evidence they had was returned. "We were starting from ground zero," Guinasso said.

Tuesday night, on the way back to the hotel, the ever-vigilant Guinasso observed D-Day sitting next to Cap. "They were engaged in a conversation that I thought was regarding the responsibilities of the foreperson," he said. "I was soon proven wrong."

At the hotel Guinasso showered and returned to the common room. But Jackson wasn't there. As the night progressed, no one saw him. The following morning, Jackson was not at breakfast. Sheriff's deputies, however, discovered a note attached to the former foreperson's door saying that he would make the bus. When he did, he was gloomy. "We all entered the deliberation room on Nov. 10, 2004, for a new beginning. But we were ambushed by D-Day with a statement that he wanted off the trial because of breaking the court admonishment about discussing the case outside deliberations with another juror."

The jurors wondered who had breached the prohibition with Jackson, but he wouldn't say. They soon learned it was Juror No. 6, the man who replaced him as foreman. "I said to him, 'this is tit for tat, D-Day,'" Guinasso said. "His face turned red as he glared at me. I then had a flashback to the bus ride where both of them were sitting next to each other after Cap became foreperson. D-Day wanted to derail the process and cause a mistrial. He didn't want to be part of something he had no control of. He was so childish."

A sense of dread settled over the room. Each juror feared the worst. They too might be removed for talking. The ritual for the ouster of the juror began once again. Jenne first took Greg Jackson to the judge's chambers. Then it was Steve Cardosi's turn. Then D-Day was called back, and as the two men passed, they gave each other dirty looks.

During the trial, Cardosi would ride his bike from Half Moon Bay to Redwood City to stay in shape. Now when he re-entered the deliberations room, he was furious, and to dissipate his anger he jumped down on the floor and did 50 push ups.

"Cap realized he was part of a conceived plan by D-Day," Guinasso said. "Everything was flashing back, the absence at dinner and breakfast and the announcement at the deliberation table that he wanted out. If anything, D-Day certainly had the qualities of a stealth juror for the defense, one who would cause a mistrial by deliberate means."

The doctor-lawyer's departure was quick. Jenne knocked on the door and requested D-Day's stack of notebooks. They returned to the courtroom, and suddenly the alternates saw that Juror No. 5's seat was vacant. They knew the drill. Dennis Lear, Alternate No. 3, was called to become the third Juror No. 5.

"These guys had been deliberating for days," Dennis Lear said. "Then all of the sudden they threw me into the pile and said, 'You're ready.' That was shocking. Remember we're sitting down there as an alternate. We didn't know what was going on. All we knew was that we could see reporters running back and forth. Every time they started running we figured something was up, but we were in the dark. You talk about mushrooms."

The transition from the minor leagues to the majors was fast. "The bailiff came down and said, 'Gather your stuff together.' And boom, ten minutes later I'm sitting in the jury room deliberating with these guys."

As frightened as Lear was, he wanted to be part of the decision. "You sit there for five months, you want to be part of the deal," he said. "You know what you feel but you want to see what everybody else feels. But then there's the dread, the other side of it. I sort of thought this was a done deal and I'm not going to have to make any decisions."

But he did.

"I was wrong," he said. "As alternates we didn't know anything about the doctor-lawyer business. Suddenly you have a man's life in your hands. You're dealing with life and death."

But Guinasso now was fed up. He wanted off. "We were to start from the beginning again. This was going to be the third time we started all over again, and each time I was losing pay from my employer by the minutes, hours, and days. I was thoroughly frustrated."

Guinasso wrote another note to the judge asking to be excused because of financial hardships. He handed the note to Jenne and was quickly summoned to Delucchi's chambers for what he hoped would be the end of his jury duty. Inside were Geragos and Fladager. Delucchi rejected the request. But if he had to pay his bills, a deputy would escort him. Guinasso agreed. The judge scheduled an abbreviated day on Friday, Nov. 12, to allow Guinasso to transfer money into his checking account.

		REMITTANCE ADVICE		CHECK NUMBER	205155
VENDOR NUMBER TJ084433		**County of San Mateo**			
		Redwood City, California		CHECK DATE	10/05/04

DATE	INV/REF	ACCOUNT	DESCRIPTION	AMOUNT
10/01/04	IJUO014A11		STATEMENT OF JUROR EARNINGS DAYS:17 MILES: 171.36 FEE: 15.00	426.36

The members of the jury were paid once a month for jury duty. Pay was $15.00 a day, and $10.00 travel one way, which equated to $25.00. This pay stub was for 17 days in court.

With the departure of Jackson, and with Cardosi as foreman, and with the addition of Lear and Nice, the deliberations moved rapidly. "This day was one of our best days of the deliberations, in that these two new jurors participated with great interest and debate about the evidence," Guinasso said. "Cap did a masterful job to facilitate the process to a point where there was more progress on this day than on any other day."

But the deliberations halted once again. On Thursday, the jurors had a break for Veteran's Day.

* * *

Outside the courtroom, another controversy had surfaced. But this time Geragos was the instigator. Frustrated that he could not introduce evidence from his own tests on Peterson's boat, he put his own boat in a parking lot attached to a building he owned not far from the courthouse, which passersby could not help but notice.

He put a headless, 150-pound mannequin filled with rocks, representing Laci's dead body, inside the aluminum craft. This crude stunt, possibly a misguided effort to influence the jury, backfired, cheapening Geragos' image. Redwood City residents poured onto the streets in outrage, turning the boat and its contents into a shrine for Laci, complete with lighted candles, flowers and signs denouncing the defense attorney.

"What is taking place here with the public is the outpouring of support for Laci and Conner Peterson from all over the world," said Vinnie Politan, who at the time was the host of Court TV's *Both Sides* and present at the parking lot vigil. "The flowers are coming from everywhere. People are expressing their love for Laci and their hatred for Scott."

The visitors to 849 Brewster St. showed their dismay at Geragos for what many believed was a publicity stunt that had turned ugly.

"Monster," said Rena Russ, a soccer mom from Redwood City. "Don't be in my Starbucks."

"Do you know what a sleaze is?" asked Georgia McNulty, a Redwood City housewife. "He needs to practice that swagger somewhere else."

"It's disgusting, it's grotesque," said a former San Mateo County criminal prosecutor who practices law in Redwood City. "Geragos had already turned lawyers in Redwood City against him with his arrogant manner."

The Peterson jurors, however, were never aware of the parking lot fiasco. They kept to the jury rules and would never allow any discussion of the trial to permeate their lives, despite the cynical belief by many lawyers that jurors rush home each night and turn on cable TV talk shows that yammer about the trial. Friends, relatives and co-workers didn't breach the wall of media silence.

But critics of Geragos' tactics believed he wanted someone to crack the code of silence, sending the case into a mistrial or even subtly influencing the outcome by getting a piece of evidence into the trial that Judge Delucchi refused to allow.

"It is a diversion from the trial," one court insider said at the time. "This is exactly what he wants so he can get a mistrial. It adds to the circus atmosphere that can lead to a mistrial."

Residents who attended the vigil left messages to Geragos about what they thought of him inside the boat. "He is a true rat," one read. "I want Mr. Geragos disbarred." Another said, "Throw him in the Bay." One more pleaded, "We don't want a sleazy lawyer in our county."

Gloria Allred, the lawyer for Amber Frey, called a news conference the following day, and hammered Geragos. "This was within a block or two of the courthouse," she said. "I think it is very disrespectful to the family of the murder victim. I think it's in very bad taste, and I think Mark Geragos owes an apology to the murder victims."

* * *

On Friday, Nov. 12, Guinasso had a premonition. "I had a different feeling than I had for any other day," he said. "I wakened with great optimism, something not evident on any previous day. My grumpiness was soon replaced by the thought that there was light at the end of the tunnel."

Guinasso's thoughts were prescient. There were no delays. After a few hours, Cardosi asked if the group had come to a decision. They had. Cardosi tore 12 pieces of blank paper and explained that the first vote was whether or not the fertilizer salesman was innocent or guilty of murdering Laci. The jurors complied. Cardosi unfolded the torn pieces that were tallied by one of the jurors. The tension mounted.

"We have a unanimous verdict," Cap said.

The next order of business was whether the jurors would find Peterson guilty of Murder One or Murder Two on Laci. Murder One meant that Peterson would be eligible for the death penalty. Murder Two would keep him alive. Once again, the foreman tore 12 pieces of paper and handed one to each of the jurors. Once again, the vote was 12-0 for Murder One.

Now the jurors would have to deal with the issue of Conner. They found Peterson guilty, just as they did for Laci.

The next step became more difficult: the degree of murder for Conner. Nice believed that the child, like his mother, deserved a Murder One conviction. Others disagreed.

"Common sense tells one that if you kill the mother of an unborn child, that child would die too," Guinasso said.

But the law came into play.

Under the law, Conner, the unborn baby, was separated from his mother and classified as a human being. They had to deal with him separately. They had to decide whether there was enough evidence of forethought for Murder One for Conner.

Richelle Nice, a mother of four, said she wasn't ready for the vote and needed further deliberation. Initially she was adamant about Murder One. But Juror No. 3, Lorena Gonzalez, insisted there was not enough evidence of premeditation and that Conner was not a fully formed baby. After further deliberation Nice and Belmessieri relented for Murder Two.

"This conclusion was based on a lack of evidence of fore-thought to kill Conner and a lack of malice of tool marks on Laci's uterus," Guinasso said.

Belmessieri and Nice were the last holdouts on the contentious issue. "How can you not kill the baby?" Nice said, pointing to her stomach.

Belmessieri asserted that the murders were more directed at Conner than at Laci but in the end he relented. "I thought there was a possibility I could be wrong," he said. "I was the last one. I said, 'Okay, fine.'"

The issue of fetus versus a living child also came into play for some jurors, but not for Richelle Nice. "That was no fetus, that was a child," Nice said. "Everyone heard I referred to him as 'Little Man.' If he could have been born, he would have survived. It's unfair. He didn't give that baby a chance."

Belmessieri agreed. "He was a living, breathing entity," he said.

After five-and-a-half months of trial, 12 jurors, six men and six women, had reached a verdict. They were now ready to let the judge know. But before they did, Dennis Lear raised one more issue—the quick verdict, which had taken less than a full day of deliberations to reach. Was it too fast? Was it too quick? Lear wondered aloud.

Guinasso, ever blunt, said, "I don't give a damn what the media thinks. You have to live with yourself and if we all deliberated hard and fair, what does time have to do with it?"

The foreman filled out the special documents provided by the court and the bailiff was informed that the group had reached a verdict on Peterson.

* * *

The inevitable question is why was Peterson found guilty, particularly in a circumstantial evidence case in which there is no murder scene, no eyewitness, no smoking gun, and even in this case, no murder weapon? To the outsider, this was a tough case. But for the jurors, the verdict was beyond a reasonable doubt.

"There were a whole lot of whys, whys, whys, whys, whys," said Belmessieri. "It wasn't just one thing. There were so many different things. We came to the conclusion about what was important and why we believed that Scott Peterson was guilty."

Beratlis agreed. "You couldn't say it was one thing, and sit there and assume how he killed her. It wasn't one thing. It was everything."

Everything included the arrogance of Peterson who thought he could get away with the perfect crime. Instead he got caught in his own web of lies, in which he convicted himself. With his own words, he placed himself on the Bay where the body of his pregnant wife was dumped. Laci and Conner's remains surfaced two miles from where he said he went fishing.

"I don't know how he did it," Belmessieri said. "I don't even care how he did it. I just know he did it. I know he had the motive, the ability, the desire, and the access. He had it all. I'm looking at it in retrospect. Okay, they found blood. It would make sense. A soft kill, defensive wounds. He did have scars on his hands. He said he worked around farm equipment. No. He sells fertilizer. There were other issues. Like the cement anchors used to weigh down Laci's body. I think we all agree that he was making anchors."

Belmessieri, like others, did not make the decision on the verdict until they went into deliberations. "We started tearing the case apart. I'm saying, let's put this all together. That's what we did. We did the timeline that gave her only 10 minutes to get ready, walk the dog, and get kidnapped. We started getting deeper into things. Every one of us had questions about things. The timeline was very significant."

The little things helped doom Peterson, like a tarp that he used to cover the boat and which could have been used to conceal Laci's body as he towed the boat to the marina. The tarp could have contained DNA evidence. To destroy any possibility of trace evidence, Peterson stored the tarp in a shed. On top of it was a gasoline powered leaf blower that spewed gasoline onto the tarp.

"Wait a minute," Beratlis said. "This is not the kind of guy who would pour gasoline all over a tarp. When we were in deliberations you could still smell gasoline on the tarp even though it was two years later."

"Why didn't he just keep the cover on the boat?" Belmessieri asked.

Further implicating himself were the videotapes he appeared in. The first that caught their attention was the videotape of Det. Brocchini's interview with Peterson and the cell phone call from Amy Rocha. Instead of asking if there were any developments in the search for Laci, Peterson blithely answered the phone.

"Hey, what's up?" said Nice. "My first thing would be, hey, did you find her?"

Telling Brocchini that he would be needing grief counseling further hurt him. How would he know that? the jurors wondered. "That's what sold us," Belmessieri said.

There were also the interviews that Peterson did with Diane Sawyer and other TV journalists in which he claimed that he had told the police about Amber Frey on the night Laci vanished. His crocodile tears did not go over well with the jurors.

If jurors had doubts about certain issues, they would go over them together. "If Greg or Tom, whoever, had doubt, we would pick that topic and all just hash it out, go over it, think about it, talk about it," Nice said.

The photos of Laci and Conner brought the reality of their gruesome deaths to the jurors. For Belmessieri, he had a flashback. "When I saw Laci's body, it reminded me of a young Marine I saw killed by a grenade," he said. "These pictures were the closest thing I've seen to that. There was nothing left from the waist up. Nothing. Just pieces. We had to put the pieces in a poncho."

Some jurors believed Peterson did not want the responsibility of being a father. "He didn't want this child," Beratlis said. "When Laci got pregnant, there's this cute woman and all of a sudden she's lost that. She's going to have a baby, a burden."

"This guy was now trapped," said Belmessieri.

Additional parts of the puzzle were Peterson buying the boat with cash and never telling anyone and then searching the Internet for boat launches and deep water currents. He had fresh water tackle for salt water fish, but the tackle was never used, and on the night he claimed his wife vanished, he couldn't remember what he was fishing for. Some people testified that he told them he was playing golf. At the same time he was telling others that he was fishing.

And then there was Geragos, his cocky defense attorney. He promised that by the end of the trial the jurors would conclude his client was "stone cold innocent," which hung over the case for months but proved nothing more than an empty boast, helping destroy the case's credibility. Some of the jurors felt Geragos had misled them by suggesting that the police failed to interview other suspects such as sex offenders.

"Geragos would say something like how come you didn't check these people, the 290s [sex offenders]," Beratlis said. "I'd sit there and go, wait a minute. I have pretty good eyesight. I was looking at the paper they put on the board. They never gave us that paper. But I'm looking at some of the ages of these people. I think I saw a birth date of 1926. I said, I can see why the police didn't look at that guy. He's nearly 80 years old."

One of Geragos' biggest blunders was calling Dr. Charles March as his medical expert, only to watch him turn into a laughing stock when he began to beg the district attorney to "cut me some slack."

"Maybe Geragos would have been smarter if he had gotten somebody who had a little more expertise," Belmessieri said.

The revelation that Peterson was an adulterer hurt his character but didn't make him a murderer. Peterson's lying, manipulating and dissembling in the police tapes that Amber secretly recorded of their conversations, however, went beyond merely showing that he was an adulterer and helped the jurors conclude that it was a stone cold killing.

"It's all about Scott," Belmessieri said. "We took a look at the whole situation. He showed no remorse. He showed no remorse because there was no remorse to show. That's when the light bulb went on for us. He's carrying on this torrid love affair with Amber Frey over the phone at his wife's vigil. He's lying to everyone, including his mother. He said I'm in one place and he really isn't. This man is twisted."

CHAPTER 12:
AT HOME AND
THE OFFICE

"The problem with jury duty is the loss of freedom.
The judge rules your life. I had finally achieved
retirement freedom and he took it away."
—Dennis Lear, Juror No. 5

Three months into the trial, Mike Belmessieri's youngest son, Dominic, headed off to boot camp at the Marine Corps Recruit Training Depot in San Diego.

"I was not at peace with him becoming a Marine Recruit," Belmessieri said. "We are a nation at war, and Marines have historically enjoyed the worst part of a terrible situation."

But when Belmessieri heard the reason why his son wanted to join, he could no longer stand in his way. "Dad, when I saw the towers fall in 2001, I knew that I had to do something to make a difference," his son told his father.

"Having said the same thing to my father in 1967 regarding my decision to put my college education on hold and to join the Corps, I realized that he was going to do it and I had better just accept it," he said.

The thought of his son's wellbeing weighed heavily on Belmessieri. In 2006, Dominic was stationed in Fallujah, in Iraq's Al Anbar Province, where many Marines lost their lives in some of the fiercest fighting of the war.

Time didn't stand still for Belmessieri or the other jurors just because they were serving on the Scott Peterson trial. They had to deal with aging parents, snoring spouses, and dying pets. Having a son in harm's way puts everything else in perspective. But in many ways the jurors did have to put their lives on hold.

"During the trial some of the 'normal' things that my wife and I did prior to stopped," Belmessieri said. "We no longer shared discussions regarding my day's experience. We no longer sat down together to watch the nightly news broadcast. For the first time in our marriage we were presented with something that we could not talk about, and, as it evolved, we could not share in. All discussion regarding anything that even remotely could be connected with the trial was off limits."

They hadn't asked to serve on the high-profile trial in which they would have to decide whether Scott Peterson should live or die. But once they were sworn in on May 27, 2004, they agreed to uphold their oaths. By the time the case was over on Dec. 13, 2004, their service gave new meaning to doing your civic duty. Some suffered emotionally, physically, and financially. That service tested relationships at home and in the office. All for $15 a day.

"I was not aware of the magnitude of how the six-and-a-half months were going to change my life," John Guinasso said. "These were the most trying times in my life."

Each day, Judge Delucchi admonished them not to talk about the case amongst themselves, or with their spouses, relatives, friends or acquaintances. They were ordered not to watch TV or radio broadcasts, or to read newspapers, books, or magazine accounts. They were not allowed to form an opinion about the case. It was as if all of them had been placed in individual bubbles. They couldn't talk about the trial, and yet they were on public display in the jury box. Jury consultants, lawyers, bailiffs, reporters, and the public scrutinized their every sneeze, sniffle, and snooze.

The jurors had to live double lives. Everyone was talking about the trial around them, but they couldn't listen. They heard the testimony but they couldn't form an opinion. It took a toll on them.

"I remember coming home sitting in my room all alone processing all the information I had just taken in for the day," Richelle Nice said. "How I was a part of this and how serious this is. Could I do it? Can I be fair? All those thoughts ran in my head. What the hell am I in? I had no idea until after the trial was over what an impact this would have on me, us. I thought mostly how sad this whole thing is turning out to be."

On May 28, 2004, their profiles (without their names) appeared in newspapers across the country. Guinasso's brother Raymond, a letter carrier in Pacifica, read a profile for Juror No. 8 that appeared in the *San Francisco Chronicle* and wondered if it was John.

"It resembled me except for the age," he said. "They had me in my sixties [Guinasso is in his forties]. They had my occupation as a truck driver [Guinasso is a parking lot facility supervisor], and some other trivial discrepancies. My answer to him was that I could not confirm or deny it. I told him to sit back and time would tell. He laughed as he hung up, knowing deep down inside that I was one of the jurors."

Guinasso followed the judge's orders to the letter. He didn't talk about the case with anyone. But acquaintances ranging from his dentist to his bank teller sat in the public seats in the courtroom and immediately recognized him.

"Once these people knew, it was like wildfire," Guinasso said. "It didn't take long for someone to know that you were a juror on the most sensational case ever to hit San Mateo County."

It was certainly a small world. Belmessieri discovered that he, Guinasso, and Zanartu all attended El Camino High School in South San Francisco, at different times. His cousin sat in a desk next to Greg Beratlis at PG&E. Beratlis and Lear had both served in the U.S. Navy. And of the 12 final Peterson jurors, seven were of Italian ancestry, and 10 had been raised as Catholics. That doesn't even count Judge Delucchi and Rick Distaso, who became a superior court judge after the trial.

The jurors followed Delucchi's admonitions, except for Justin Falconer, who was dismissed for discussing the case, Fran Gorman, who was dismissed during the deliberations for conducting research on her home computer, and Greg Jackson, who talked about the case on the bus to the Crowne Plaza.

Each morning as they made their way to the courthouse the jurors were tested as they ran the gauntlet of media trucks.

"After Falconer, we all made sure that we didn't put ourselves into any situation that could cause any problems," Beratlis said. "It was like walking a tight rope. You went outside to walk and there would be reporters at the coffee shop or the diner. The reporters were obviously right outside the courthouse so you made sure that you hurried through the courtyard for fear of being filmed or seen in the same vicinity as somebody that was for or against the trial."

Some contend that jurors watch TV all the time, but the Peterson jurors were serious about avoiding the coverage. They wanted to give Peterson a fair trial. The case had already been transferred from Modesto because of media saturation there. The jurors' significant others played vital roles in keeping the jurors honest.

"My wife would mute the TV if it even looked like Scottie was coming on," Dennis Lear said.

Julie Zanartu sat with her remote control at the ready. "I would watch the TV like Clint Eastwood with a gun and snap it any time I heard the words 'Scott Peterson,'" she said. "If I was in the other room and it would come on any time, my husband would start going, 'La, la, la, la, la, la' really loud."

But sometimes they had to deal with people who felt it necessary to try to pop their bubbles. At Genentech, where Zanartu works as a biotech clinical trial inspector, a female co-worker asked, "Is Scott as hot in person as he is on TV?"

"I turned and walked away like I didn't hear it," Zanartu said. "I'm not even going to dignify that one."

Beratlis, the father of two teenage boys, talked about sports with friends and family. If someone brought up the trial, he would walk away.

"I had a couple people at the office who felt they needed to give their opinion on the case," he said. "I just told them to get out of my cubicle and actually had management make an announcement to not talk to me unless it was business related."

One time Beratlis was watching a football game and a teaser came on about the case. "I went into a panic trying to find the remote control," he said. "I just ran out of the room. My family was very supportive during the case. I would come home after a lengthy day of testimony and just be drained."

Most of the jurors received full pay during their jury service and didn't suffer financially. Zanartu's employer accommodated her schedule. Beratlis actually made extra income by working on Saturdays to catch up on his work, but found the six-day workweek wore him down. Tom Marino, a postman who has since retired, only had to work one day a week.

"Most of my co-workers would just stare at me," Marino said. "No one said much. I did have quite a few law firms on my route and some of the attorneys said that they would love to speak with me after the trial was over."

Others suffered significant financial hardships. Steve Cardosi, the paramedic-firefighter, went to court Monday through Thursday and worked two 24-hour shifts, and in some cases additional mandatory overtime, over the weekend.

"I had to make ends meet," Cardosi said. "The trial cost me a lot."

Guinasso, who had held down two jobs at a time since he was 18, was the only juror whose employer didn't pay for jury service for the extended length of the trial. He was used to working seven days a week, especially during baseball season, when he managed a parking lot at AT&T Park, the home of the San Francisco Giants. During the trial he would often work from 10 p.m. until 6 a.m., and start jury service at 9 a.m. If he was lucky he'd get fours hours of sleep during a 24-hour period. Between his jury service and his work as a parking lot facility supervisor he was logging 100 hours a week.

"I was rarely at home," he said. "I needed to work to pay my bills. I had no social life during this period. My social life was replaced with sleep when feasible. I was tired. I was cranky. I was drained."

Cardosi suggested that he should get off the trial. "You are not going to make it through," he told Guinasso.

"But we weren't the best of friends at the beginning," Guinasso said. "We clashed all the way through, mainly because Cap is very opinionated and he was one of the younger ones."

Early in the trial, Jenne, the bailiff, pulled Guinasso out of the line. "Your eyes look pretty heavy," she told him.

"I'll drink more coffee," Guinasso responded. "I am a big guy. If I lean back my chin is going to go down. But you know what? You've got to look at my head movements. If my head's moving, I am awake. I am paying attention."

From then on, Guinasso, who wore a blue windbreaker over his uniform to cover up his name, "John," and to protect his identity, was always seen holding a cup of coffee.

Jenne pulled Guinasso out of the line several other times.

"Jenne was looking at our mannerisms and marking them down in a notebook," he said. "It was almost like she was documenting a race horse. I was pulled out for my facial expressions. I explained to her, 'laughter is spontaneous and so is frowning.' You respond. It's not something that's planned. I was also pulled out because my note taking was too predictable."

* * *

Dennis Lear thought the ordeal might never end. In Sept. 2003, he had retired as a United Airlines mechanic after 36 years. He had been living in Montara, which is why he chose that as his nickname. But after he was selected as a juror, he and his wife bought their dream home, a ranchette in Coarsegold, a small town near Fresno. Lear agreed to continue his jury service. From Sunday night through Thursday, he would stay in Redwood City and return to Coarsegold for the weekends.

"The problem with jury duty is the loss of freedom," Lear said. "The judge rules your life. I had finally achieved retirement freedom and he took it away. We bought our own lunch. How much can you afford when they're only paying $15 a day? Then at the end of the trial we got 1099s and they included the gas as wages. Explain that to the IRS."

The judge agreed to pay $55 a day for Lear's motel room, which doesn't go far in San Mateo County. "They sent me to this fleabag motel on the Redwood City-Atherton border," he said. "It was gross. Even the no smoking room was filled with smoke. It was the kind of place where you wouldn't walk across the floor without shoes, never mind socks."

After a day, he told the bailiff he needed a change of venue but the bailiff said that was the only place he could stay. He asked to see Judge Delucchi. "They finally said I could stay anywhere but they were only going to pay $55 so I went to the Comfort Inn, a respectable place, for $10 more out of my pocket."

After weeks of arriving at the same time each Sunday night, the night manager asked why he was there. Lear explained that he was with "the trial."

"Which one?" the night clerk asked.

* * *

In addition to seeing his son become a Marine, Belmessieri had to deal with a change in his work status. He had worked as a manager for a major corporation for 30 years. But the company shut down his facility shortly before he became a juror.

When he reported to the new facility in April 2004, he was given a menial assignment "which required skills and knowledge more in line with the job of a clerk or temporary clerk as opposed to someone with 30 years of experience in labor relations.... Despite my disappointment with the new assignment, I performed it as best as I could, and often found myself with more time on my hands than work."

He is now a night shift production supervisor, working 9 to 12 hours a day, five to six days a week. He plans to work in his present capacity until he retires in four or five years. "I do not see any opportunity for advancement within the organization or even a return to my status prior to the trial."

* * *

Richelle Nice had quit her job with the Stanford Credit Union shortly before becoming a juror. Her youngest son took ill and she was missing work as she shuttled him back and forth to the emergency room.

At the beginning of the trial she was living on $400/month in child support from the father of her two youngest children. But another juror informed her that the credit union may have violated family-medical leave statutes. The credit union agreed to pay her salary and medical benefits for the duration of the trial.

The trial was difficult for the highly-emotional Nice. But in a way it provided a welcome refuge. Her relationship was crumbling. One of her sons was almost killed during the trial and his best friend was shot in a drive-by shooting across the street from her four-bedroom house in East Palo Alto, which she describes as "a very rough area."

"It was almost like I didn't have to deal with my life outside the courtroom," she said. "I had too much on my mind to even deal with my own life. That was good in a way because my life wasn't the best, so I didn't have to deal with that for seven months. I almost had to become something else, someone else."

But when the trial ended, she was lost.

"Where do I go now?" she asked. "What am I going to do? I don't trust anyone now. I didn't really to begin with but now, after seeing a beautiful family like this can be taken down by something so hurtful to so many, I had so much anger, so much hurt. I didn't know what to do with my life. I seemed to have lost myself during this trial."

Nice leaned on jurors like Guinasso and Cap for support.

"Going to the courthouse daily. Being treated like we weren't even there. No one could talk to us or look at us, so we all formed strong bonds between each other, friendships that will last a lifetime. I know first hand."

In just one example, Nice needed money or she would lose her pickup truck. When Guinasso heard about her predicament, he was happy to give her $1,000, despite his own financial woes. "I just told her to get back on her feet," he said. "If you want to pay me back some day that's fine but I am not asking for it."

* * *

Belmessieri was also impressed by the simple decency of the jurors.

"Wonderful people," he said. "If I were on trial, they are the type of people who I would want to decide my fate. I will always be proud to be associated with them and the trial. They are honest, committed, and courageous people."

The jurors represented America: a postman, an airline mechanic, social workers, a doctor-lawyer, an engineer, a parking lot supervisor, county employees, homemakers, a paramedic-fireman, a Marine, and high-tech workers. Twelve distinct and strong personalities whose only common bond was the trial, something they couldn't talk about.

They were given a number and selected nicknames to keep their real names from leaking out to the press. Even after the trial, they continue to refer to one another by their nicknames: Zane, Mario, Crystal, Treadhead, Kekoa, Cap, Leilani, Bill, Joe, Sean, Tracy, Juliet, D-Day, Ricci, Montara, Shannon, Jazz, and Neo. Most of them identify themselves with their juror numbers.

Perhaps the most distinctive personality was Richelle, who began dying her hair red about two months before the trial; it's become a trademark for her.

"I've always dyed my hair," she said. "It's been red, it's been pink. It had blue in it. I just like to be different."

As a child she didn't like Strawberry Shortcake, the character she became identified with, but "she's grown on me." She now owns several Shortcake dolls.

When it comes to Ricci, there is no middle ground.

"Ricci became one of my favorite jurors just because of oddities," Guinasso said. "She would dress different than most, but deep down, she is very intelligent. She called me 'her rock.' My favorite quality about Ricci is her openness and her candidness. You know where you stand with Ricci at all times. To this day, we speak about life. She is a dear friend."

She was all too much for Dennis Lear, especially when he asked a question about the boat evidence during the deliberations. "She jumped up and paced the length of the table, pointing her finger and screaming 'fuck this and fuck that,'" he said. "The room went silent and most everyone ignored her. She loved to play the

'Drama Queen.' You saw how she was dressed. Attention was everything. My question, 'Is she color blind?'"

Ricci was part of a clique that included Cap, Fairy Sorrell, the juror who Guinasso described as being "no nonsense" with a great sense of humor, and Kristy Lamore, the blonde-haired Juliet. They lunched together daily. Another clique included Lear, Beratlis, and Marino who took walks during breaks and talked about restaurants, golf and how to make Martinis. "I was a novice at this and after being on the trial, martinis became my favorite cocktail after a long day," said Beratlis.

For Guinasso, Treadhead became his favorite juror because he was down to earth and compassionate. "He spoke about others more than he spoke about himself. He was very modest."

At first Guinasso didn't fit in. "John was not interested in being anyone's friend," Lear said. "He was there for business."

After Justin Falconer was kicked off, Cardosi (Cap), called him a "rat." But during deliberations Guinasso nominated Cap to serve as foreman, and the two grew to respect one another.

"He was intelligent beyond his years," Guinasso said of Cap. "He was a motivated individual. That is why I nominated him to be foreperson. He did a tremendous job. His facilitation kept everybody on track, and to a point in which it was comfortable for one to make a decision about the case."

Greg Jackson, who spent most of his lunch breaks reading *The Wall Street Journal* and checking e-mails on his hand-held Blackberry, never found a way to fit in, even when he was wearing his Giants cap and tattered jeans during deliberations. One day, Belmessieri invited both Guinasso and D-Day to lunch. They went to a Redwood City pizza parlor. "Treadhead and D-Day carried on most of the conversation," Guinasso said. "It was probably the only time D-Day had lunch with a juror. Most of the time he isolated himself."

The court was ill-prepared to deal with a high-profile case and made few concessions for the jurors. It was a makeshift setup. At first the jurors lined up in the third-floor hallways and found themselves face to face with prosecution witnesses, such as the Peterson's maid. At one point the whole Rocha family walked by.

"The hallway was strewn with office material, such as partitions and three chairs, one of which had no back," Beratlis said. "I thought nothing of it at the time. Only after a couple of days did I realize that these were going to be our accommodations for at least the next few weeks. We stood out there at times for over a half hour because the judge and lawyers were in chambers discussing issues."

Later the jurors assembled across from the courthouse and were taken into the courthouse through a tunnel. They were warned not to look at any of the reporters or camera operators. Later on, they went through the metal detectors. They had to take the stairs or the elevator up to the courtroom, where they often ran into Geragos, Pat Harris or the Peterson family.

"We were all under the microscope," Beratlis said. "There was a feeling of paranoia that we were the ones on trial for being jurors. It was not comfortable. Nobody wanted to screw this up so we all watched our backs."

Eventually the ice broke and most found ways to pass the time.

"Jurors spoke about anything and everything pertaining to life except the Peterson case," Guinasso said. "We spent our time in the break room drawing on the chalkboard, telling jokes, sleeping, making microwave popcorn [supplied by an alternate juror named Sharon McNeal, a.k.a. Jazz, who made trips to Costco] and finding out how many kernels did not pop. It was boring, but laughter could be heard from the break room on most days. Zane [Beratlis], Juror No. 1, is a Greek man who kept everybody loose with impersonations, jokes and satirical remarks."

Cardosi also had Pat Harris' mannerisms down. He would drag two fingers of his hand across the table in the same way that the defense lawyer from Arkansas would.

By Sept., Beratlis, like the others, desperately needed an outlet. That month, one of his friends invited him to coach Pop Warner football again.

"I jumped at the opportunity and really believe it helped keep my sanity," he said. "I could go on the field and put all of my focus on the children and leave the trial for a little while. That became my sanctuary where nobody bothered me."

As the trial reached its conclusion, the jurors felt more and more confined, both by the court's admonishments and the media.

"There were people outside in the parking lot watching as you came and went," Beratlis said. "Sometimes these people would follow you home. You didn't know who they were. It was very unnerving. I knew I was on a very big trial but I didn't want my family or home to be in danger. They didn't do anything wrong."

Somehow through all the turmoil, the jurors found Peterson guilty of murder. But other troubling issues would surface during the penalty phase. Near the end of deliberations, Tom Marino provided the jurors with a welcome diversion: a glimpse of his wife and the outside world.

"I was looking out the window of the jury room during a break and I did see my wife with our dog walking across and down the street. I pointed her out to a couple of jurors. It was a pleasant diversion for us. The deliberations were very intense."

CHAPTER 13:
THUMBS DOWN

"He was a manipulator."
—Greg Beratlis, Juror No. 1

*"I saw the graphic nature of sea life that had burrowed their way
into her torso, and the areas of the torso that were eaten by sea life,
and the area of the upper arm that was chewed on by
the pack of dogs upon discovery."*
—John Guinasso, Juror No. 8

It was now a matter of death or life.

The jury wasn't finished with Scott Peterson. After an 18-day break, the jurors returned to the Redwood City Courthouse on Nov. 30 to face the final stage of the Peterson trial—the penalty phase. There were just two choices for someone convicted of Murder One and Murder Two in California—death by a lethal injection or life in prison without the possibility of parole.

The jurors would soon deliberate after hearing witnesses calling for Peterson's death because of the horrifying nature of his crimes and others extolling his redeeming virtues to save him for a life behind bars.

But once again, the Peterson trial was in jeopardy and the outside world was unaware of what was quietly transpiring in Judge Delucchi's chambers. John Guinasso was at the center of another hurricane, and he was called in for questioning.

It was no secret that Geragos had repeatedly maintained that Guinasso was his feared "stealth juror," who had been ready to convict Peterson ever since the trial began. Geragos could have vetoed his presence in the jury box before the trial began, but he didn't. On that Tuesday morning, Guinasso would soon be "on trial." The jurors gathered on the third floor of the courthouse and the bailiff escorted them to a break room on the second floor where they engaged in small talk.

Suddenly, Jenne knocked on the door. Judge Delucchi wanted to see Guinasso in his chambers. Inside, he sat between Geragos and Dave Harris. Delucchi was pleasant and asked him to answer some allegations lodged against him.

"Juror No. 8, you drink before you come to jury duty every morning?" Delucchi asked.

"No, Your Honor," he answered.

"Juror No. 8, you mentioned to a bartender that jurors had secret notebooks?" the judge asked.

Again, Guinasso said, "No."

"Juror No. 8, you have spoken to a local bartender about the trial?" Delucchi asked.

Negative, once more.

Delucchi sent Guinasso back to the break room.

After a two-and-a-half hour delay, the bailiff told reporters and family members on both sides of the trial that the matter had been settled. When Delucchi resumed the sentencing phase in his courtroom, the only clue to what had transpired was when he disclosed the matter was an evidentiary issue, or more specifically a "serious 402" matter. A 402 could also include jury misconduct.

The jury was back in the courtroom ready for the penalty phase. Prosecutor Dave Harris walked over to the defense table and pointed at Peterson as he asked for the death penalty, eliminating any chance that the prosecutors were going to be lenient or sympathetic. The jury could come back with a vote for life, Harris said, but the prosecution wanted a lethal injection to take the convicted killer's life, based on Peterson's crimes.

Judge Delucchi didn't mince words. If the jurors came back with a recommendation of death, that is what it meant. Peterson would die, as California law prescribed.

As painful and as stressful and as bizarre as the process to reach a verdict was, the jurors would once again be plunged into uncharted territory. None of them had ever served on a capital case. Their job would not be as quick as in the days of ancient Rome when Emperor Nero adjudicated life or death to a fallen gladiator with a thrust of a thumb. The six men and six women would deliberate, disagree, vote and then disclose their verdict. Once again the courtroom would be filled with sorrow and tears.

No one truly ever knows what goes through the mind of someone who is legally required to ponder such nightmarish issues. Several members of the jury had their brush with death. Steve Cardosi is a paramedic and fireman in Half Moon Bay. His job is to rescue people from death. Dennis Lear was an airline mechanic. An oversight on a maintenance item could doom a jetliner.

When deliberating on death for someone like Peterson, which is really the worse fate for a country club golfer? Spending his life in a small cell, or Death Row at San Quentin, where it might take 20 years or more to exhaust his appeals before the executioner raps on his cell?

But if the executioner does call, just how painful would that death really be, compared to the anguish Peterson caused, or any killer causes, to the families and friends of the victims? Jackie Peterson, whose father was murdered, knew the consequences of what happens to the families of loved ones. After her father's death, she and her siblings wound up in an orphanage. The Rochas were becoming aware, too. Every Christmas Eve would horrify Sharon and her family, ruining their holidays. Mother's Day would become a nightmare. Her daughter's death would ripple through generations.

Residents of Modesto, however, didn't seem to have any trouble deciding the fate of Peterson. They left crude signs outside the Peterson house. "Hi Scott, I am coming for you. Luv 'Bubba,'" read one of many hand-painted signs of hatred.

As the penalty phase began to unfold, the prosecution announced it would call four witnesses compared to 147 called during the trial. Geragos called only 14 witnesses during his losing case. For the penalty phase, he would call 39 witnesses. Was quantity now quality?

The most powerful witness for the prosecution was Sharon Rocha, Laci's mother. Harris saved her for last. Sharon's companion, Ron Grantski, who helped raise Laci, would be called and so would her brother and half-sister, Brent and Amy Rocha.

"She just lit up a room," Grantski said in tears. "I miss her. I miss the grandson we were supposed to have.... You don't realize a lot of things until they're gone. There are things you wished you would have said differently or things you wished you could have said at all. And now you can't."

A sobbing Amy Rocha explained the loss of Laci to her family. For Laci, family was everything. It was Laci who was the party planner after their grandmother died. She threw all of the parties on the holidays at her home and always remembered family birthdays.

"I miss my sister very much," she said. "I try to remember good memories we have with each other, but they are overshadowed all the time by how she died, by who, maybe her knowing who did it. ...I miss her terribly."

Now it was time for Laci's mother. The prosecution wisely stacked its lineup to build for maximum emotion. Sharon Rocha, who quietly sat in the courtroom for most of the case, became the conscience of the trial. She would tug on the emotions of the jury. Only a mother could explain the loss of a child, and she would soon paint terrifying images of what Peterson had done to her daughter and to her unborn grandson and the rest of her family. She shrieked at a man who had once called her "mom." It was the primal scream. Spectators in the audience wiped away tears as Sharon talked about the loss of her daughter.

"She always wanted to be a mother; divorce was always an option," she screamed at Peterson. "Murder is not."

As the search for her missing daughter visibly ripped apart the Rochas, Scott merely watched the horror unfold.

"There was someone who knew all along and wouldn't tell us," Sharon glowered at Peterson. "Instead, you made us go through this every day."

After Laci's remains were discovered, Sharon learned that her daughter had no head. Such a thought never entered her mind. But as she learned more, she felt the villainy of her former son-in-law. She painted a vivid picture of his crime.

"Laci had motion sickness very easily, and that's the place you took her, the Bay. You knew she'd have motion sickness for all eternity," Sharon sobbed as the impassive Peterson sat at the defense table.

The most vivid word picture Laci's mother painted were her thoughts as she said goodbye to her daughter, armless and headless in her coffin and alone forever with her baby.

"I knew she was in the casket," she said. "And I knew her baby was next to her, but she didn't have arms to hold him."

Jim Hammer, a former San Francisco prosecutor who followed the trial for Fox News, was overwhelmed by her remarks about Laci in her coffin.

"In death, she could not hold her child," he said. "This is one of the most haunting images I have ever heard."

A former San Mateo County prosecutor agreed that the image of the armless mother would be a powerful image for a jury to consider as it voted for life or death.

"I counted eight jurors weeping openly," he said, "and they listened and understood that her life and the life of her family would never be the same. For all eternity, she will never be able to hold her child. She had no arms."

After hearing Sharon Rocha, Guinasso could not help but recall the horror of seeing the autopsy photos of the remains of Laci and Conner.

"The autopsy photos during the penalty phase of deliberations were even more disturbing," he said. "We had a chance as a juror and jury to hold these photos and examine them in the most intimate nature. Some jurors held them longer and closer than others, but all jurors viewed them during deliberations. Juror No. 7 [Nice] and Juror No. 12 [Kristy Lamore] were crying. Other jurors had demonstrated emotions of disgust and anger during the viewing."

Guinasso has never forgotten what he saw.

"These visions would haunt me for the duration of the penalty phase," he said. "Matter of fact, I am still haunted by these photos periodically during the course of an average day."

Grantski touched Guinasso.

"Ron Grantski's testimony," he said, "was one that expressed anger and rage. He said he never knew what Laci saw in him. He called Scott a coward, a liar, and finally stated, 'Scott, you never knew anything about fishing.'"

Amy Rocha's testimony was short and concise. "She cried throughout the duration," he said. "She spoke about how Laci's death would affect her. I was on the verge of tears listening to this young woman speaking about her loss."

"Brent's testimony was one of anger," Guinasso said. "He called Scott a liar. He pointed at Scott and stated I trusted you with my sister, and you betrayed my family and me. He left the stand with the comment that he would pay for the murder of his sister."

But it was Sharon Rocha's haunting remarks that devastated Guinasso.

"She pointed at Scott as she wept, and then raised her voice to blurt 'divorce was always an option,'" he said. "He did not have to kill Laci. She then held a white tissue with tears pouring down her face describing to Scott that Laci could not even hold her son Conner, because she had no arms."

It got worse for Guinasso.

"She proceeded to tell Scott, with a slight pause in her voice, that Laci could not even see her son, because she had no head," Guinasso said. "It brought tears to my eyes as I listened. It was hard to fathom the degree of pain that Sharon Rocha possessed. It was very hard!"

The impact of what transpired didn't dissipate once the trial day ended.

"I left stunned; no one said goodbye to one another as we left," he said. "That was the only time in six months that happened. Some of the other jurors as they left were still wiping tears from their eyes."

As he walked to his Chevy Blazer, Rocha's wail echoed inside his brain.

"I drove home and Sharon's words still echoed," he said. "I went to work that night and it was still hard to focus. I had never experienced this state of mind, and worst of all, you could not talk to anyone about it. It was as if you were alone in this world. It ate at me daily until we reached deliberations on the death penalty."

Greg Beratlis was also affected by Sharon Rocha's word paintings that evoked the staggering sense of loss she suffered.

"She drove it home," he said. "Scott took her to the sea that she was deathly afraid of when she was alive. Laci lost her arms and her head and would never hold her baby because she had no arms. Who could not feel that? It was heart wrenching. You could see what she said and imagine it. We saw these bodies and what was left of them."

Sharon's loss of Conner was compelling.

"Laci was her oldest daughter and she was pregnant," Beratlis said. "I think Sharon wanted that baby, too."

Mark Geragos and his team were in trouble. The jury already found his client guilty of Murder One and Murder Two. The job of saving his client's life seemed to be slipping away after the powerful cries of Sharon Rocha.

On Dec. 1, Pat Harris opened the penalty phase for the defense. He was polite. He didn't attack the jurors for finding Peterson guilty.

"He acknowledged our decision, but said he disagreed with it," Guinasso said. "I thought it was a humble beginning to the opening statement. He said there would be family members, friends, neighbors, and a professor who would testify on Scott's behalf. Pat Harris said after we heard all the witnesses, we would know that Scott's qualities as a human being would be one that warranted life in prison and not death. I waited anxiously for the beginning."

Like the prosecution, the defense called a father to the stand to save his son. Lee Peterson said Scott is his best friend and he told of his own history, growing up in poverty in Minnesota and then turning to business in Southern California where he ran a successful packaging company in the San Diego area. It was as if Frank Capra had written this rags to riches script.

Scott, Lee related, was their golden boy. He and Jackie gave him a comfortable life. The family lived in exclusive Rancho Santa Fe. There were trips to Europe and country club memberships. Scott was a championship golfer in high school and went on to play on the Arizona State golf team, one of the best in the country, where

Phil Mickelson played. He led an enviable life. He lived in a world of charm, hardly someone worth pitying. He wasn't a poor kid who was abused or led a life of crime as a young boy, accelerating to murder as an adult.

Lee Peterson suggested that his Scandinavian roots may prevent him from being "emotional on the outside," something his son might have inherited if his attitude during the trial suggested like father, like son.

"I'm frightened and depressed," Scott's father admitted.

And he was sad, first about the death of Laci, but now about the possibility that his son's life might be taken from him.

"It's beyond belief," he said. "It's something I never thought I would have to go through."

Guinasso was moved at what he was hearing.

"He expressed his love for his son, and told us in no uncertain terms that putting Scott to death would devastate him and his family," he said. "I noticed Scott, for the first time in any testimony by a defense witness, cry uncontrollably. Mr. Geragos put his arm around Scott to comfort his client as if he was his father. It was the first genuine emotion shown by Scott. It surprised me."

Scott's father painted a portrait of a happy family with older sisters and brothers doting on their baby brother, especially during vacations and holidays. It was as if the magical child renewed his family.

"Scott brought our extended family closer together," he said.

The defense called 38 other witnesses, the last of which would be Jackie Peterson, who would try to match the emotional power of Sharon Rocha. Many of the ensuing witnesses would repeat the chant that Scott's death would destroy the family, especially Jackie, whose father was a murder victim.

The defense called the owner of a Morro Bay restaurant where Peterson waited tables. Abbas Imani, the owner of Pacific

Café, told the jury Peterson was the "the politest and most courteous person I ever met."

Robert Thompson, one of Scott's professors at Cal Poly, San Luis Obispo, called Peterson a standout student, and he had remained friends with him and Laci over the years. Thompson also played golf with his former student.

"I've been grieving ever since," he said. "I was close to Laci, and she was such a warm, just lit-from-within type of person. At the beginning of all this, like everyone, I had my doubts about whether Scott could do such a thing. ...I have eight years of experience with this fine young man...and I have to go with what I know and not what the media says."

The chorus to save Peterson kept singing the same song. Scott's older sister Susan Caudillo said, "I don't think my parents will make it if he goes." Joe Peterson, Scott's older brother, said the fertilizer salesman wasn't a murderer. "No way," he said. "Not my brother. Absolutely not. My kids can't believe something like this can happen. They ask about how their uncle can be locked up. They ask, why would somebody think he could do this?"

Some of the witnesses, like Abraham Latham, Peterson's cousin, criticized the jury for making a mistake by bringing in a guilty verdict, which was another uncalculated error for a group of people who had carefully weighed their decision and were poised to make another.

"There is not a violent bone in his body," Latham said of his cousin.

David Thoennes, Scott's golf coach at University of San Diego High School, chipped in with another golf ball defense, saying, "I just can't imagine anything like this from the young man I knew."

Sandra Bertram, who was one of Scott's bosses at the Rancho Santa Fe Country Club, echoed those sentiments with her putt. "I do not believe Scott is guilty of this crime," she said. "The child who I knew, who I saw daily, could not have done this."

"There were 37 other witnesses sandwiched between Lee and Jackie Peterson," Guinasso said. "These 37 witnesses were ineffective in their testimony. Most of them spoke about Lee rather than Scott, and when they spoke about Scott, it was about his golf swing and not his character."

At one point, Guinasso thought he would become ill if he heard any more testimony about Scott, the great golfer.

"It became boring listening to what a great golfer he was," said Beratlis. "It became wearing. It was redundant."

Geragos' strategy sputtered.

Jackie Peterson took the stand on Dec. 6, 2004, and Scott looked at her with tears in his eyes. She took two routes in her attempt to save Scott's life. The first was to explain the impact of Scott's death on her family, which by now had jurors dialing out, and the other was to take pity on Jackie for her own Dickensian child-hood. But she would also unfold a life of luxury in which her pampered son lived.

"We would lose a whole family," she said, sobbing. "Both Sharon and I would lose a whole family...I beg you to consider that."

"It was the first time in any testimony where both of the families were portrayed as friends and not adversaries," Guinasso said. "It concerned me, because I did not know if it was genuine on Jackie's part. It appeared to me it was only for the benefit of saving her son's life."

Most of the Peterson clan was in the courtroom and so were friends. But the chill between the families was obvious. Sharon Rocha, sitting near the jury box, had no reaction to Jackie's plea.

Jackie told the jurors, "We all lost Laci. I know how much we all loved her."

The credibility of this remark would be questioned later in her daughter Anne Bird's book, *Blood Brother: 33 Reasons Why My Brother Scott Peterson Is Guilty.*

Hiding from the media at his half-sister's house in San Francisco, Peterson had been found flirting with Bird's attractive babysitter, Bird wrote. When Jackie called the Bird house, Lorraine, the babysitter, answered the phone call.

"Oh, Lorraine," Jackie purred into the phone. "This is Scott's mom."

"Oh, hi," the babysitter said.

"I wish Scott would meet someone like you," Bird quotes Jackie as saying.

Jackie was a sympathetic figure, physically. She used a canister of oxygen to help her breathe. Her life story was sadly compelling, too.

Geragos asked her to tell the jury about her life—possibly hoping that her tragic upbringing might persuade the jurors to spare her son. Juries are supposed to reject such potentially sympathetic stories when considering the death penalty, but Geragos hoped Jackie would vibrate the emotional strings of the jurors like a fiddler playing a sad song.

Jackie told her tale of sorrow and survival. Catholic nuns begged for food door to door for the orphans. Her mother died soon after Jackie graduated high school; two unwed pregnancies followed for Jackie and, like her mother, she gave up her babies. This time it was for adoption. One of the babies was Anne Bird.

The usually emotionless Peterson dabbed his face with a tissue as her story moved forward. In 1966, she had another child outside of marriage, whom she raised as a single mother. Jackie finally found hope in 1971 when she married Lee Peterson, a businessman. Their only child was Scott, who was born a year later.

"He was a joy from the moment he was born," she said.

But Scott didn't live at "Bleak House." Lee's packaging company was humming, and Scott led a charmed life, which his mother, however, said he never took for granted.

"In high school, he tutored the homeless in the evenings," she said. "Once he came home and said, 'Mom, those kids don't have shoes that fit them.' He noticed their needs and wanted to help them."

Once again, extolling the virtues of a poor little rich boy was a questionable strategy. It's tough to feel sorry for the rich.

"The country club stuff had become patronizing," Beratlis said.

Then came Jackie's pitch about Laci. Jackie loved her, she said, although Bird's book was filled with instances in which her mother complained about her daughter-in-law. Jackie said she was thrilled that Laci finally got pregnant after three years of trying. When Laci vanished and returned from the sea with her son, it was a blow to her.

"We mourn for Laci and [baby] Conner," Jackie said. "We've lost Scott and them. I really feel if you were to take Scott away from us, it would be a whole family wiped off the face of the earth."

Unlike Sharon Rocha, Jackie Peterson appealed to the minds of the jury, not their hearts or their guts.

"In this trial you heard about his wife and baby being ripped from him, how he was stalked by the media, harassed by the police and painted as a devil to the public," she said. "He's not that and has never been that."

Guinasso, devastated by Sharon Rocha, was unmoved by Jackie Peterson.

"Jackie's testimony was not as overpowering as Sharon's, and at times, it seemed pitiful as she had the oxygen tank next to her," he said. "I was sad to see her put in such a position. I knew she had no choice."

Closing arguments for the prosecution and defense began Dec. 7, 2004, and lasted two days. Prosecutor Dave Harris said Peterson, who killed his wife and unborn son, deserved the death penalty. He was, Harris said, "the worst kind of monster."

Pat Harris led off the summation for the defense, and he seemed shaken by the guilty verdicts as he approached the jury box. He wanted the jurors to get to know the real Scott Peterson.

"There was a tear running from his eye when he was telling us that Scott is not this monster," Guinasso said. "He reminded me of an evangelist on a Sunday morning pleading for a cause."

After Harris summarized Peterson's redeeming values and asked for leniency, Guinasso doubted his sincerity.

"I sat there wondering if what I had just heard was scripted or genuinely from the heart," Guinasso said. "I reserved that thought for deliberations."

Geragos played a wild card when he followed Harris and approached the wooden railing along the jury box. He apologized for not being present at the guilt phase verdict, but then he continued apologizing. He knew the penalty phase had gone badly for Peterson. He had not prepared for one because he believed so much in his client's innocence.

"He followed up by stating that it may even be called malpractice on his part," Guinasso said. "I thought immediately that he might be stating that, to create an appellate issue after the conclusion of our verdict, if at the time it was a 'death' verdict."

Always glib, Geragos painted his own word picture. A prison guard, he said, would come to Peterson's cell. Geragos rapped three times on the wooden banister enclosing the jury box. The guard would tell his client his mother died; six months later, the guard would knock and tell him his father was dead. Geragos concluded that executing Scott would only mean more death.

"I listened intensely to Mr. Geragos," Guinasso said. "It was the first time in a long time that I thought he had a legitimate argument."

Judge Delucchi followed, reading the jury instructions for the penalty phase in which he emphasized that the jurors should not consider how Peterson's death might affect his family and friends. The jurors could only consider aggravating and mitigating factors in their decision on life or death. That was the law.

The bailiff escorted the jurors into the deliberations room for the remaining two hours of the day. The mood was dark.

"There were no jokes or kidding around before we started deliberation," Guinasso said. "The seriousness of the matter was evident."

Guinasso nominated Cardosi as foreperson again and there was a second and a third. The fireman took charge. The white board was wheeled to the front of the large rectangular glass covered table. Kristy Lamore, Juror No. 12, who liked to pace, remained seated. Cardosi divided the white board into two columns, one aggravating, and the other mitigating. The board quickly filled with their thoughts.

"We had a lot of people in that room who had feelings that went one way or the other, but we were never disrespectful about each other's opinions," Belmessieri said. "Never once did we say now wait a second my opinion is that we shouldn't have the death penalty. What we said was what does the law require us to do?"

This became one of the key issues in the death penalty deliberations.

"I know we all had our own demons dealing with this," the Marine said. "Greg [Beratlis] felt sorry for Scott and wanted to help him and that's the kind of person he is, but he overcame that and asked what does the law require us to do? What do the people of the state of California, who we were serving, require us to do here?"

Housekeeping was over. A knock soon sounded at the door and the group, instead of being transported back by a hotel bus, stepped into Sheriff's Department vans that were used for transporting prisoners.

"I noticed ankle cuffs attached to the bottom of the seats as I looked behind the front seat to the back seats," Guinasso said. "All I could think was wasn't it ironic that Scott Peterson himself probably was transported from Modesto to Redwood City in one of these? And here we are as jurors taking seats in place of prisoners."

They had become prisoners once again. During deliberations, their break time outside was in the exercise yard located on the roof of the courthouse and surrounded by cyclone fencing.

"It was one giant cage that you would see at the zoo," Guinasso said. "I felt like an animal at times. I had that built up frustration of wanting my freedom. But for this period of time, I could only think about it."

Back at the Crowne Plaza, the old routine resumed. Their bags were already in their rooms. The same four channels on the TV sets were still programmed. It was business as usual. No one was happy.

"For me, I was miserable and cranky for both sequestrations," Guinasso said. "This time, I contracted the flu and was more irritable than normal."

Dinner was in the common room, but not every juror showed up. The impact of the upcoming decision had taken its toll on their appetites. And salmon was once again on the menu.

At 6 a.m., there was a knock on every juror's door. Guinasso was already awake and getting sick. He hadn't slept well.

"I was breaking down," he said. "My resistance was at an all time low. Jurors were passing out cold and flu medicine. We were all breaking down emotionally and physically."

It was Friday, Dec. 10 and many of the jurors hoped they would reach a verdict. The foreman started the process by selecting a fact from the white board and it would be debated, sometimes heavily. It would become a battle of aggravating factors versus mitigating factors.

"We as jurors put a lot of weight on Laci and Conner being on the bottom of the Bay until April 13th and 14th and Scott knowing about it," Guinasso said. "More than 100 days elapsed while Laci's family suffered not knowing where she was at or what happened to her. This outweighed any mitigating factors by tenfold."

Geragos' golf ball defense flopped, as did testimony about Peterson being a charming waiter.

"Scott's golf swing, or hospitality at the Pacific Café had little value as mitigating factors," Guinasso said.

Amber Frey's tapes became a powerful tool for those seeking the death penalty.

"These tapes exposed him as a man who planned events to accomplish a devious and heinous goal," Guinasso said. "When we were in there deliberating on the death sentence, you had to think about the 39 witnesses that the defense had during the penalty phase talking about mitigating services that might have saved his life. Most of them spoke about his game of golf, most of them spoke about his reading a book to their niece or his niece or doing a neighborly deed, but the real Scott Peterson was exposed in those tapes and that weighed more than any mitigating circumstances the defense offered."

Guinasso's vision of Peterson from the word pictures he painted of himself was chilling. The tapes revealed the darkness inside him.

"He was somebody that if you were looking for different things for first-degree murder, you could find them and the first was he had to plan it, obviously. Even with Amber Frey—he planned on seducing her that first night with his champagne and strawberries. He had everything planned."

The debate raged, but the lunch break stopped the proceedings and the jurors were escorted into the courtroom to eat. Perhaps in deference to the judge, only Delucchi's chair was not used. All the other chairs were occupied, especially at the prosecution and defense tables.

Guinasso was not hungry, but opened a potato chip bag and pulled a chip from it and held it so Cardosi could see it and said, "Vegetable."

"I thought Cap was going to fall out of his seat from laughter, as he was a food conscious being, and I was completely the opposite," Guinasso said. "It sort of lightened the atmosphere for the moment."

The deliberations continued until court ended for the day. The foreman wanted a straw poll to see where the group was. The vote was six for death, four abstentions, and two for life—Beratlis and Marino. It was back to Club Med until Monday.

"We were stalemated," Beratlis said.

Beratlis said he had to go through the rules about premeditated murder and mitigating and aggravating circumstances. The group went over them again.

Nice, Belmessieri, Zanartu and Guinasso were among those who voted death on the first round.

"I said death, but I don't think any of us were so dug in that we wanted to just go out and say that's it," Belmessieri said. "We wanted to be sure we were making the right decision."

Nice explained the process. "There were people who had some doubt about certain areas like Greg and he needed to go over these areas," she said. "We would help him go over it or Tom, whomever. We would pick a topic and hash it out again and talk about it."

Marino, the devout Catholic, was concerned about whether Peterson deserved the death penalty, even though it was a double murder. He needed more time.

Beratlis also needed the weekend to process this. "I was exhausted," he said. "I didn't want to decide on death; I needed to think. Mario [Tom Marino] said he needed time. When I went back to the hotel, I began picking it all apart in my mind. This was a man's life."

Guinasso, Beratlis said, wanted the death penalty. "He was clear," Beratlis said. "But nobody was going to force me to make a decision."

But after six months, Beratlis knew one thing for sure about Peterson. "He was a manipulator," he said.

He said when anybody had doubts about what was transpiring, Guinasso was ready to read the rulebook on the deliberations.

"We were not going to be a lynch mob," Beratlis said. "There would be no rush to judgment.... After the trial, my son and I would discuss the decision and he would ask how the death penalty was justice by taking another person's life. Who am I to be playing God? I was no better than Scott Peterson. I said I was following the letter of the law."

It was a pro football-viewing weekend at the Crowne Plaza and the jurors made football squares that cost $1.00. These squares had numbers on them for each team, and the winner took the pot.

"It was something we did to amuse ourselves," Guinasso said. "We were all bored. One thing did happen as we watched the Raiders versus the Atlanta Falcons on Channel 5, the CBS-owned outlet. There was a *60 Minutes* promo that advertised an upcoming story about an accused killer who was sent to death row and who might have his sentence overturned by the Supreme Court.

"I thought that was very telling, and asked the sheriff's deputy to note that, so I could speak to Judge Delucchi," Guinasso said.

Guinasso took up the issue once he returned to the courthouse on Monday, Dec. 13. He handed Jenne a note addressed to Judge Delucchi about the *60 Minutes* commercial. Impatient for an answer, he asked Jenne if Judge Delucchi was ready to see him. Once again, the Teamster sat between Geragos and Dave Harris.

"I told Judge Delucchi what I had witnessed on the television," Guinasso said. "He asked me if it might change my thought process regarding this phase. I said it might. As soon as I said that, Judge Delucchi stated, 'Juror No. 8, death is death, and life is life. Whatever verdict is arrived at, that is what it will be.' In common terms, it meant go into the deliberation room, follow the law, not a commercial on television."

Once deliberations resumed on Monday, events moved swiftly. Cardosi asked for the autopsy photos of the headless and armless Laci and the gelatin-like remains of Conner. He put the autopsy photos next to Laci's photo of her in the red satin outfit sitting in the chair at a Christmas party that she attended without Scott.

Belmessieri picked them up and looked at Laci in her red dress that appeared in her missing posters.

"This is Laci before Scott dumped her into the Bay and let her family wait all that time so we can see Laci after Scott Peterson," Belmessieri said. "And by the way, when everybody is standing around talking about their grandchildren, this is the only thing Sharon will see. Let's talk about what Scott has as a redeeming value."

Richelle Nice was the first to look at them, and she burst out crying, uncontrollably saying that Scott was supposed to protect Laci and Conner, not murder them. The photos were passed to each juror for comparison.

"I was hysterical," Nice said.

Dennis Lear and Tom Marino had seen enough and passed. The foreman called for another vote. It was now 11 to 1 for death. The postman, Tom Marino, Juror No. 2, identified himself as the hold out.

Marino now wanted each juror to say why he or she chose death over life. He needed convincing; he also wanted to make sure everyone was certain about the vote, just as he had done during the verdict phase.

Marino listened carefully. They asked if everybody was ready for the final vote. Something strange seemed to come over Marino. Before the final vote was taken, he pulled his chair away from the table to the corner of the room near the window.

"I saw him pressing his two hands together in a prayer mode mumbling something under his breath," Guinasso said. "I reminded him that his religious views could not be considered according to the law, and that only aggravating and mitigating factors could determine the verdict."

Marino was ready. So were the others.

"This is the reality of it," Belmessieri said. "Okay, what have we heard, so far, that says this man has value? We went through the whole thing. It is expected that a mother and father would beg for his life, his sisters and brothers, too. We had to dismiss that and take into consideration what he brought to society."

The foreman tore off pieces of paper for the ballots.

"The room became very quiet," Guinasso recalled. "It felt as if you were in a vacuum. Juror No. 1, Greg Beratlis, was complaining of chest pains. Other jurors were shaking as they surrendered the torn pieces of paper to Cap with their decisions. Others started to cry from the pressure that had mounted."

Cardosi began reading the tally. Guinasso awaited Marino's vote for life.

"Cap," he said, "counted off death, death, death, death, death, death, death, death, death, death. And death! Mario had changed his mind."

It was a unanimous verdict, 12-0.

Marino, the last holdout for life, eventually found what he heard on Amber Frey's tapes to be one of the reasons that Peterson should be recommended for the death penalty.

"The tapes showed that he seemed unconcerned about his missing wife as if he knew what really happened to Laci and thought he could get away with it," the postman said. "Why was he still interested in Amber?"

The tapes showed something else during the penalty phase because the instructions to the jury were to weigh the mitigating and aggravating circumstances when considering the death penalty.

"The tapes showed Scott's actions and attitude to be one that shows a lack of respect and concern for all parties involved," Marino said.

"I think John (Guinasso) said it best when he said off the cuff, 'Tom, why are you going to get your religion involved in this case?'" Belmessieri said. "'You have a duty and an obligation.' That's how I see it. It is a matter of duty and obligation, not a matter of personal opinions and personal causes."

As the foreman filled out the paperwork for the court, Kristy Lamore broke down crying. Others fell back in their chairs taking a moment to regain their composure. After completing the paperwork, the foreman told Jenne that the jury had reached a decision.

Within an hour, the families, lawyers, media, sheriff's deputies and Modesto police began making their way to the courtroom. Once everybody was seated, the jurors were ushered into the courtroom single file and they took their respective chairs.

Peterson was at the defense table talking to Geragos and Harris in what seemed like just another day in court for him.

"This decision was not going to faze him," Guinasso thought. "It seemed as if he was in his own little world and nothing would affect him. It was odd behavior for a young man who was just about to get the death penalty."

Judge Delucchi asked the foreman to give the clerk the document he had completed. Marylin announced the decision to the packed courtroom.

Sharon Rocha collapsed into Ron Grantski's arms crying. Other family members sobbed. Scott showed little emotion.

"It seemed odd," Guinasso said.

Judge Delucchi asked the defense if they wanted the jury polled; they did.

Then came a chorus of yes, yes....

"Scott almost looked desensitized," Beratlis said. "There was no emotion. It was as if he was looking through us. The Petersons looked numb as if it was all a dream. Peterson would now pay the ultimate price."

Others saw a different reaction. "I saw him laughing," Zanartu said. "That's when I started crying. How dare he do that to his own family and not even care."

Outside, the jurors began hearing cheers at their verdict from a gathering of people who had waited outside to hear the news of Peterson's fate.

"It was sickening," Beratlis said. "I felt nauseous. What if we had reached a different verdict? How would they have reacted? Then I thought justice was served; the judicial system worked. Maybe that is why they were cheering."

SUPERIOR COURT OF CALIFORNIA, COUNTY OF SAN MATEO
HALL OF JUSTICE
400 COUNTY CENTER
REDWOOD CITY, CALIFORNIA 94063

ALFRED A. DELUCCHI
Judge (Ret.)

December 13, 2004

John Guinasso

Re: *People v. Peterson*
    Case No. SC055500

Dear Mr. Guinasso:

On behalf of the Superior Court and the citizens of this County, I wish to thank you for your recent service on jury duty.

I greatly appreciate your patience, your time, your effort and your commitment to our community. The right to a jury trial is a most fundamental right in our society and requires the involvement of everyone in order to assure the system works for everyone.

I am mindful of the personal sacrifice you had to make to serve as a juror and I commend you for your participation. It is this kind of involvement that ensures we may all continue to live in a free society.

I wish to convey to you my appreciation for your diligence and attentiveness and compliment you upon your earnest consideration of the evidence and arguments of the respective lawyers, together with your painstaking deliberations prior to agreement upon the verdicts. As a good citizen you have performed an indispensable civic obligation.

Thank you again for your time and effort.

Very truly yours,

Alfred A. Delucchi

Alfred A. Delucchi, Ret.
Judge of the Superior Court
For the County of San Mateo

On the day the jurors recommended the death penalty for Peterson, Judge Delucchi sent the jurors a letter of thanks for their civic service.

CHAPTER 14: WHY?

"If she disappeared, he could be a victim. He could say,
'I lost my soul mate. Now, my life is incomplete. I have to find someone.'
And here comes Amber who is very vulnerable and she is treated
like a queen. It would all be poor Scott."
—Greg Beratlis, Juror No. 1

There was no bullet, no knife, no blunt object or poison that took the life of Laci Peterson. In all likelihood, she was strangled or suffocated—"the soft kill," authorities have said.

All murders are horrific, but imagine this death scene. An eight-and-a-half-month pregnant woman, whose womb was filled with her baby boy, is grabbed and strangled or suffocated. If she was sleeping, she might have stirred, only for a moment.

If she was awake, there might have been a struggle, her arms and legs flailing as her attacker, the man she loved, took the breath out of her life. There may have been screams, horrible gasps for breath, hands desperately reaching back to grab at her killer. Either way, she was no match for her bigger and more powerful attacker. She would die, and soon after her son would die from a lack of oxygen.

Her last thoughts could well have centered on one question: Why?

Nobody knows how Peterson really killed his wife, but the jurors, after spending six months of their lives on the case, couldn't keep from wondering why he did it.

Beratlis believed that Peterson did not want the responsibility of fatherhood, but divorce was out of the question. Scott was the golden boy in the Peterson family. He had to be perfect.

"Perfection painted him into the corner," Beratlis said. "In the back of his mind he always thought he might be given up like his mother's other children. I think he was insecure about his personality and learned early in life how to please people. Then he marries Laci who was full of life."

Ironically, he feared his life would change when she became pregnant and literally full of life.

"He is in this relationship with his wife who has been having trouble getting pregnant," Beratlis said. "He never intended for her to get pregnant, but she did and his world came crashing down. She was a bubbly personality, and she brought the limelight to him, but now she was pregnant and heavy and he was going to be a father. His son wasn't a dog that you put in a kennel. This was a responsibility. He would never have Amber. He never had any responsibilities with her. Her daughter was not his responsibility. She was not his daughter, and he was not the bad guy if they separated."

But if Peterson divorced Laci, he would become a bad guy, a man who ran out on his wife and his infant son. That was intolerable. Murder became a viable option.

"What do I do now? I am a heel if I get a divorce, a bad guy and I don't know how to be a bad guy; the only option is for her to disappear," Beratlis said. "If he got divorced, it would be like a blemish on his life."

But there was more to this killing, Beratlis believed, and it would play into Peterson's narcissism. In his twisted world, Laci's disappearance would make him the center of attention.

"If she disappeared, let's say she was kidnapped, he could be a victim," Beratlis said. "He could say, 'I lost my soul mate. Now, my life is incomplete. I have to find someone.' Everybody would feel bad for him. The perfect marriage and now the perfect ending. He goes through the grief and then looks for a new partner. And here comes Amber who is very vulnerable and she is treated like a queen. She was so naïve and she was clay in his hands. It would all be poor Scott."

John Guinasso looked at Peterson day after day in the courtroom and after six months of watching how the defendant responded, he wondered why. Now the reasons seem clear.

"I believe Scott Peterson was scared of one word in life, 'failure,'" Guinasso said. "In his warped mind, killing Laci and Conner without getting caught would have prevented the ultimate failure in his life, a divorce. Without Laci and Conner in his life, it would have opened the doors to conquering and pleasing his desire for conquest. In my opinion, Scott fed off his womanizing conquests, and in turn fueled his mind with the word 'success,' not 'failure.'"

Beratlis said one of the reasons Peterson received a second-degree murder conviction for Conner's death was that Conner wasn't an intended victim. Laci's death was an act of great planning.

Guinasso thought Peterson killed his wife on the evening of Dec. 23, 2002, after they left Salon Salon, where Amy Rocha gave Peterson a haircut and taught Laci how to use a curling iron on her hair.

"Scott's pizza invitation to Amy at Salon Salon was going to be another facet of his alibi if she had accepted," Guinasso said. "Remember, Laci had called her mom at about 8:30 p.m. that evening. That was probably when she was getting ready for bed."

Like other jurors, Guinasso believed that Peterson murdered his wife and unborn son to escape the responsibilities of being a parent.

"Freedom, he wanted the single life," he said. "In my opinion, he was a sexually addicted person. Amber might have been the next one he would kill. My final reasoning of why he committed the murders of his wife Laci and his son Conner is due to one word, 'selfishness.' In my opinion, Scott thought the world revolved around him, and if he wasn't put at the pinnacle of any situation, he would abandon it, or go even to the extreme—murder."

Tom Marino also believed Peterson wanted to snuff out a part of his life represented by Laci and Conner. But Marino feels that Peterson was in denial about his actions.

"Deep down inside me, I think he did it because he wanted to erase his marriage and anything else that came with it [that being the baby]," Marino said. "It was almost like he wanted to delete that chapter of his life and somehow I think he rationalized this horrible event by convincing himself that somebody else really did do it."

"Why did Scott do it?" asks Mike Belmessieri. "Freedom! He wanted to live a single playboy like lifestyle. Paying an ex-wife spousal support and child support would have created a bit of a problem for him."

As it did for all of the jurors, the question why resounded in the minds of Julie Zanartu and Richelle Nice. It is a mystery locked in the mind of the man who now sits on death row.

"He is the only one who knows why he did it," Zanartu said. "I don't think anyone else will ever know for sure. We can only speculate. I wish I knew what was going on in his mind."

Nice doesn't know how Peterson killed his wife and son, but she can't understand why he would do such a heinous act.

"All day long I used to think of Laci and the Little Man," she said. "Scott, why did you do it? That was never answered for me at the trial. Will we ever know? She was so beautiful and full of life. Why would you want to do that? Only Scott has all the answers."

SUPERIOR COURT OF CALIFORNIA, COUNTY OF SAN MATEO
Hall of Justice and Records
400 County Center
Redwood City, CA 94063-1655

PEGGY THOMPSON
COURT EXECUTIVE OFFICER
CLERK & JURY COMMISSIONER

(650) 363-4516
FAX (650) 363-4698
www.sanmateocourt.org

December 29, 2004

John Guinaoso

Dear Mr. Guinaoso:

We received an inquiry for counseling services. The court does not offer these services. However, if you are interested, you may contact Lynda Frattaroli, Unit Chief of the San Mateo County's Access Team at (650) 573-2276, and she will advise you of the resources available.

Should you decide to contact Ms. Frattaroli, please identify yourself as a juror who sat on the Peterson case.

Should you have any questions regarding this correspondence, please contact Mel Toomer, Deputy Court Executive Officer at (650) 363-7881. Thank you.

Sincerely,

Peggy Thompson,
Court Executive Officer

cc: Mel Toomer, Deputy Court Executive Officer

Despite the post-traumatic effects that a capital case such as this may have on the jurors, San Mateo County does not offer them counseling.

CHAPTER 15:
AFTERMATH

"If you spend three months or six months or a year on a trial, your emotions are going to be attacked. You have feelings and memories and if you have these feelings, it means you are a kind and caring human being."
—Dr. Jesse Hanley, expert on stress disorders and author of "Tired of Being Tired"

When Howard Varinsky, the veteran San Francisco jury consultant who had just come off helping prosecutors convict Martha Stewart in New York, was asked about what happens to jurors in a murder case, he gave pause for thought. They, like retuning GIs in Iraq, have a lot in common.

"People will come away from a trial like this as if they had been in a battle zone," said Varinsky, the prosecution's jury consultant. "They will be very changed people. These people will become victims when they have to decide on the death of someone."

There are no courses to study about being a juror at a murder trial; there are no hospitals that treat juror-victims. Maybe there's a therapist who can talk to them or who can prescribe medications to help them pass the time until their memories fade away, if they ever do.

What was unfortunate in the Peterson case was that San Mateo County doesn't provide counseling for jurors. Some of these victims may not understand how they have been affected as they try to cope unknowingly with the emotional impact of a trial that has left them with flashbacks and nightmares. At war, GIs at least get combat pay. Nobody was paying these combatants for hazardous duty.

Julie Zanartu thinks about the case every day. Greg Beratlis always finds someone bringing the subject up, despite his wish to move on with his life and put the trial behind him. Mike Belmessieri still thinks about the autopsy photos of Laci and Conner, which brought him a flashback from his military service. John Guinasso has nightmares, too.

"I just see the picture of her torso, the one in which she was chewed up by a dog and eaten by sea life, no head, a little bit of an upper arm and no legs. It's just overwhelming," Guinasso said.

Dr. Jesse Hanley, an expert on stress disorders and the author of *Tired of Being Tired*, said it is not surprising that the Peterson jurors are suffering from the effects of being on the long murder trial.

"It's normal," she said. "If you spend three months or six months or a year on a trial, your emotions are going to be attacked. You have feelings and memories and if you have these feelings, it means you are a kind and caring human being."

"An emotional trial like the Peterson case, especially because it had such vivid and horrifying autopsy photographs, affects the stress hormones in the brain, which makes people more vulnerable emotionally," she said. "It would not be surprising that the jurors might sleep poorly, overeat, crave sugar, have mood swings and have irregular menstrual cycles."

"It's normal to be upset by traumatic events and it is not just the people who came back from Vietnam and now Iraq," Hanley said.

What a long trial like the Peterson case does, she said, is to reach back into past memories and rekindle them and not just once, but constantly. Mike Belmessieri's sudden flashback to seeing a fellow Marine's death is not unusual.

"Being in court everyday reinforces this," she said.

There are ways to treat such stress disorders. Medications like Xanax offer temporary relief. Curtailing the intake of sugar helps and so do vitamins and supplements. Therapists who specialize in stress disorders are also helpful. Relaxation techniques may offer relief. And there is time, which, as they say, heals all wounds.

"It's a healing process," Hanley said.

The scars from the Peterson trial become evident when jurors talk about the case and their involvement.

RICHELLE NICE

Richelle Nice is "Ricci," but to the millions of Americans who watched the trial unfold, she is "Strawberry Shortcake," the nickname the media gave her during their coverage of the case. She even has used the sobriquet on her telephone answering machine.

Nice, the most flamboyant member of the jury, started out as an alternate, but her unique looks and crimson hairstyle made her a darling of the media. Since the end of the trial, this single mother of four returned to the spotlight when *People* magazine revealed that she had been corresponding with Scott Peterson as a pen pal. So far, she has received eight letters and an Easter card, all of which she keeps in a manila envelope stashed in a bedroom drawer. She initiated the letter writing campaign, she says, with the hopes of getting the wily Peterson to confess. So far, he has not.

Peterson, ever the manipulator, writes her back in a neat cursive handwriting, the kind that kids at Catholic schools are always taught. The fertilizer pitchman says he didn't kill his wife and unborn son and asks her for tips about spending time in his cell on San Quentin's Death Row. Ever the self-promoter, he tells Nice that the Modesto cops bungled their investigation and he likes visits from family members and friends. Taking a page from his seduction file, he inquires about her days as a juror, why she convicted him and sent him to death row.

Nice's therapist suggested that her emotionally frail client, who had suffered two breakdowns since the end of the trial, tell Peterson about her life on the edge of sanity. Initially, the plan was to write the first letter and mail it with no address. Nice rolled the dice and sent it to San Quentin. She never thought Peterson would reply. He did and his letters, not surprisingly, were emotionally distant. It was as if he was back at the defense table, cool and calm and out of touch with what had happened.

This has become a cat and mouse game. Peterson tries to convince Nice that he didn't kill Laci and Conner. Nice is trying to convince him to admit his guilt. It's like a tango that twists into a pretzel.

It usually took two to three weeks to get a letter to Peterson. He would then reply.

"In his letters, he was asking me more about how I was, and how the trial affected me and my family and how hard it must have been for me having to view the autopsy photos," she said.

Ever the hustler of women, Peterson, she said, told her, "You guys were forced to look at them, but he can't. He said he would stare at a spot on the wall and basically shut down. So I realized he would not confess. I had to change the direction of my letter writing and ask how his life was now."

Life has not been easy for Nice and her children. Abused as a young girl, she suffers mood swings and talks about her own death. A family member has been keeping an eye on her to make sure she doesn't hurt herself when she drives her truck.

She says she has no romantic interest in Peterson. She reiterates that and believes that her correspondence with the man she helped put behind bars will eventually succeed in achieving the result she wishes to achieve.

"He is going to admit it to me," she insisted.

When Beratlis heard the news that Nice was corresponding with Peterson, he became noticeably upset with her. He could not imagine why she would dwell in the past.

"I don't want to be involved anymore at all," he said. "I'll see the other jurors at some point in my life again but that was one phase of my life and it is time to move on."

Beratlis thinks Peterson's execution will pale in comparison to the suffering he has caused the Rochas and even his own family.

"What happened to the Rocha family will go on and on," he said. "Christmases will be tarnished forever. It is like what happens when a child is abused. The cycle goes on and on and that is what happens to the ones we know about. What about the ones we don't know about? What are they going to do?"

Nice said she doesn't have the emotional makeup of Beratlis.

"I'm not like Greg by any stretch," she said. "This trial has consumed my life. I mean I ate, drank and breathed and slept it. Like Greg said, I handle things differently now. I look at things differently now. I didn't know how or where to release my feelings and I told my therapist about writing Scott and she said, 'Well, do it.'"

She admitted she felt sorry for Peterson, but that doesn't change her mind about the verdicts.

"We did justice, but that is another life that is going to be lost, period," she said, "point blank and, you know, it didn't have to be that way. It's sad that he chose to end his wife's life and his son's life and his own life. It's sad. It's a waste of three lives."

Nice said Peterson couldn't give up his playboy lifestyle because of his son's impending birth.

"The more she grew bigger, it really hit him," she said. "He's such a Casanova and all of that. It probably would not have stopped him completely but he would have had to slow down and I think that wasn't an option."

The debate over Murder Two about the killing of Conner, the "Little Man," as she called the unborn child, centered over the issue that "there was never anything that showed he was trying to kill Conner. Mike and I were saying, well, you can't kill a pregnant woman without killing the baby unless you take the baby out of her womb and he didn't."

Nice, like the others, has nightmares.

"I sometimes wake up at night crying," she said. "What is wrong, I think? What went wrong in my life? What happened to me? That is why I am on so much medication."

In Dec. 2005, she had a "major" breakdown at one of her children's schools. It was nearly a year after they recommended the death penalty.

"I couldn't get out of my truck," she said. "All I knew is that I was done with my life; it was over. I wanted to slam my truck into the wall, slam it while I was driving. I couldn't care less about me, but my kids, I had those kids so I feel an obligation to take care of them. They keep me going."

She's haunted by Laci's murder. During her classes for cosmetology, she found herself writing letters to Peterson.

"I'm thinking of Laci when songs come on," she said. "You know everyone knows who I am. There are a lot of girls in my college classes who are 18 or 19 years old, and their moms are telling them to get my autograph. It's like man, you know, I just convicted this guy for killing his wife. I'm now his fucking pen pal. What the hell is going on?"

JOHN GUINASSO

For two years John Guinasso, who was "Bill" during the trial and still signs his correspondence with "Juror No. 8," has lived in agony. The dates and images of the trial trigger flashbacks. The San

Francisco Bay that once served as a backyard during his childhood is now a constant reminder of the tragedy.

"The San Francisco Bay used to represent serenity," he said. "But now it beckons with the hollow cries of Laci and Conner Peterson. All I can think of is Laci's head still on the floor of the San Francisco Bay looking up to God and asking, 'Why?'"

Guinasso, a gentle soul in a lineman's body, gained weight during and after the trial. At 280 pounds he is heavier than he has ever been. The stress shows no sign of abating. The flashbacks haunt him.

"All these flashbacks begin with the gruesome photos of Laci Peterson's torso wedged in the rocks of the eastside shoreline of the San Francisco Bay and young Conner lying in the shallow tidal pool surrounded by debris," he said. "These flashbacks always start out with these visuals and then end with a young man who had apparently everything going for him, Scott Peterson, pictured with a dastardly grin that conceals his murderous deeds."

Guinasso shudders when he drives over the Bay Bridge to the East Bay and sees the exit for the Berkeley Marina. "My mind becomes obsessed with the autopsy photos, and Sharon Rocha's painful dramatic testimony of the loss of her beautiful daughter," he said. "Sometimes it does not stop there. It continues throughout the day. Sometimes people will ask me if I am okay, and I respond yes. I do this only to appease their question because it is hard for someone to relate to your mental state if one has not been through such a stressful process."

Certain dates disturb Guinasso: Dec. 9, when Peterson began to hatch his plot to kill his wife and unborn son, and Dec. 23 and 24 when he executed his plan. Christmas is no longer joyful.

"These last two Christmas holidays, I tried to enjoy the company of family and friends, but my mind would not let me," he said.

Guinasso, a throwback of sorts, has not sought counseling. Instead, he has relied on his girlfriend and brother for counsel. Since he was 18, he has sought refuge in his work, but even more so now.

"San Mateo County does not provide counseling to any juror that may be suffering mentally after such a horrific experience," he said. "I find that shameful after witnessing countless delays during the trial that added up to thousands of dollars to the county. The county protected us jurors as pieces of fine China during the trial and deliberations, and then disposed of us like paper plates at its conclusion. It sent mixed messages to our brains."

People who never heard the evidence still question the verdicts.

"Men especially ask me how could you convict Scott Peterson if there wasn't any physical evidence?" Guinasso said. "I try to explain to them that circumstantial evidence carries the same weight as direct evidence. On the flip side, the majority of the women thought our verdict was correct, and that we did a tremendous job as jurors on such a tough trial."

Unlike the general population and the county, the victims' family was grateful for the jurors' service. Two months after the trial they met Sharon and Dennis Rocha and other members of the Rocha family and prosecution at the Canyon Inn in Redwood City. "The pain was still evident, especially for Sharon and Dennis Rocha, but for all of us at this stage it was about starting the healing process," Guinasso said.

But so far healing has not come. It is a process that, for Guinasso, might take a lifetime as Peterson's case wends its way through the appeals process.

"I thought there would be closure after Judge Delucchi sentenced Scott to death in March 2005, but there has not been any," he said. "I believe closure will actually be obtained on the day I turn on the TV and the news anchor states, 'Scott Peterson's death sentence has been carried out by lethal injection, with members of the Rocha family present.'"

JULIE ZANARTU

Julie Zanartu identifies so much with her juror number—9—that when she found a shirt with her number on it, she had to buy it. After all, for months she had been known to the outside world and to her fellow panelists as "Juror No. 9." Even her friends got into the act. Her good friend Larry played the Beatles' song, "Revolution No. 9," each time he saw her. "Number 9, number 9, number 9, number 9," the lyrics drone on. The gag got old after a while.

When first asked about how she has been affected by the trial, Zanartu says it hasn't changed her life. She hasn't experienced the same kind of post-traumatic stress that she has heard other jurors talk about. She feels funny about that.

"I still do my normal things, like go to work, hang out with my friends and my husband," she said. "I remember telling my friend Gina there must be something wrong with me because I don't feel any different. I don't have nightmares. In the first couple of days I would cry sometimes. It was a traumatic experience. That was once in a while, just at first. Maybe one day I'll just completely crack or something."

But a day later, she realizes her life has been affected profoundly. "I haven't celebrated one Christmas since then," Zanartu said. "I just can't get into it."

On the first Christmas following the trial, she and her husband visited her mother. The decorations on a neighbor's house didn't bring Christmas cheer.

"I just got really sad looking at the Christmas decorations," she said. "Everything happened with Laci and her poor family at

Christmas. It just bothered me. After that, Christmas didn't make me happy any more. I stay home. I don't buy presents. We don't get a tree. Nothing."

At work, Zanartu has a daily reminder of the trial and the tragedy. The Genentech offices, where she works as a biotech clinical trial inspector, are situated on the San Francisco Bay. Zanartu takes walks along the shore during her lunch breaks.

"I can't do that walk without thinking about where they found the bodies," she said. "Especially when I see a boat. I think about what he was thinking about when he put her in the boat. One day I saw a pickup truck backed up to the dock. It was similar to his truck. It made me wonder about how he did it. What was going through his mind? How did he get there?"

Like the others, she has had to deal with ignorant and unpleasant comments from people.

"My favorite one is, 'Do you really think he did it?'" she said. "Of course, I know he did it. I don't think he did it. Some people are ignorant about the justice system. They say, 'Are you one of those who voted for the death penalty? Doesn't it have to be like 7 to 5?' I'm like, 'No, that's not how it works.' I just think they're kind of dumb. They just don't understand. I think they think it was a vote, like an election, and I got outvoted."

Other people have expressed their disdain for the verdicts. She usually ignores their comments—"I'm not going to argue. It's over and done with"—but sometimes she feels she has to respond. "Out of everybody in this room, mine is the only one that matters," she told one woman.

A girl at work said she was hoping the jury would let Peterson go. "You guys let O.J. go," she said.

"It's as if there's only one set of jurors who go around and do all the trials," Zanartu said. "I had nothing to do with O.J. Sorry."

She doesn't have flashbacks from seeing the gruesome autopsy photos, but they had one culinary impact: she no longer eats ribs.

"It just bothers me now," she said. "When they talked about the dogs chewing on Laci, that was disturbing. Seeing the baby's face really got to me. Every once in a while I see the little baby. It had a little face. It wasn't just a fetus, it was a person."

The deliberation process for guilt was more trying for Zanartu than the penalty deliberations, but both were difficult.

"I think probably life in prison is worse than the death penalty," said Zanartu, whose first husband was murdered while serving time in San Quentin. "To me, Peterson is going to die there regardless, whether by injection or old age or by somebody killing him. So either way it's not going to be a nice thing. To me the hardest thing was finding him guilty or not guilty. I knew it was going to be devastating for the Peterson family. But you can't consider that."

During the trial Zanartu struggled to keep her emotions in check. But after the death penalty verdict, she allowed herself to break down. "I'd cry to my husband because I was so emotionally drained," she said. "I didn't cry during the whole trial. I wanted to. But I was there for a reason and it wasn't to be emotional. At the very end, I allowed myself to cry because it was all over. I felt terrible for everybody involved, both families."

She was struck by the Rochas when she met them at the Canyon Inn. Zanartu, who is shy, peeked into the restaurant. Dennis Rocha saw her.

"He came over and picked me up and grabbed me and hugged me," she said. "Nobody's ever hugged me like that before. That was emotional for me."

And then there were ladybugs. At the party, Zanartu overheard Sharon Rocha talking with prosecutor Dave Harris about ladybugs. Laci loved ladybugs. The day the jury reached its guilty verdict, the prosecutors saw ladybugs land on a windowsill at their hotel which overlooks the San Francisco Bay. Zanartu told Sharon and

Harris that a ladybug had landed on her the day before she was selected to be a juror as she was walking along the path by the Bay.

"That ladybug always stuck in my mind," Zanartu said. "Maybe it was one of life's coincidences. Then on Laci's birthday in May, I was walking on the trail and sure enough a ladybug came right next to my head."

These days her sorrow and tears are over the death of her father a few years ago and coping with her mother, who has Alzheimer's. Those two personal tragedies bring her tears. While most of the others do not want to serve as jurors on another trial, Zanartu was excited when she received a summons for jury duty in 2006 for another murder trial.

"I was hoping they would pick me," she said. "I was all excited. Everybody said can't you get out of it? My doctor said, 'I'll write you a note to say you're too stressed out and you can't go.' But I wanted to go. I always wanted to be on the jury before this. I think it's interesting."

DENNIS LEAR

Dennis Lear credits his wife, who has a degree in psychology, with helping him cope with the stresses of the trial. He hasn't suffered from nightmares or relationship issues. The retired United Airlines mechanic lives 100 miles away in Coarsegold in the San Joaquin Valley. He no longer has the daily reminders of the Bay or the Redwood City Courthouse.

Lear, who describes himself as someone who sees a lot of grays in life, seems to have taken his jury service as one of life's difficult experiences. You get through it and you move on.

"It's not something I'm proud of," he said. "We did what needed to be done."

Nevertheless, he is more skeptical of the world around him.

"One of the things that bothers me from time to time is that if a kid like Scott could do such a crime, anyone is capable of something similar," he said. "I think I look at people around me with a more critical eye."

He is also critical of the system that kept him and his colleagues cooped up for more than six months.

"Having done a major trial, I don't need to do another," he said. "When I think of all the wasted time during this trial, it's no wonder people avoid jury duty."

He has the usual encounters with people in restaurants and in the community. One time an avid trial watcher introduced herself and said she was in the courtroom every day. He had little idea what she wanted from him. "I guess she wanted to tell her friends," he said.

Lear understands that the Peterson saga is a story that won't die. The cable shows continue to repeat the interviews done with jurors, witnesses and other trial participants over the last two years. The shows are a constant reminder for Lear.

"This trial proves the power of the press," Lear said. "They still repeat the interviews and people still watch. Who would have thought this would still be going on?"

But will the Peterson trial and the verdict meted out be a cautionary tale for other would-be wife murderers? Not likely, Lear said.

"Hopefully some guy who's out there thinking about murdering his wife will have second thoughts but I really doubt it," Lear said. "They all think they won't get caught!"

With time, the impact seems to be receding from Lear's consciousness.

"Not to say I haven't woken up thinking about the trial," he said, "but as I analyze things I know we made the right decision. I decided a long time ago not to let hindsight affect my decisions. You make a decision and stick with it. We made a decision and we get to live with it for the rest or our lives. It's not something we will ever forget. Just don't put it on my gravestone."

TOM MARINO

On Dec. 13, 2004, the day the jury recommended the death penalty, a reporter showed up at Tom Marino's home in San Carlos. Relieved that the trial was over, the postman, then 55, fought to hold back his tears.

"The experience had been really difficult, harrowing and horrible," he said. "We need to get on with our lives and put this horrid thing behind us."

Marino was conflicted about his views on the death penalty before he became a juror. His parish priest advised him to follow the laws of man. He did his earthly duty and followed the letter of the law, but he still struggles with the decision.

"I don't care who you are," he said. "It's not an easy decision to live with. To make the decision, you're following the rules of the court. That's not difficult. But after you do it, now you have to live with the fact. I don't care who you are. It's got to bother you. It did bother me. Nobody wants to take a life."

Marino, like Lear, has tried to put the whole experience behind him.

"I'm doing well with it," he said.

But there are constant reminders: a news article or TV segment, a replay of Sharon's heart-wrenching statements, news about Peterson's appeals or his life on death row.

"It brings it back," Marino said. "Then you're going through what went through your mind at the beginning, when it first happened. It's not like you can totally forget it. But I don't relive it. I haven't lost sleep over it."

He hasn't sought medical or psychiatric help. He continues to go to church, where he sees his priest all the time. In some ways, the experience has helped Marino appreciate what he has. He continues to golf regularly, despite a painful auto-immune disease called Retroperitoneal Fibrosis that affects the gland that separates the intestine and stomach. He looks forward to Christmas, unlike other jurors.

"I enjoy it even more," he said, "knowing that my kids are still here and that we have a grandbaby. It's even more important because they are here. We feel much more fortunate. I felt the Rochas' pain. If it was a family member or one of my children, I couldn't imagine how it would affect me. Then you put it in perspective. How lucky I am. I still have my kids."

The photos of Laci and Conner's remains didn't convince him to vote for death.

"My feeling was it wasn't like Scott was a hatchet murderer and mutilated someone terribly like some killers do," he said. "It wasn't like he chopped her up in a bunch of pieces and buried her somewhere. It might have been strangulation, it might have been an argument. But he didn't put those bodies in that condition. The San Francisco Bay did."

The soft-spoken Marino, the last holdout during the death penalty deliberations, came to that decision based on the letter of the law. He did have some relatives, more religious than he, who questioned his role in imposing the death penalty. "They couldn't understand it," he said.

He tends to downplay the lasting impact of the trial, but his questions linger, and will for a long time.

"I don't know if I'll be alive if and when they do execute Peterson," he said. "I know it's right, but I still don't know how I will feel about the execution then."

GREG BERATLIS

Before the trial, Greg Beratlis thought that someone who looked like Scott Peterson could not have committed these murders.

"People think evil looks like some shady figure cloaked in darkness," he said. "People think that if a person is clean-cut and good looking, has a nice smile and is fairly intelligent that they must be trustworthy."

Ruling on a life or death matter challenged Beratlis to reassess his belief system. He realized he had been looking at life through his own values. He wasn't as open-minded as he thought he was.

"We think that people are just like us," he said, "That nobody in his right mind could plan out and commit this crime without some emotional breakdown or remorse."

That is exactly what he found in Peterson. "When he killed his wife, he was in essence killing his own blood, his son," he said.

Beratlis was a trusting sort before the trial. No longer. He is cautious now about whom he will let into his house and whom he will let into his life. The trial changed almost everything for him, except for his love for his family. Through it all, his wife and sons have provided stability. "My relationship with my family is much closer now," he said. "You never know who could take away what you love most."

Beratlis still has to protect them from crazies. Some of them, it turns out, go to school with his children.

"After the trial my youngest son was badgered at school," he said. "He was told that his father was a killer for sentencing Scott Peterson to death."

Greg's son had told him that it did not bother him.

"But when a whole group of your peers are yelling at you that your father is a killer, it has to hurt. It hurt me that my son would have to go through this. With time, it subsided."

He still discusses the final verdict with his oldest son, who opposes the death penalty. "He believes that taking a person's life will not bring justice," he said. "I explain that I was given the parameters that if the crime warranted the punishment, then I must follow these guidelines and that this decision was not taken lightly. We still don't agree to this day."

It was only after the trial ended that he discussed it with his wife, who did not watch or listen to news of the case while it was going on.

"My wife never asked how the trial was going or brought up anything that was told to her at work about the trial," he said. "My family kept it in check."

Beratlis had no idea what was in store for him after the trial ended and he took part in the jury press conference on Dec. 13, 2004. Beratlis, who became instantly recognizable as millions watched the telecast, became another victim of the media pack who waited like wolves at his door, demanding his time.

"It was overwhelming," he said. "The lights, the bookers, the reporters all wanted a piece of my time. There were cars parked outside my home all night. The next morning these same cars followed me to a meeting place to do their interviews. Inside the house was just as crazy. The phone rang off the hook from TV bookers and reporters. We finally took the phone off the hook."

One of those calls was from a man who threatened to kill him and his family.

"What did my family have to do with this?" he asked. "What kind of person makes this kind of a threat? I felt like I should be the target of whoever did not agree with my decision, not my family."

Two nights later someone lit a candle and left it on his driveway. "These were scary times," he said. "I even received death threats in the mail, but I also realized that not all people are going to agree with our decision."

But he found there were others who had served as jurors in capital murder cases who lent moral support by sending letters and e-mails.

"They knew what I was feeling right after the trial," he said. "They understood the emotional toll it took on us. I wrote back to a few of them. It was good for my well being."

Beratlis kept himself busy. Too busy. He didn't want to miss any opportunities in life, as he had put his life on hold for months. He eventually burned himself out. He knew he needed help to get his life in check. He was remodeling his house, which added stress. His diet was out of whack. He had gained weight during the trial. His sleep was chaotic.

"I would wake up numerous times in the night with chest pains which started during the guilt phase of the trial and carried on for at least six months after the trial," he said. "I was lucky if I slept more than an hour straight."

He joined a self-help program called Chi Fountain in an effort to regain control over his life. Through the program, he lost weight and alleviated his anxieties that started during the trial. But two years later he is still searching for the equilibrium he had before serving as a juror.

"I think that my life is still not back together completely," he said. "I find myself getting emotional about things that seem unimportant at the time. I have not been able to figure out what triggers these emotions. It does seem to be getting better."

People in the community still approach Beratlis and offer their opinions about the case.

"The one that really blows my mind is when they ask if he was really guilty," he said. "I look at them and I ask, 'Do you think that you could make a decision about a man's life if you really did not believe in your decision?'"

Through it all, Beratlis, who received another jury summons in 2006, feels the case has had a broader impact.

"Many people feel there is no justice in America, that it was bought and paid for. Now many of them feel that justice has been served. I just did what I believe was fair to the system. I listened to the facts and then made my decision. I would hope every person in America would do the same. I would do it all over again if I were in the same situation," he said. "I feel that the system needs to have people who are willing to listen to the facts before making a judgment."

MIKE BELMESSIERI

Like the other jurors, Mike Belmessieri is haunted by the autopsy photos of Laci Peterson. Laci's destroyed body was such a powerful image that it brought back his experience where he recalled seeing a young brother Marine's body shattered during a grenade attack.

After nearly two years, Laci's horrifying photographs still affect Belmessieri, especially when he has to drive past San Francisco Bay on his way to work each day.

"I can't look at the Bay without being reminded that part of Laci is still out there," Belmessieri said.

Because of the attention he has gotten from the trial, Belmessieri often comes face to face with people who want to discuss the case. He no longer feels as if he needs to defend his decision, and the decision of his colleagues.

"I don't try to convince anybody of anything," he said. "I don't want to convince anybody that he's innocent or guilty. People are going to believe what they want to believe. I just want to communicate what we went through and what many others will or have gone through. That's what it's about. I want people to understand the process."

On the home front, Belmessieri is hopeful that Dominic, his son in the Marines, will return to the United States in May 2007. Belmessieri has some idea of what his son will be going through.

"My son will leave Iraq, but Iraq will never leave him," he said. "When he and I speak I will avoid asking him about it. If he volunteers I will very attentively listen and understand the very personal pain that he wishes to share with me and be very honored that we are close enough for him to do so."

Belmessieri drew on his own experiences as a Marine to help him deal with the aftermath of the trial. But there are some things about his service that he does not like to talk about.

"I'm proud that I served this country as a Marine," Belmessieri said. "That's a title one earns for life. I'm a Vietnam era Marine, but I don't want to be asked about it because then I'll start getting all emotional, and I need to get away from that sort of thing. It's just too painful."

FRAN GORMAN

Even though Fran Gorman did not cast the final votes for guilty or the death penalty, she too came under enormous emotional stress. To set the record straight, she told members of the media who gathered at her driveway after the verdict that she was in complete agreement with it.

"This is the right verdict; this is the correct verdict; it's how I would have voted," she said.

After the trial, Gorman took time off for vacation. Although family and friends were understanding, they were unaware of what she endured. Unlike the other members of the jury, she no longer had their emotional support because she had left the panel.

"A week after being dismissed I broke down completely," she said. "I went to Kaiser for Xanax and sought help through counseling. My counselor concluded that I was suffering from post-traumatic stress and offered to write me a disability note. That was a wake-up call. I'd never been on disability in my life and wasn't about to start now. I went back to work but continued going to counseling."

She was in Boston when the death penalty decision was announced. She was alone with her emotions.

"There by myself I was away from family, from my counselor, from everything that was familiar to me," she said. "Anxiety attacks came in waves. On the way home I tucked myself into a remote corner of Logan Airport and cried myself stupid."

She later reconnected with some of the members of the jury, including Richelle Nice, Mike Belmessieri and Fairy Sorrell. But she still yearned for some form of closure. That, she hoped, would come at Peterson's sentencing. When she entered the courthouse, she held on to Belmessieri. In the jury box, she sat next to Nice, drawing a quizzical glance from Jenne who could have removed her, but didn't. She tensed up during Sharon Rocha's heartbreaking tirade against Scott.

As Laci's family greeted the jurors, she wondered how they would react to her.

"What would they say or do? Then it was my turn. I stepped forward into a warm hug from Sharon and a bear hug from Dennis. The anxiety I'd felt for months suddenly lifted. I'd found closure."

Certificate of Appreciation

JOHN GUINASSO

has rendered an important civic service as a

JUROR

for the *People v. Scott Peterson*

Superior Court of California – County of San Mateo

This certificate is awarded in recognition of the conscientious performance of this important duty of citizenship and the rendering of a valuable service in the administration of justice to the people of the State of California.

WITNESS WHEREOF, I have hereunto subscribed my name and affixed the seal of the Court on this date:

December 13, 2004

HON. ALFRED A. DELUCCHI
JUDGE OF THE SUPERIOR COURT, Ret.

Certificate of Appreciation to Guinasso, received by all the jurors.

CHAPTER 16:
THE LONG ROAD AHEAD

"I do not feel there will be any closure for me until there is a ruling from the appellate court in which the jury's verdict and penalty are held to be the just and appropriate punishment."
—Mike Belmessieri, Juror No. 4

On March 16, 2005, ten jurors, two alternates, and one dismissed juror filed into the courtroom for one last time, but they were not there to weigh the evidence. They had already done that. They attended the sentencing hearing to show their support for one another and for the Rochas. They wanted closure. But they also knew that in many ways this was just the beginning of a long journey.

"The sentencing by Judge Delucchi did bring a certain degree of closure, but not to the extent that I had hoped it would," said Mike Belmessieri. "It simply finalized the first phase of the experience, but there was so much more to come, and so much more involved."

Some felt awkward as they took their old seats in the jury box. Dennis Lear didn't know where to sit at first. "I had moved around so much," he said.

Greg Beratlis felt both comfortable and confined as he took his seat. "I was nervous not knowing what to expect," he said. "Sitting in the jury box was familiar but then again being on stage in front of the people was scary."

For Richelle Nice, the sentencing represented not only an end to the trial, but also the breakup of her surrogate family: the

231

other jurors. She had fears about leaving her "comfort zone" and leaving "the people I became so close to." A jumble of thoughts raced through her mind as she sat in the box.

"Are we supposed to just forget each other and go back to our normal lives, like we didn't just see how this man killed his family? Will our friends and family understand? How can they understand? Only others who have been here understand."

Like the rest of the jurors, she came to see Scott Peterson's reaction to his sentence. "Today is Scott's day to find out his fate," she said.

During the trial, Peterson was always sitting at the defense table when the jurors entered the courtroom. But on this day, the bailiffs brought him in shackles and leg irons. He still wore a dark suit but his wrists were cuffed and shackled to his body.

The jurors were apprehensive. Would Judge Delucchi sentence Peterson to death, or would he grant his motion for a new trial? That 135-page motion targeted specific jurors, most notably John Guinasso. It alleged that he engaged in misconduct and claimed that the judge erred when he dismissed Justin Falconer and Greg Jackson.

Guinasso, who had played such a critical role throughout the trial, was conspicuously absent. He accepted an offer from ABC's *Good Morning America* to appear on March 16 and 17 and flew to New York. He reasoned that the media would focus on the jury as a whole, "if I remove myself from the jurors that are attending the sentencing."

But on that day, he found himself sitting in a hotel room, 3,000 miles away from where he wanted to be; his opportunity to appear on *Good Morning America* had fizzled out. It didn't feel right.

"I was now regretting my decision," he said. "I wanted to be back in Redwood City for the sentencing. I should not have gone to New York. I wanted so bad to be there."

What's more, Fran Gorman was sitting in his old seat. That didn't feel right either.

Judge Delucchi quickly rejected each of the 13 claims in Peterson's new trial motion and declared that he had received a fair trial.

Guinasso, who received a blow-by-blow e-mail account from a reporter in the courtroom, felt relieved. "I released a big sigh knowing that we had followed the letter of the law," he said.

Delucchi, who has a kind demeanor, looked at Peterson. With a faint quaver in his voice, he acknowledged that he did not have a prior criminal record and that he came from a "caring family," but he called the murders "cruel, uncaring, heartless and callous." Peterson had betrayed his wife's trust. Conner "was not even permitted to take a breath on this earth," he said. With that, he sentenced Peterson to death.

"When the judge upheld the penalty, it validated our verdict," Beratlis said.

Once again, Tom Marino felt the weight of their decision.

"Even though I was almost assured from the news media that Judge Delucchi was most likely to give his affirmation to the death penalty and subsequently did give the death penalty, a chill ran through my spine," Marino said. "It almost took my breath away as he said the words. I thought to myself, we did the right thing and now it's over."

Or was it?

"The realization is that I have to deal with the fact that for the rest of my life, I was a participant in having to make a life or death judgment about another human being," Marino said. "Ultimately, I have played a small part in pulling that switch."

The Peterson family asked to make victim statements, arguing that they had lost their grandson. "It was not their daughter who was murdered," the judge said, turning them down.

It would be the Rochas' turn to vent, and they did. Brent, Amy, Dennis, and Sharon Rocha and Ron Grantski, among other family members, unleashed their fury on Peterson, an outpouring of grief and anger unlike anything the jurors had witnessed before. The emotions were raw. The lawyers couldn't object to what they said.

Once again, the only one who didn't show any emotion was Peterson, who appeared vacant, detached.

"He still had the same expressionless face on," Lear said. "I think he enjoyed the attention."

Brent Rocha went first. He said he had purchased a gun shortly after Laci vanished and thought of killing his brother-in-law. "I chose not to kill you myself so you would have to sweat it out and not take the easy way out," he said.

He lashed out at his brother-in-law's duplicity.

"You slept in the same bed with Laci for two weeks knowing you were going to kill her," he shouted. "You ate the food she cooked for you knowing you were going to kill her."

"That's not true," Jackie Peterson said.

"You're a liar," Lee Peterson shouted when Brent said that Peterson had confided that his fertilizer business was failing and that he wasn't looking forward to becoming a father.

Delucchi warned the audience to refrain from outbursts.

Lee Peterson stood up and walked out of the courtroom and was soon followed by Jackie.

Zanartu witnessed everything and cried for both families. "I wasn't there to judge or to do anything," she said. "I felt the Rocha family's emotions towards him. I was a spectator."

"Dennis Rocha was cussing Scott out the whole time as he sat in the gallery," she said. "I heard him say, 'You're going to rot in hell.' I thought Dennis was going to run over there and kill him. He looked like he wanted to. When he got up there he really laid into him. He got up and yelled, 'You piece of shit.'"

"You're a monster," Amy Rocha shouted at Peterson.

Once more, it was Sharon Rocha whose anguished cries hit the jurors and the rest of the courtroom observers. She looked at Peterson.

"What are you doing?" Sharon asked, channeling Laci's voice. "You know how much I love you? I thought you loved me too. ...Scott, I want to live.... Please stop, I don't want to die."

Then Sharon invoked Conner's voice. "Why are you killing mommy and me?" she said. "I don't know you yet, but I love you. Please daddy, don't kill me."

"Did she know you were killing her?" Sharon asked in her own voice, staring at Peterson. "Did she look at you? Did you look at her? Was she alive when you put her in the Bay?"

"Why did you murder Laci, Scott?" she continued. "Because of you I will never meet my grandson. I'll never know what color his eyes would have been. Would he have had dimples like his mother? I'll never have that opportunity to know because of you. I know you're nothing but an empty, hollow shell. ...You deserve to burn in hell for all eternity."

At one point, when Sharon said that Peterson killed Laci, he shook his head no.

"Yes you did!" Sharon screamed.

For the first time, Zanartu noticed what other jurors had seen: Peterson's arrogance. "He seemed really cocky that day," she said. "He was smirking. I guess he knew what was coming. But no reaction, despite the things they were saying to him. He just sat there. He just took it and looked at them."

Delucchi asked Peterson if he wanted to make a statement, but after consulting with his defense team, he declined.

After the hearing, Laci's friends, the Modesto detectives, and prosecutors thanked the jurors. The judge made a point of thanking them personally.

"The judge was pretty emotional, tears and all," Lear said. "He thanked us as we left and told us we were the best jury he ever had."

The judge had validated their verdict by sentencing Peterson to San Quentin's Death Row. But the jurors knew that wouldn't bring any conclusion to their saga.

"I do not feel that there will be any closure for me personally until there is a ruling from an appellate court in which the jury's verdict and penalty are held to be the just and appropriate punishment," said Belmessieri. "Should there be a reversal in the conviction or the penalty by an appellate court, closure may be long in coming. Should any court's reasoning to reverse the decision be based on jury conduct, or anything regarding our actions, closure as a matter of my conscience may never come."

Birgit Fladager, who was sworn in as the Stanislaus County district attorney in July 2006, is confident that the verdicts and sentencing will be upheld, largely because of Delucchi's rulings.

"Judge Delucchi was so conscientious about dotting the 'i's and crossing the 't's, handling everything appropriately so that the likelihood of legal challenge would be minimized," she said. "I think that's his goal to do everything right legally so that there is not a challenge down the road. We have complete confidence and faith that this case will withstand appeal. That is in no small part due to Judge Delucchi and his rulings."

The prosecutors watched them carefully. They knew who was listening attentively, who wasn't, who was taking notes, and who wasn't. In the end, they were impressed with the quality of the jurors.

"Everyone commented that Mr. Guinasso didn't take many notes compared to the other folks," Fladager said. "But he also appeared to us to be very attentive. We chatted with him afterwards. It was very clear he had very good recall without having taken all the notes. Each juror obviously took this seriously, worked very hard.

We had a lot of faith in them. We were extremely gratified that they came to the right result in both phases of the trial."

Fladager isn't surprised that the jurors are still coping with their service two years later. She worried about how the trial would affect them.

"I brought it up with Judge Delucchi to ask if there wouldn't be something available for the jurors after the fact," she said. "In terms of having someone who could talk to them after the fact and debrief them about what to expect and how this might affect them and how they could deal with it. I was told there wasn't anything available for them. That's something that has to be considered in major cases like this."

It is hard to fathom what the jurors went through, Fladager said.

"I don't think anybody really can truly understand how difficult the situation would have been for them," she said. "From our perspective obviously it was difficult for us but at least we could talk about the case all the time. That's pretty much all we did 24 hours a day. The idea of having to sit and listen and process that information and not be able to discuss it...that's incomprehensible, I think, for most people."

Fladager plans to bring the issue of helping jurors after they serve in high-profile trials before the California District Attorneys Association to try to get legislation passed.

"They tend to be forgotten," she said of the jurors.

Fladager almost suggests that the fates, or a higher power, played a large role in the outcome of the case. There were so many twists and turns, ups and downs. Laci and Conner's bodies washed up on the Richmond shore months after their disappearance. Three jurors were dismissed. What would have happened, for instance, if the doctor-lawyer had remained on the jury?

"There is no telling," Fladager said. "We look at it that everything happened for a reason. When it happened and how it happened, it happened for a reason."

Years from now, as Peterson's appeal works its way through the system, the defense may want to interview the jurors again and get sworn affidavits.

"This will be maybe 10, 15 to 20 years from now," Fladager said. "So there's a little concern about what might happen down the road. We were grateful for the hard work the jurors put in. We know that it was hard on them."

In California, death penalty cases are automatically appealed to the state Supreme Court. To date, the transcripts from the trial and other records have not even been certified. It could take 20 years before Peterson is put to death, if ever.

"It is conceivable that the law clerks who will be assisting in Peterson's final appeals were not yet born at the time that the crime was committed," said Loyola Law Professor Stan Goldman. "One of the reasons it takes so long is because there is such a short list of lawyers in California who handle death penalty appeals and the writs of habeas corpus that it takes sometimes years to find someone to take on the case."

On Feb. 25, 2005, Mark Geragos fired the opening salvo in the appeals process, with his unsuccessful motion for a new trial.

Among the 13 points cited, Geragos argued that Judge Delucchi should not have dismissed Justin Falconer or Greg Jackson. Senior Deputy Dave Harris filed a rebuttal on March 9, 2005, claiming that Peterson and his lawyers had taken such liberties with the facts that it had "created a claim out of whole cloth."

Geragos also argued that Beratlis and Jackson should not have gotten into the boat during deliberations. He felt the jurors conducted an unlawful experiment that went beyond the evidence, while Harris argued that the jurors did nothing more than closely examine the evidence.

"Certainly Geragos raised the boat as an issue," Fladager said. "Appellate counsel will raise it too. We frankly don't see it as an issue."

* * *

The dismissed jurors will likely be brought up in any appeals. After Delucchi questioned Falconer about the Brent Rocha incident on June 21, 2004, he decided to leave the original Juror No. 5 on the panel. But two days later, Guinasso sent a note to the judge complaining that Falconer continued to talk about Det. Brocchini's testimony, the Modesto police, the prosecution, and that his girlfriend told Falconer that the blonde anchorwoman on Court TV (Nancy Grace) had called him "a loose cannon" and "gregarious." As a result of the note, Delucchi interviewed all 12 jurors and six alternates.

Guinasso had confronted Falconer, but that did not solve the problem, he told Delucchi.

"He keeps saying if anybody has a problem with this, they should be man enough to come up to him," he said. "Well, I have, but what am I supposed to do? I can't be physical with him."

In his motion, Geragos argued that the other jurors and alternates did not back up Guinasso's claims when they talked to Delucchi. But even in the transcripts provided in Geragos' motion, several jurors told the judge that they heard Falconer commenting on the evidence.

Greg Jackson, Alternate No. 1 who would take Falconer's seat, heard him talk about Court TV.

"Yes," he told Delucchi. "He said specifically that his girlfriend apparently was very upset with a reporter for Court TV, and I remember specifically him saying that she said she was going to kill this reporter, that she wouldn't tell him what it was that had made her so upset, but she had recorded it or had otherwise made a copy or would tell him later, presumably after the trial was over, and that she was keeping these types of records."

Michael Church, Alternate No. 6, reported that Falconer talked to him about the anchor and the prosecution's performance.

Even Falconer had a hard time denying the charges, according to the prosecution's rebuttal.

"Are you denying that you made comments on Brocchini's testimony?" Delucchi asked.

"I—I don't think I did," he responded.

Mike Belmessieri told the judge: "I went to lunch with No. 5 [Falconer], No. 6 [Cardosi], No. 7 [Gorman] and a couple of the alternates yesterday and we went into the jury room. On the way to the jury room [Falconer] asked me if I got anything out of Det. Brocchini's testimony. I said yes."

Delucchi had heard enough. He noted there had been the Brent Rocha incident at the screening station, and that Juror No. 8 [Guinasso] and Juror No. 3 [Lorena Gonzalez] had complained about his talking about the case.

"He's like a bull in a China shop in there," Delucchi said. "...I have the testimony of Juror Number 8, and I'm more inclined to believe Juror No. 8 than I am to believe Juror No. 5."

"Juror No. 8 is a head case," Geragos said.

But Delucchi held firm.

"If I leave this guy in there, I'm leaving a cancer in that jury room," Delucchi said of Falconer. "...This guy is not following the Court's admonitions. ...He's talking about this anchor. I don't care who brought it up, but he's apparently taking the position that he knows about this. I think that's detrimental to your client. That would indicate to some of these other jurors that maybe these anchors were used to weigh down Laci Peterson. ...So that's the way I feel about this guy. I think that he's a total cancer in this jury. And I find that there is good cause to remove this juror. ...So I think he's going to be unhappy about this. But so be it. We have a trial to worry about here."

Geragos shot back: "If there is a cancer in the jury, the cancer is No. 8. That is where the cancer is."

"You should be happy then," Delucchi said.

"Why? You should bounce eight," Geragos said. "Bounce eight."

Three weeks into the case, Geragos had identified his enemy: Juror No. 8.

After reading the motion, Guinasso was incensed. "How can such a high profile lawyer as Mr. Geragos be affected by a juror who was reporting several violations of the court's admonitions by another juror? Isn't the judicial process about delivering a true verdict through a fair and non-biased interpretation of the facts? Apparently Mr. Geragos is all about winning even if fairness isn't a factor."

"He has also referred to me as a 'stealth juror,'" Guinasso continued. "Didn't the defense have the ability to remove me as a juror during the selection phase? Wasn't he the one that asked me the question during *voir dire*, 'If I had made a decision regarding the verdict, could someone persuade me from it?' I responded, 'Absolutely not!' I told him that I was hard headed and that no one could change my mind after I had made a decision. Apparently Mr. Geragos didn't know that I was a juror who demanded that his client get a fair trial."

* * *

In his motion, Geragos also argued that Delucchi should have kept Jackson on the panel. On Nov. 10, 2004, Delucchi received notes from Jackson, Juror No. 5, and the new foreman Steve Cardosi, Juror No. 6.

In his note, Jackson admitted approaching Cardosi outside of the deliberations. But Cardosi, in his note, said he thought Jackson approached him outside of the deliberations because he wanted to smooth out any hard feelings.

In chambers, Jackson told Delucchi he wanted off the jury and acknowledged talking about doctors DeVore and March with Cardosi on the bus.

"You tell me what happened, doctor," the judge began.

Jackson told the judge that he had changed his opinion as a result of the conversation.

"The reasons are probably irrelevant," Jackson said. "But it was a good discussion and an interesting discussion. And I continued to want to pursue this line of discussion. ...We did go back and forth a little on the bus. And when I wrote in the second note there that I changed my opinion based on the conversations on the bus, that's true. ...And the weight that I was giving those two experts did change as a result of that conversation."

Jackson also talked about the maelstrom swirling around him. He felt hostility from the others.

"It's created some extraordinary consternation, frustration, hostility in the jury room," Jackson said. "Everything from the fact that Cap is now the new foreperson, and I'm trying to take him down, and I've wanted off the jury now for quite some time. There is just an enormous amount of hostility now focused at me because of this."

He didn't feel safe.

"I have not been threatened bodily, but the comments, the looks...."

Delucchi wondered who was making the threats, but Jackson wouldn't say.

"Your honor, I prefer not to...go there, except to say that I have tried mightily," he said. "I think I'm at an end of what I can do reasonably with this jury to weigh this evidence fairly. I don't think I can weigh it fairly any longer."

The judge brought in Cardosi. He asked the new foreman if there was any hostility toward the doctor-lawyer, and he said no. Cap was mystified about what was happening, but did acknowledge that the doctor-lawyer wanted to talk more than the others.

"I can't really explain why he feels that way, other than speculation, where he wants to talk a lot more than other people," Cardosi said. "We're trying to give people fair and equitable time to voice their thoughts, and everything else. And he tends to take a very long time. But, other than that, everybody gets...a certain amount of time to make their point and then they get cut off. That's the only thing that I can think of.... This hit me this morning out of the blue. I have no idea where it came from."

Jackson returned to the judge's chambers and told Delucchi he could no longer be fair.

"As you sit there now, do you feel, if you were to continue to deliberate in this case, that you could be a fair and impartial juror in this case?" the judge asked.

"No," Jackson responded.

With that, Delucchi decided to remove the third juror from the panel. But before he dismissed Jackson, he called him to his chambers again. He would be put "back outside" into the real world. But the judge wondered why the doctor-lawyer felt the way he did.

"When I took the oath, I understood it to mean that I needed to be able to weigh both sides fairly, openly," Jackson said. "And given what's transpired, my individual ability to do that I think has been compromised to a degree that I would never know personally whether or not I was giving the community's verdict, the popular verdict, the expected verdict, the verdict that might, I don't know, produce the best book.

"I'm not going to speak to the media. I don't ever want to personally profit from this case in any way, directly or indirectly. I think I'm going to get on an airplane if you grant relief, literally.... But, your Honor, I did my level best."

Jackson noted that the deliberations were continuing efficiently. There was a "healthy, ongoing debate going on," he told the judge. "And the new foreperson is superb in making sure [that] anybody who wants an issue on the white boards, it goes up without question...I think they are doing a superb job."

But it was clear to the judge that Jackson could no longer remain.

"Juror No. 5 wanted to get off this case from the second day [of deliberations]...I don't know what's going on in here, but there is a real problem with this one particular juror now," Delucchi said. "He says he cannot be a fair and impartial juror for whatever reason."

Two days later, the jurors convicted Peterson.

In his motion, Geragos argued that the doctor-lawyer revealed there was improper outside influence affecting the jury. But Dave Harris pointed out that Jackson was simply having a hard time fitting in.

"The doctor had a different style than that of the other jurors and was unhappy with how they conducted deliberations," Harris wrote. "The new foreman denied there was any hostility being directed towards the doctor."

For Belmessieri, it was a bit of an understatement to say that D-Day didn't fit in.

"D-Day could not handle being challenged by the reasoning of individuals who had lesser academic discipline in areas he considered to be his expertise," he said. "Suddenly his status in the group changed. He became just another fish in the fish bowl. The final blow to his ego was when John, a Teamster-parking lot attendant (and someone who does not take a lot of notes) made a motion to replace the doctor-lawyer with a paramedic-firefighter, and he was voted out as foreman. It was too much of a blow for him to accept."

As Guinasso contemplated the back room machinations and the filings by Geragos, he wondered why Geragos made an issue about the ousters of Falconer and Jackson, but did not get upset when Fran Gorman was dismissed.

"As he sat in chambers, wasn't it me who told Judge Delucchi that if Fran Gorman remained on the jury, it would taint the process?" he asked. "That's right. Geragos may have thought that she was pro prosecution, and maybe that's why he didn't vigorously object to her removal."

In his heart, Guinasso believes Peterson received a fair trial, and that is what matters. But he will carry his decision with him for the rest of his life.

"The evidence spoke for itself," he said. "Every piece of circumstantial fact that was presented pointed toward Peterson. He was the cold-blooded murderer that took his wife and baby's lives."